Extravagant Affections

"A ground-breaking contribution to both feminist and sacramental theology, brimming with insights that result from cross-fertilizing the two. Written with engaging style and supple argument, it makes brilliant use of the ambiguity of women's experience of sacraments, both positive and negative, to rethink basic meanings and practices. The result is an extravagant feast for the mind and heart that proves beyond doubt the power of feminist discourse to clarify and transform central tenets of Christian faith."
— ELIZABETH A. JOHNSON

"To read Susan Ross's *Extravagant Affections* is to get a rare glimpse into the sacramental life and theology of many Catholic women today, but also into what the future should be and is likely to be. For some decades, we have learned increasingly to begin our theological reflection from the shared faith experience of believers, but Ross points out — rightly — that for the most part, we have neglected to take account of the gendered dimension of women's religious experience; and as a result the sharing has been truncated. Beyond this criticism, she goes on to suggest creatively how family (in the broad sense) may be the context within which best to discover the way in which gender affects the sacramentality of human life. This book deserves a wide readership."
— BERNARD COOKE

"Susan Ross has put together a critical and constructive feminist contribution to sacramental theology. The attention she gives to learning by celebrating, to embodiment, to a broad notion of sacramentality, and to developing fresh sacramental paradigms offers something that will allow the general reader good insight into the issues at stake, and ought to draw other sacramental theologians into conversation."
— DAVID N. POWER, O.M.I.

Extravagant Affections

A FEMINIST
SACRAMENTAL
THEOLOGY

SUSAN A. ROSS

Continuum

New York • London

2001

The Continuum International Publishing Group Inc
370 Lexington Avenue, New York, NY 10017

The Continuum International Publishing Group Ltd
The Tower Building, 11 York Road, London SE1 7NX

Printed in the United States of America

Library of Congress Cataloging-in-Publication Data
Ross, Susan A.
    Extravagant affections : a feminist sacramental theology / Susan
A. Ross.
        p.   cm.
    Includes bibliographical references and index.
    ISBN 0-8264-1320-X (paperback : alk. paper)
    1. Sacraments – Catholic Church. 2. Feminist theology.
3. Catholic Church – Doctrines.   I. Title.
BX2203.R65 1998
234'.16'082 – dc21   98–25997

In Memory of
John B. Ross, Jr. (1948–1996)
and
Ann O'Hara Graff (1950–1996)

and for
Bill

"We must not deprive ourselves, our loved ones,
of the luxury of our extravagant affections."
Mary Gordon
Final Payments

Contents

Introduction

In Mary Gordon's novel *Final Payments,* Isabel Moore comes to a profound realization about her life, her desires, and her religion. After a struggle to find her own way in life following her father's death, she comes to see that Jesus' statement, "the poor you will always have with you" does not mean that we are "to justify the excesses of centuries of fat, tyrannical bankers," but that the costly jar of ointment, which the apostles thought should be sold for the poor, must be broken open and enjoyed. Isabel comes to realize that she must "open the jar of ointment" and live her life fully, accepting both the joys and the risks of loving.[1]

This book proposes that the jars of ointment of the church, the sacraments, need to be broken open, by all people, but especially by women. The horror of Jesus' disciples at his allowing a woman to anoint him with costly oil is echoed today by the refusal of magisterial Roman Catholicism to allow women to preside at the Eucharist and to act as sacramental ministers. Beneath this refusal is a complex set of reasons and traditions, but these reasons and traditions serve to contain and protect what lies within these jars of ointment: God's own extravagant affections for humankind. In this book I explore these reasons and traditions, along with the experiences of women who are challenging them.

This book has been a long time in the making. It began around a series of questions I began asking as I was completing my dissertation over fifteen years ago: How is it that a tradition, claiming to venerate the physical, material, and bodily, through its sacramentality, is so hostile to the reality of women's bodies? How can Catholic women, who feel both nurtured and

---

1. Mary Gordon, *Final Payments* (New York: Ballantine Books, 1978) 298–99.

betrayed by their tradition, continue to worship? Is a feminist sacramental theology a contradiction in terms? These questions have been more than academic ones for me. My interest in the arts, particularly music, originally led me to work in sacramental theology. The sacraments are, in a way, "works of art" for the church — works that are at the same time ordinary and extraordinary, celebrating the transcendent within the immanent. Like music, the sacraments say in gesture, sound, rhythm, and word, that which cannot be said otherwise. I have always felt a deep connection with these ancient rituals, even in my most nonobservant years, making sure that I did not miss that most extraordinary of rituals, the Easter vigil, with its frankly sensuous light and darkness, incense, bells, and music.

But this deep connection has always included a sour note. My femaleness means that I am, to some extent, an interloper in these rituals. Of all the sacraments, only one requires the presence of a woman. All the rest depend, implicitly of course, on women: to give birth to the infant, to bake the bread, to raise the child, to reconcile, to care for the sick. But this dependence is not really acknowledged. And one sacrament, while ostensibly the least dependent on women, would not be at all possible if women did not give birth to men. This "sour note" can take a number of different expressions, some of which will be explored further below: that women cannot have direct sacramental access to God but must go through a male mediator; that sacraments do what women do, only on a higher and more sacred level; that the sacraments express a desire on the part of men to separate from women. This note also leads to a dilemma expressed to me a number of times especially by groups of women religious: for years — indeed, for centuries — women have found in the sacraments, especially in their daily Mass attendance, a confirmation of the sacredness of their dedicated lives and a definition of their piety. But now, energized and angered by a new awareness of the injustices in sacramental theology and practice, some women are abandoning traditional eucharistic liturgies for women-led celebrations, to the dismay of some of their sister members. How can religious communities of women, torn by their loyalty and their anger, worship together? How can women who have families pass on a tradition that both nurtures and alienates? How can single or childless women find sustenance in a tradition that both encourages their journeys to sainthood yet barely acknowledges their existence, save as potential mothers?

I have come to believe that there is, at present, no one simple answer to these questions. There is no one clear path to a feminist sacramental theology. The answer is rather one of complexity and ambiguity. Women who continue to participate in the sacramental system, and those who have abandoned it, have more in common than they may realize. For those who participate in it may well be changing it from the inside, while having one foot outside it, and those who have abandoned it may find that they are still connected to it. Ambiguity is, I will argue, a component element of sacramentality itself, and is also characteristic of women's involvement in the sacraments. Thus, I advocate neither adaptation of the existing sacramental system nor wholesale exodus from it. Rather I argue for ways of expressing this ambiguity, within and alongside the sacraments.

I wish to emphasize the particularity of this project — that is, the relatively narrow scope of what I have set out to do: that is, to provide a feminist analysis of some of the main dimensions of sacramental theology — those having to do with the body, with symbols, and with ethics. And these analyses are themselves partial, focusing on some alternative ways of construing the sacraments. This book is not a comprehensive feminist sacramental theology, in which each sacrament receives a detailed history, analysis, critique, and reconstruction. Nor do I attempt to cover the complexities of liturgical theology. It will be evident early on in this book why I think a feminist approach to sacramental theology is fraught with difficulties. But I am convinced that sacramental theology is in need of some kind of feminist response. This book is an attempt to provide one, partial and incomplete though it may be.

It is more than evident to any participant or observer of what Janet Kalven of the Grail terms "women-defined" theologies that to speak of "women" as a homogeneous group is seriously problematic. As is well known and as I will indicate in chapter 2, the terminology surrounding women's efforts to do theology is very much in question. So to undertake a theological project in which the categories "women" and "women's experience" are central is to invite criticism. Not only is the diversity of the experiences of women a concern, but so is the very issue of gender identity itself. But traditional sacramental theology, as I will argue here, operates out of an implicit, and sometimes quite explicit, set of conceptions that assumes an "essential" and "natural" quality to gender. While I intend to challenge many of these categories, my aim is to respond to the ways in which women as a whole, because of our capacity to give birth, and because of the perceived "order of nature," are given a place on the margins of, or outside, the sacraments. In other words, the given categories of gender in the tradition of sacramental theology will provide a starting point. Further, my own theological sympathies are more in the direction of what is coming to be known as a "critical realism," or a "revised natural law" approach that does not dismiss altogether the category of gender or the significance of human bodiliness as givens. These points will be developed in more detail in chapters 4, 5, and 6.

The first part of the book, chapters 1, 2, and 3, is intended to provide an introduction and some methodological considerations before the more substantive concerns of the subsequent chapters are developed. The first chapter sets a context for such reflection, offers a brief overview of "sacramentality," and develops some themes in sacramental theology that are hospitable to feminist thought. The second chapter attempts a correlation between feminist theology and sacramental theology, and develops a set of criteria that will guide the rest of the book. The third chapter takes up the difficult concept of ambiguity and attempts both to show how ambiguity is a meaningful theological concept and how it can be useful in developing a feminist sacramental theology.

The second part of the book, chapters 4, 5, and 6, take up, respectively, the issues of body, symbol, and ethics. Each one of these issues, I argue, is deeply rooted in gendered conceptions of reality. Some of the assumptions about gender in these conceptions are quite explicit, as in the Roman Catholic symbolism of the bridegroom and bride as model for Christ and the church, clergy and laity. Other conceptions, such as those relating to the role of symbols, the nature of sacrifice, and the role of the sacraments in relation to ethics, are not as explicit about gender; indeed, I will argue, there is a denial of gender, to some extent, in how these issues are generally understood. Opening up these conceptions to a feminist analysis reveals how gendered assumptions — for example, concerning the role of symbols in relation to God, and the place of the sacraments in relation to the public — are operative. Once revealed, these assumptions are open to challenge and reinterpretation. I attempt such a reinterpretation by turning to feminist theories of the family as providing what I call the "embodied context" for sacramentality. These theories are loosely related to each other, and provide a way of construing sacramentality as both rooted in the "natural" and as constructed by the "social."

The final chapter concerns women's role in sacramental practice — that is, the worshiping community and women's roles in worship. Here I draw explicitly on some of the interviews that I conducted with women who are involved in sacramental ministry, as well as theoretical work in ritual. My aim in this chapter is to challenge the distinction between women who remain in more traditional church situations — for example, parishes —

and women who worship in what have come to be called "alternative" worship communities. While necessarily suggestive, this chapter argues that women's "strategies of ritualization," to use Catherine Bell's term, are similar in both situations, and that their theological concerns also reveal common patterns.[2] But women who continue to be involved in parish sacramental life offer important insights into sacramental theology through their commitment to the wider community.

My own concerns are both critical and constructive. The tradition, I believe, has all too often come to interpret, preach, and practice the sacraments in ways that constrict their grace-filled potential: by stressing strict divisions between clergy and laity, divine and human, men and women, by turning to legalistic conceptions of reality at inappropriate points, and by maintaining a rigid conception of gender roles that is both limited and limiting. As the gifts of God's "extravagant affections," and our own for God and for others, the sacraments provide opportunities for Christian women and men to express, play, celebrate, and live out the "riotous plenty that is God." My hope is that this book will help us take a step closer to receiving graciously and sharing abundantly this extravagant and riotous love of God.

I could not have completed this book without the very generous assistance of many others. The Louisville Institute awarded me a Christian Faith and Life sabbatical grant for 1997–98, which gave me more than a full academic year to write, and during which time most of the book was written. The timing of the grant was especially felicitous, and I am deeply appreciative for their support at a time when I doubted that this book would ever be completed. Thanks to James W. Lewis, executive director of the Louisville Institute, and to Kathleen Cahalan of the Lilly Endowment, for their generous support.

I am also grateful to John McCarthy, chairperson of the theology department, and Kathleen McCourt, dean of the college of arts and sciences, both of Loyola University Chicago, for their support of my work, as well as my colleagues in the theology department and the women's studies program, whose encouragement and interest helped along the way. During the Spring of 1994, I was a faculty fellow in the Center for Ethics Across the University, and did much of the reading and research for what eventually became chapter 6. My thanks go to David Ozar, the director, my

---

2. Catherine Bell, *Ritual Theory, Ritual Practice* (New York: Oxford University Press, 1992).

colleagues in the seminar, and my colleagues in the Society of Christian Ethics who heard a very early version of chapter 6 at the annual meeting in January 1995.

Earlier versions of chapter 7 were presented at the annual meeting of the Catholic Theological Society of America in June 1997 and at the annual meeting of the American Academy of Religion in November 1997. I am grateful to all those who were present at these sessions for their comments.

Over the last eighteen years, since I began teaching, I have given occasional parish talks and more formal addresses to various groups, including religious communities of women, to whom I presented some of the ideas of this book in much earlier, and often rather undeveloped, forms. I am grateful to all of these groups, who listened intently and often questioned me vigorously. The Sisters, Servants of the Immaculate Heart of Mary (IHM), the Sisters of Charity of the Blessed Virgin Mary (BVM) and the Sisters of the Living Word deserve thanks for their invitations to me to meet with their communities on the issue of women and the Eucharist and for the opportunities I had to think through some of these issues. The parishes are too numerous to name, but it was in those church basements and parish centers that I became aware of the numbers of women engaged in parish work, and of their love and energy for their communities and for the church. I am convinced that these women truly represent the future of ministry.

Special thanks are due to those women who gave generously of their time, and of their ideas, when I asked to interview them for this project. These women, who are pastoral coordinators, pastoral associates, directors of liturgy, directors of religious education, ministers of care, and faculty members, opened their doors and their hearts to my questions. They provided ideas, responded enthusiastically to mine, and gave me the opportunity to share time, meals, and concerns. I am deeply grateful to them for their interest in and enthusiasm for my work.

In 1990, the Women's Constructive Theology Seminar of the Catholic Theological Society of America began meeting formally at the time of the annual meeting. Elizabeth Johnson and I were the first two presenters. Her work, since published as *She Who Is: The Mystery of God in Feminist Theological Discourse* (New York: Crossroad, 1992), has helped to move forward the task of feminist critique and retrieval of the tradition. She and the other members of the seminar have continued to be very supportive of my work. I am grateful for the opportunity to have benefited from their comments on a much earlier version of the ideas developed here and to have participated in the ongoing work of the seminar. Another group,

Women Doing Theology, of Loyola University, responded to a draft of the first two chapters of this book, and I am grateful to them as well for their generous comments.

Many of my family, friends, and colleagues deserve particular mention for their help along the way. My mother, brother, sisters, and in-laws were kind enough to ask periodically how the book was going and to give encouragement. Many friends, too numerous to name, gave their encouragement and support, with meals, conversations, concerts, informal playing sessions, and generous ears. Carolyn Farrell and Fran Glowinski offered friendship, support, and feedback. Marcia Kurzynski and Laurie Cassidy were wonderful graduate assistants and were of invaluable assistance in suggesting and finding resources. Justus George Lawler has been a supportive and attentive editor. Anne E. Patrick generously read chapters 4 and 6 and provided helpful comments. Anne E. Carr graciously read the entire manuscript and gave encouragement as well as constructive criticism. Two close friends, and happily, colleagues as well, were more than generous in reading and responding at length to drafts of various chapters. I am deeply grateful to Patricia Beattie Jung of Loyola University Chicago and Cristina L. H. Traina of Northwestern University for their friendship, good humor, thoughtfulness, and critical insight.

This book is dedicated to the memory of two people close to me who died just as the writing was getting underway, and to my husband. My brother John fought a valiant battle with cancer and although he lost that battle, his courage, humor, and determination "never to give up" were an inspiration to me, his wife, friends, and our entire family, especially during the last months of his illness. My friend Ann also lost her brief battle with cancer. We had shared years of friendship, support, and theological reflection since our days together in graduate school. Ann was the coordinator of the Women's Constructive Theology Seminar and had encouraged me in my project for many years. I regret that she is not here to continue her own promising work.

My husband, William P. George, has been supportive of me and this work in more ways than I can count. He read much of the manuscript, and his theological insights and questions pushed me to think and rethink many of my ideas. We have not agreed on everything, but we have both learned much. His considerable editorial skills have contributed greatly to whatever clarity this book may possess, and his love, support, and encouragement have been immeasurable.

Chicago, May 1998

Women and the Sacraments: Method and Criteria

CHAPTER ONE

Sacraments and the Need for a Feminist Perspective

At the time of Lewis and Clark, setting the prairies on fire was a well-known signal that meant, "Come down to the water." It was an extravagant gesture, but we can't do less. If the landscape reveals one certainty, it is that the extravagant gesture is the very stuff of creation. After the one extravagant gesture of creation in the first place, the universe has come to deal exclusively in extravagances, flinging intricacies and colossi down aeons of emptiness, heaping profusions on profligacies with ever-fresh vigor. The whole show has been on fire from the word go. I come down to the water to cool my eyes. But everywhere I look I see fire; that which isn't flint is tinder, and the whole world sparks and flames.

— Annie Dillard[1]

Sister Margaret L., 52, is about to celebrate the twenty-fifth anniversary of her profession in her religious congregation. The usual practice in her community is to mark the anniversary with a Eucharist, followed by a reception with her community, family, and friends. But Sister Margaret, who works with immigrant families in the inner city, decides that instead of a traditional Eucharist, presided over by a priest, she wants to have a "banquet of thanksgiving," with her clients, congregation, family, and friends, in which she will give thanks to all for their support of her vocation and ministry. Preceding the banquet will be an informal, noneucharistic liturgy, prepared by her closest friends. Some of the sisters in her religious community are shocked that there will be no traditional celebration of

---

1. Annie Dillard, *Pilgrim at Tinker Creek* (New York: Harper & Row, 1974) 9.

Mass, and they arrange to be out of town on the weekend that Sister Margaret's anniversary party is scheduled. Sister Margaret is saddened, but not surprised, at their absence. Some weeks after the anniversary, the community gathers together to discuss the role of the Eucharist in their religious life. They can come to no resolution, and they decide to ask a feminist theologian to come and speak with them about this issue.

*   *   *   *   *

Anne M., 68, a widow, breaks her hip in an accident at home. A Roman Catholic, she is brought to the community hospital where she has surgery to set the broken bone, and where she will stay until she is transferred to a rehabilitation center. The hospital has a staff of chaplains from different denominations who share duties visiting patients. One day, Lisa P., an ordained Lutheran pastor, stops by Anne's room. They talk about Anne's life, her relationships with her deceased husband, her children and friends, and how she will cope with her broken hip. Lisa visits a few more times, and on their fourth visit, Anne finds herself confiding in Lisa some of her own failings in relation to her husband and children, as well as her hopes and concerns. Lisa listens, they pray together, and Lisa ends their visit by laying her hands on Anne's head and saying that God has forgiven her. For the first time in a long time, Anne feels touched by God's forgiveness, and later on she tells her daughter that her experience with the Lutheran pastor was her best confession ever.

*   *   *   *   *

At a national conference on Hispanic ministries in the U.S., the concerns of women expressed in preparatory documents are not included in the conference's official program of action for the future. Outraged by this omission, a small group of women decides to meet outside the cathedral where the closing liturgy is to take place. They gather together and begin reciting the rosary. As the conference participants arrive for the liturgy, almost all the women and many of the men join the women on the steps. Those inside the cathedral find that they cannot begin the liturgy until the gathering outside the front doors has finished the rosary. All of those on the steps outside feel energized by this decision, and walk into the liturgy determined to carry out their recommendations despite the official

conference's action. Many of the women involved in the rosary's recita-
tion felt that their action made the strongest liturgical statement of the
conference. As one participant put it, "the sacred was now outside with
us while we prayed in protest. And it was not until we marched inside
the church singing, until we brought the sacred inside with us, that the
planned opening prayer inside the church was able to start."[2]

* * * * *

A group of women from St. Scholastica's parish have met monthly over
the last seven years about issues that concern them. In the last few years,
the issue of women's ordination has been a particular concern. They have
read widely, and have invited members of the parish, including a feminist theologian (who is also a member of the group) to speak about the
theological and pastoral implications of official teaching. After the "Responsum" issued from Rome in November 1995 that declared the teaching
against women's ordination to be part of the "ordinary magisterium," and
thus infallible, the group decides to hold a vigil outside the church. They
gather on a cold Wednesday night, and read passages from the gospels
that include the resurrection appearance of Jesus to Mary Magdalen, the
anointing of Jesus by the unnamed woman, and selections from the writings of women from the past and present. Carrying lit candles, they then
recite the names of women who have been supportive or influential in
their lives. After the readings are over, each woman extinguishes her can-
dle. The local news stations carry a short report on the vigil, and the next
morning the pastor and his associate (a nun) receive a number of phone
calls asking when the group will next meet as well as calls denouncing the
group's action.

* * * * *

The story is told of a young priest who visits a religious education class
in his parish. "Does anybody know how many sacraments there are?" he
asks. "I do," "I do," the children cry out, waving their arms. The priest

---

2. The story is told by Ada María Isasi-Díaz, "*Mujerista* liturgies and the Struggle
for Liberation," in *Liturgy and the Body,* ed. Louis-Marie Chauvet and François Kabasele
Lumbala, *Concilium* 1995/3 (London and Maryknoll: SCM and Orbis Books, 1995) 107.

calls on a little girl to answer his question. She responds, "Seven for boys, and six for girls." The priest is speechless.

What this little girl knew, and what the women in the stories above know, is that one's gender makes a difference when it comes to the sacraments. *How* gender makes a difference is not the same in every case, but there is, in all these stories, both recognition of and resistance to the fact that the sacred is overwhelmingly, in Roman Catholicism, officially mediated through clerical men.[3] The issue of ordination is important in all these stories, but it is not the only factor. Many have come to see that there is something lacking in the institutional church's traditional sacramental celebrations. Many women (and men) are now finding ways of celebrating the presence of the sacred outside the official sacraments. While Margaret has a deep love for the church and for the Eucharist, she resents the fact that, unlike men's religious orders, women's congregations need to bring in someone who is not a member of their community for a eucharistic celebration. The Eucharist no longer symbolizes for her the unity of the church, but rather its divisions. Anne is a devout Catholic, but the pastor of her parish is a busy man, and not particularly comfortable around women. Her experience with Lisa's ministry got her thinking more about the ordination of women, an issue that she had thought before to be something that only "radical feminists" wanted. The women at the rosary protest are all churchgoers and active in ministry. Yet the failure of the conference to address their issues revealed to them how empty the closing liturgy would be without some kind of acknowledgment of their presence and concerns. By claiming ritual power, they challenged the traditionally central role of the Eucharist. And the women at the parish vigil realized that they needed to give witness to their pain and anger at the "official" church in a public way. Lighting the candles, reciting the names of remembered and forgotten women, was, like the action of the Hispanic women, a way of showing that their concerns were shared, public, and ritualized.

* * * * *

---

3. I say "overwhelmingly," but not completely, because lay persons can, in cases of emergency, administer the sacrament of baptism, and in the case of marriage the spouses administer the sacrament to each other. But the point is that clerical presence is assumed to be necessary for sacramental validity.

This book explores the difference that gender makes in relation to the sacraments, and to sacramental and liturgical theology. Informed and inspired by the insights of feminist theology, as well as some of the developments in post–Vatican II sacramental theology, my aim is to raise critical questions and to suggest creative possibilities for reflection on and celebration of the sacred in our lives, especially the lives of women. For nearly two millennia, women have been in the background of sacramental and liturgical celebrations. Prevented from assuming liturgical leadership roles because of misogyny and ideas of pollution and propriety, women are now claiming the public spaces of liturgy. And as women become more active in the sacramental life of the church and raise the cry for equal participation in all ministries, magisterial Roman Catholicism has hardened its position against women's full liturgical participation, now claiming that women's exclusion from ordination is part of the "infallible" teaching of the church.[4] Clearly the stakes are very high. Yet many public dissenters and private questioners are not willing to leave the church for other, more liberal, denominations.

One reason for their remaining in the tradition is a conviction, borne of the spirit of Vatican II, that *"we* are the church" — that the church is the whole people of God, and that the role of the laity (for all women, including nuns, are laity) is to be active participants in their church. But another reason, I will argue here, is a connection to the sacramental tradition of Roman Catholicism, a tradition that has always been larger than the official liturgical traditions, that finds the holy in the humblest of places, and that has always resonated within women's lives. This "hidden" or "implicit" sacramentality that women have long known and experienced is now becoming public. Along with the critical and constructive insights of feminist theology, it has the potential to subvert as well as to transform the sacramental life of the church.

Meanwhile, the institutional church is in a time of transition in relationship to the sacraments, due in large part to the "shortage" of ordained

---

4. See "Responsum to *Dubium* on Ordaining Women to the Ministerial Priesthood," *Origins* 25/24 (November 30, 1995). The statement issued by the Vatican on November 13, 1997, "Some Questions Regarding Collaboration of Nonordained Faithful in Priests' Sacred Ministry," (*Origins* 27/24, November 27, 1997) confirms the clear divisions between the ministries exercised by the faithful and the sacerdotal priesthood, and even forbids the "nonordained faithful to assume titles such as *pastor, chaplain, coordinator, moderator*" (article 1/3).

priests, but also due to a less legalistic understanding of the sacraments, a changed relationship to the institution, and a new sense of ritual power on the part of the laity. In the industrialized world, fewer and fewer men are entering seminaries or religious orders. The National Conference of U.S. Catholic Bishops has devised rubrics for "communion services" to be conducted in the absence of a priest.[5] Women are being appointed as pastoral coordinators and administrators in parishes where there are not enough clergy to staff full-time. While not ordained, they preach and distribute communion. And more and more women, and many lay men, inspired by the vision of Vatican II that all share together in the common priesthood, are studying theology in hopes of ministering in the church.[6] It is clear that how and why the church celebrates the sacraments, and understands its own sacramentality, is in the midst of great change. And women are at the center of this change.

The experiences and reflections of women pose fundamental challenges and opportunities to sacramental theology and practice. Theology from women's perspectives, as it has developed over the last thirty years, provides both vantage points from which to reinterpret the sacramental tradition, and plentiful resources for its transformation. In turn, a reinterpreted sacramental theology can provide important resources for feminist reflections on the body, worship, the nature of church and of human community.

SOURCES AND METHOD

Sacramental and liturgical theology are vast fields, complex, and often abstract. Until recent years, they were two relatively distinct areas of

---

5. See "Directory for Sunday Celebrations in the Absence of a Presbyter," *Origins* 18 (1988) 301–7.

6. *Lumen Gentium,* the dogmatic constitution on the church, *Vatican II: The Conciliar and Post-Conciliar Documents,* ed. Austin Flannery, O.P. (Collegeville, MN: Liturgical Press, 1975), #10: "Though they differ essentially and not only in degree, the common priesthood of the faithful and the ministerial or hierarchical priesthood are none the less ordered one to another; each in its own proper way shares in the one priesthood of Christ." What "sharing in the common priesthood" actually means is a topic of much debate. See, e.g., Susan Welch, "Priestly Identity: Sacrament of the Ecclesial Community," *Worship* 69 (March 1995) 109–27; Lawrence Welch, "Priestly Identity Reconsidered: A Reply to Susan Wood," *Worship* 70 (March 1996) 307–19.

scholarship. They have also been largely male-dominated fields. Feminist theological concerns have played an even smaller role in these disciplines than in other doctrinal areas, such as christology, theological anthropology, or moral theology.[7] Sacramental theology was, until relatively recently, tied more to canon law than to liturgy, and liturgy, in turn, was more concerned with rubrics than with ecclesiology.[8] The fact that sacramental liturgy is performed by clerics and requires episcopal approval for changes is one factor that might contribute to isolating sacramental theology from feminist concerns. It is also important to note that sacramental and liturgical theology are much more explicitly tied to the institutional church, where women have virtually no official voice or established authority. The most creative work in feminist theology has been in the academic fields of biblical, moral, systematic, and historical theology, as well as spirituality, where there are opportunities for women to participate fully in the disciplines. The narrow focus of the traditional concerns of sacramental and liturgical theology has broadened considerably since Vatican II, but there is still a long way to go before the questions that feminist theology raises are seen as central to the disciplines' self-understanding.[9] Moreover, these disciplines have only begun to explore their own fundamental theological assumptions, many of which are questioned by feminist theology.

Thus the use of mainstream Roman Catholic sacramental theology as one possible resource for a feminist sacramental theology poses serious questions: Are its assumptions about symbols, human nature, and

---

7. Catherine LaCugna comments in her introduction to *Freeing Theology: The Essentials of Theology in Feminist Perspective* (San Francisco: HarperSanFrancisco, 1993) 3: "Not all topics covered in this book are at the same point of development in terms of current scholarship, feminist or otherwise. A great deal more has been written about feminist biblical hermeneutics than about feminist sacramental theology."

8. See Bernard Leeming, *Principles of Sacramental Theology* (London: Longmans; Westminster, MD: Newman Press, 1960); Anthony F. Alexander, *College Sacramental Theology* (Chicago: Regnery, 1961).

9. A brief survey of some of the most widely used texts in sacramental theology reveals a decided lack of attention to issues of gender, apart from marriage and orders. See, e.g., Bernard Cooke, *Sacraments and Sacramentality* (Mystic, CT: Twenty-Third Publications, 1983); George S. Worgul, *From Magic to Metaphor: A Validation of the Christian Sacraments* (New York: Paulist, 1980); Michael G. Lawler, *Symbol and Sacrament: A Contemporary Sacramental Theology* (New York: Paulist Press, 1987); Joseph Martos, *Doors to the Sacred: A Historical Introduction to Sacraments in the Catholic Church* (Tarrytown, NY: Triumph Press, 1991).

the role of liturgy, valid for women as well as for men? Can they be valid if they are not so for both women and men? What texts, practices, traditions, are understood to be authoritative? What are the criteria by which sacramental practice, or reflection on practice, is understood to be authentically Christian? Such questions, and many others, suggest that any use of mainstream sacramental theology by feminist theologians needs careful scrutiny. When we turn to feminist theology as an explicit source for rethinking the sacraments, we have an additional set of issues to consider. One of the distinguishing features of feminist theology is its explicit starting point in the experiences of women.[10] In its early years, feminist theological reflection, at least in the academic context, was practiced by those who had the resources and education for such reflection — largely white, middle-class women. Their generalizations about the nature of "women's experience" revealed much about their own privileged social location, and frequently ignored the racial, ethnic, and class-related factors that impinged on the lives of most women in the world. Thus early debates over women's ordination concerned women's equality with men without fully considering the context of such equality.[11]

In the Roman Catholic tradition, women's invisibility from liturgy has become increasingly recognized as oppressive. Indeed, with the exception of the sacrament of marriage, in the official practice of the sacraments the presence of women is completely unnecessary. Of course, women have been present at liturgies throughout the church's long history, but this presence is carefully circumscribed — formerly explicitly excluded

---

10. This is a very complex issue: what experience is, and whose experience we are talking about. For some discussions of this issue, see Ada María Isasi-Díaz, "Experiences," in *The Dictionary of Feminist Theologies,* ed. Letty Russell and Shannon Clarkson (Louisville: Westminster John Knox Press, 1996) 95–96; idem, "Elements of a *Mujerista* Anthropology"; Ann O'Hara Graff, "The Struggle to Name Women's Experience"; and María Pilar Aquino, "Including Women's Experience: A Latina Feminist Perspective," all in *In the Embrace of God: Feminist Approaches to Theological Anthropology,* ed. Ann O'Hara Graff (Maryknoll, NY: Orbis Books, 1995).

11. For a representative early discussion, see *Women Priests: A Catholic Commentary on the Vatican Declaration,* ed. Leonard Swidler and Arlene Swidler (New York: Paulist Press, 1977). See also Elisabeth Schüssler Fiorenza, *A Discipleship of Equals: A Critical Feminist Ekklesia-logy of Liberation* (New York: Crossroad, 1993), especially "Should Women Aim for Ordination to the Lowest Rung of the Hierarchical Ladder," 23–38, where she argues that women's ordination ought first to be to the episcopacy, since without power at higher levels, ordained women would continue to be marginalized.

from the sanctuary, women are now, at best, a reluctant "last resort" for liturgical functions.[12]

Because of sacramental and liturgical theology's support for, or, at best, lack of concern about, women's official exclusion and invisibility, many women have not found in these disciplines the potential for inclusion, much less transformation. Instead, since the earliest groups of women began to gather together to reflect, share, and celebrate, they have turned to their own distinct experiences: bodily, familial, social, political, religious, and not primarily to church traditions. As Mary Collins has noted, feminist liturgies tend not to be text-based, but rather event-based, multiple, and particular.[13] Thus, "women's experiences" as a source for feminist theological reflection on the sacraments constitutes a multiple, diverse, and continually changing source. Unlike traditional sacramental theology, there is no clearly defined set of texts or practices that constitute a given for liturgical or sacramental reflection by and for women.

Indeed, even the term "feminist sacramental theology" is something of a misnomer, since much feminist reflection on women's rituals does not automatically privilege the sacraments as normative. As a theology of liberation, feminist theology subjects texts and traditions to a critical scrutiny for their emancipatory potential. Since the church's official liturgical celebrations have been so exclusive of women, women have turned to "unofficial" religious practices, to ways of celebrating, mourning, and remembering significant events in their lives that are on no liturgical calendar.[14]

---

12. This point is strongly reiterated in the November 1997 Vatican instruction (see n. 4, above). If clergy are available, lay men and women are not to distribute communion. And even though women are now permitted to be acolytes, there are still a few dioceses that forbid such practices, since their bishops fear that allowing girls in these roles will discourage boys from wanting to join the priesthood.

13. See Mary Collins, "Principles of Feminist Liturgy," in *Women at Worship: Interpretations of North American Diversity*, ed. Marjorie Procter-Smith and Janet R. Walton (Louisville: Westminster John Knox Press, 1993) 9–26; see also Heather Murray Elkins, *Worshiping Women: Re-Forming God's People for Praise* (Nashville: Abingdon, 1994).

14. Among the many resources available, see Rosemary Radford Ruether, *Women-Church: Theology and Practice of Feminist Liturgical Communities* (San Francisco: Harper & Row, 1985); Marjorie Procter-Smith, *In Her Own Rite: Constructing Feminist Liturgical Tradition* (Nashville: Abingdon Press, 1990); idem., *Praying With Our Eyes Open: Engendering Feminist Liturgical Prayer* (Nashville: Abingdon Press, 1995); Barbara Bowe, Kathleen Hughes, Sharon Karam, and Carolyn Osiek, *Silent Voices, Sacred Lives: Women's Readings for the Liturgical Year* (New York: Paulist Press, 1992); Diane Neu and Mary E. Hunt, *Women*

Given these considerations, the idea of proposing a feminist sacramental theology may seem to be a fruitless one. Yet I will argue in these pages that the long and rich, albeit distorted, exclusive, and misogynistic sacramental tradition is too valuable to be discarded entirely. There are dimensions of the sacramental tradition that can be, and in fact are, very much in line with the goals of feminist theology. Feminist thought has the potential not only to affirm in creative ways, but also to correct, clarify, subvert, and transform this tradition.

While my basic purpose is to undertake a feminist critique of sacramental theology, I do not intend the process to be entirely one-sided. It is surely the case that the sacramental tradition offers potential resources to feminist theology that need to be thoughtfully considered, such as a sense of continuity and tradition, a connection to the global church, long experience with ritual and pastoral practice. But the main assumption of this study is that feminist theologians are more aware of the strengths and weaknesses of the sacramental tradition than the tradition is of the insights of feminist theology.[15]

HISTORICAL CONSIDERATIONS

In Roman Catholicism, the sweeping liturgical changes following the Second Vatican Council had a profound effect on the entire church, but particularly on the laity. Influenced by the self-understanding developed at Vatican II, which emphasized that the church is the "people of God," clergy and laity found new ways — some inspired by ancient practices, some by cultural traditions heretofore excluded from "official" liturgy — of incorporating the laity in the liturgy. Yet little, if any, explicit attention was given by sacramental theology at the time to the role of women in the post–Vatican II church.[16] Women were now permitted to act in various ministerial capacities such as those of reader, cantor, eucharistic minister, and the like, which was a major shift in practice. But the

---

Church Celebrations (Silver Spring, MD: WaterWorks Press, 1990); Miriam Therese Winter, *Woman Prayer, WomanSong: Resources for Ritual* (Oak Park, IL: Meyer-Stone Books, 1987).

15. There are some exceptions to the general lack of attention to feminist theology by sacramental theologians, notably David Power. See his *The Eucharistic Mystery: Revitalizing the Tradition* (New York: Crossroad, 1992).

16. See, for example, the works mentioned in n. 9, above.

kind of thinking by and about women that has marked feminist theology over the last thirty years had, until recently, little if any influence on the liturgical changes following Vatican II. One might say that most of the *institutional* liturgical changes in both thinking and practice were put into place before feminist theology had sufficiently developed its own self-understanding and critique of ritual forms and of the assumptions of sacramental theology.

Yet as feminist theology has developed, women have been marking, celebrating, and remembering important events in their lives through new forms of liturgy, and they have been raising critical questions about traditional forms, especially the Eucharist. The development of the women's movement in both society and the churches was taking place as many of the official liturgical changes were being instituted. New ways of thinking about humanity, language, God, sin, grace, salvation, and the experiences of women have had an enormous impact on theological method and content.[17]

In the early 1970s, the question of the ordination of women brought many of these issues to a head. The Lutheran Church ordained its first women pastors in 1970. The Episcopal Church of the U.S. voted to ordain women in 1976, after the "irregular" ordination of eleven women by some retired bishops in 1974 forced the issue. Pope Paul VI responded in 1976 with the statement *Inter Insigniores,* the official Vatican Declaration on the Question of the Admission of Women to the Ministerial Priesthood, which asserted the "unbreakable" tradition of a male-only clergy.[18] Twenty years later, the issue is still provoking heated debate in the Roman Catholic tradition. Witness the dismissal of Sr. Carmel McEnroy from her tenured position at St. Meinrad Seminary in Indiana in 1995 for signing a statement calling for further discussion of the ordination of women.[19]

---

17. It would be impossible to list all the works that have been influential over the last thirty years. Some of the major works would be those of Anne Carr, Rosemary Radford Ruether, Elisabeth Schüssler Fiorenza, Elizabeth Johnson (in the Catholic tradition), and Letty Russell, Rebecca Chopp, Mary McClintock Fulkerson (in the Protestant tradition).

18. The text can be found in Swidler and Swidler, *Women Priests* (see n. 10, above).

19. See the *Proceedings of the Catholic Theological Society of America*, vol. 50 (1995) 321–22, for the society's response. See also Avery Dulles, S.J., "Gender and Priesthood: Examining the Teaching," *Origins* 25/45 (May 2, 1996) where the author urges the U.S. bishops to be stronger in advocating the official church teaching. The fact that the issue is not to be discussed raises a whole set of questions about church authority and community.

The significance of ordination and the complex history of the question notwithstanding, the point that I will be developing in this book is that the challenge of feminist thinking to sacramental theology lies not only in the argument for women's ordination. This is, to be sure, the most visible and significant way in which the challenge of feminist thinking to sacramental theology is found. In addition, the rich contributions of women to new forms of liturgical celebration cannot be understated.[20] Feminist, womanist, *mujerista,* and other forms of women's liturgical creativity have enriched immeasurably the lives of many and stretched the imaginations of the possibilities of liturgical practice. But the challenges to sacramental theology go deeper than ordaining women or having women-centered liturgies (although they involve these as well). They concern the ways in which we understand symbols, human nature, the world and how God is revealed in the world, and how the sacraments are tied to our lives as Christians in the world — in traditional Catholic terms, our moral lives. Feminist thinkers have just begun to explore the possibilities of a sacramental theology and practice transformed by feminism.

PROCESS AND RATIONALE

Thus the starting point for a feminist sacramental theology raises important and difficult methodological and historical issues. The ancient saying, *lex orandi, lex credendi,* rightly suggests that the place to begin reflection on the sacraments is in the context of worship.[21] Sallie Mc-Fague, in her *Metaphorical Theology,* argues that "the *primary context,* then, for any discussion of religious language is worship."[22] But such a statement raises deeper, more pressing questions. What or whose worship is the "primary context" for such theological reflection? The official wor-

---

For a probing analysis of this situation, see Anne E. Patrick, *Liberating Conscience: Feminist Explorations in Catholic Moral Theology* (New York: Continuum, 1996).

20. The best source here is *Women at Worship* (n. 13, above).

21. See, e.g., Kevin Irwin, *Context and Text: Method in Liturgical Theology* (Collegeville, MN: Liturgical Press, 1994) 3ff. See also Catherine M. LaCugna, *God for Us: The Trinity and Christian Life* (San Francisco: HarperSanFrancisco, 1991), and her response to J. R. Sachs in the *Proceedings of the Catholic Theological Society of America,* vol. 51 (1996) 39–44.

22. Sallie McFague, *Metaphorical Theology: Models of God in Religious Language* (Philadelphia: Fortress Press, 1982) 2. Emphasis in the original. McFague's point is echoed by many others; I will develop this further in chapter 7.

ship of the church? The liturgies designed by women's groups? For many women, *both* these worship experiences are important, yet differing theologies emerge from each. And what of the women (and men) who have become alienated from worship, in large part because of their resistance to a clericalized sacramental system?

My own starting points will involve both a reflection on what sacramental theologians refer to as a "fundamental sacramental theology,"[23] or a "general theory of sacramental life,"[24] as well as the liturgical practice of women, rather than a specific focus on the individual sacraments. My intent is to begin by acknowledging the revelatory character of the world, of human being, and deliberately to focus on the importance of the experiences of women. This starting point is also a critical feminist issue in its acknowledgment of the embodied character of all of sacramental and liturgical life.[25] In addition, the theological insights of the best of contemporary sacramental theology still need to be seriously scrutinized from a feminist perspective. What sacramentality involves, how we interpret symbols, and how we understand the experiential basis of the sacraments — all have serious implications for the lives of women.

Feminist liturgies play a very important role in feminist theory and practice. In feminist liturgical practice, reflection and liturgy go hand in hand, so the traditional distinction between sacramental and liturgical theology no longer holds firm.[26] Liturgies *are* theology, in that they deliberately give expression to relationships with others, the world, and God, and in their intentional subversion of patriarchal liturgy. Since feminist liturgies are explicitly tied to specific communities, it is impossible to make broad generalizations about any "standard" form of liturgical practice. All these factors make any kind of theological reflection on feminist liturgy a

---

23. See Louis-Marie Chauvet, *Symbol and Sacrament: A Sacramental Reinterpretation of Christian Existence,* trans. Patrick Madigan, S.J. (Collegeville, MN: Liturgical Press, 1995 [1987]).

24. See Kevin Irwin, "Recent Sacramental Theology," *The Thomist* 52 (January 1988) 125.

25. I simply note here that sacramental theology refers to human relations to God through the concrete, that is, particular objects and actions that have been designated by the church as sacred; liturgy refers more particularly to those formal and communal acts in which sacramentality is ritualized.

26. See David Power's comments on this in his review of feminist sacramental theology, "Sacramental Theology: A Review of Literature; Feminist Theology," *Theological Studies* 55 (December 1994) 657–704: "More than anywhere else, in feminist writing the boundary between liturgy and sacrament has all but disappeared" (694).

risky endeavor, and even more difficult when related to the discipline of sacramental theology. My reflections here will focus more on the nature of sacramentality than specific feminist liturgical practice, but the issues arising from women's liturgical experiences will play an important role. Thus, given the absence of feminist concerns from the side of traditional sacramental and liturgical theology, the complexity of the issues raised by appeals to "women's experience," and the diversity of new feminist liturgical practice, any attempt at formulating a feminist sacramental theology is fraught with difficulty.

But there are several reasons for pursuing such an endeavor. First, there are important connections and analogies between what I consider to be the basis for the sacraments — the sacramental principle — and the basic commitments of feminist theologians. These include a reverence for the created order and for embodiment. The pulse and energy of the created order itself eludes fixation in strict categories.

Second, feminist liturgies are, for the most part, not intended entirely to replace traditional liturgies, but, as liturgical theologian Mary Collins notes, to critique them, to offer alternative ways of reflecting on and celebrating significant life events.[27] Many Christian women remain connected, in various ways, to church communities — largely parishes, but also intentional base communities — that include men, children, and nonfeminist women, and they continue to draw on the message of Jesus as their theological basis, as well as many other traditional symbols. The work of women who are involved in parish sacramental ministry provides a source of wisdom for sacramental theology that needs to be tapped.

Third, there are a number of problematic issues in sacramental theology — the role of gender, the meaning of sacrifice, to name just two — that cannot be adequately addressed without an explicit dialogue with feminist theology. This conversation has just barely begun.[28] Without more explicit attention from feminist theologians, the discipline of sacramental theology will be impoverished, as it clings to outdated categories and practices.

And finally, the crisis of the sacraments in the church today — and I write here with particular reference to the church in the United States — is in essence an institutional and moral crisis. The crisis is institutional in the sense that personnel and morale issues are placing enormous stresses

---

27. See Mary Collins, "Principles of Feminist Liturgy," in Procter-Smith and Walton, *Women at Worship,* 11ff.

28. See Power, "Recent Sacramental Theology."

on parish and diocesan structures.[29] And it is moral in that the alienation of sacramental practice from structures of oppression continues to widen. The sacramental life of the church will wither without a full dialogue with the voices of women.

While the book's focus will be primarily on the Roman Catholic tradition, I will also draw upon the wisdom of other Christian traditions, many of which are also "sacramental" in their self-understanding and view of the world. The experiences of ordained women in other Christian denominations, especially as eucharistic presiders, can provide important clues for thinking about women's sacramental ministries. Often within feminist theology and praxis, confessional differences recede into the background when it comes to crucial issues such as the language we use to talk to and about God, justice for poor women and children, and transformation of oppressive structures in church polity. Ordination has been the issue that has generated the most heat within the Roman Catholic tradition, but this does not mean that Catholic women are "behind the times" when it comes to issues concerning justice for women. And, conversely, Protestant women have found that ordination does not solve the problems of institutionalized sexism that continue to plague even the most "liberal" of traditions.

In the background, as a further source for this work, are the conversations that I have had with a number of women engaged in parish sacramental ministry. This group does not constitute a data base in any social-scientific sense, since I am not a sociologist. But these women's thoughtful considerations of their lives and work both confirmed some of my own assumptions as well as challenged me to rethink, or think more deeply, about some of the ideas that I had about the nature of sacramentality, women's relation to the sacraments and to the institutional church. Their commitment to sacramentality, to their own local church communities, as well as to the broader world church, is truly striking.

With these methodological cautions in mind, I turn next to a discussion of what it means to be "sacramental," and how the Catholic tradition has valued sacramentality.[30] My point is intentionally to begin with a consideration of the sacrality of the world, which is what I understand the

---

29. See Tim Unsworth, *The Last Priests in America: Conversations with Remarkable Men* (New York: Crossroad, 1991).

30. By Catholic, I do not mean only the *Roman* Catholic tradition, but also those such as the Anglican and Lutheran traditions, which see sacramentality as one of their core values.

"sacramental principle" to imply. But this "sacramental principle" is, as I note below, not a Christian invention. It is grounded in a reverence for the world that is common to all religions, in one form or another, and is crucial to feminist thought, and recently, as well, to ecofeminism.

SACRAMENTALITY

It has long been acknowledged that sacramentality is a distinguishing dimension of the Catholic tradition. In his book *Catholicism,* Notre Dame theologian Richard P. McBrien remarks that "a major theological, pastoral, and even aesthetical characteristic of Catholicism is its commitment to the *sacramental principle.* . . . Everything is, in principle, capable of embodying and communicating the divine."[31] On the most fundamental level, the sacramental principle means that creation is sacred: all of life — human, animal, vegetable, mineral — is potentially revelatory of the divine and is to be treated as such. Such diverse theologians as Irenaeus of Lyons, Hildegard of Bingen, nineteenth-century poet Gerard Manley Hopkins, and David Tracy have described a "world charged with the grandeur of God" that acknowledges the inherent sacrality of the earth and its people.[32] Over the course of history, Catholicism has looked to the world to find "traces" of God. Thomas Aquinas wrote that we come to know God through God's "effects" in the world. His Franciscan contemporary Bonaventure referred to the "footprints" of God.[33] The tradition has long held a reverential place for the concrete ways in which God can be manifest through the material. Thus one can point to the "sacramentals," the historical veneration of

---

31. Richard P. McBrien, *Catholicism* (Minneapolis: Winston Press, 1980) 731. Emphasis in the original.

32. For Irenaeus, see his "The Refutation and Overthrow of the Knowledge Falsely So Called," in *Early Christian Fathers,* ed. Cyril C. Richardson, volume 1 of the Library of Christian Classics (New York: Macmillan, 1975); for Hildegard, see *Scivias,* trans. Columba Hart and Jane Bishop (New York: Paulist Press, 1990); for Hopkins, see "God's Grandeur" in *The New Oxford Book of English Verse,* ed. Helen Gardner (New York and Oxford, 1972) 786; for David Tracy, see *The Analogical Imagination: Christian Theology and the Culture of Pluralism* (New York: Crossroad, 1982).

33. For Thomas Aquinas, see *Summa Theologiae,* I, q. 2, a. 2: "Hence the existence of God, in so far as it is not self-evident to us, can be demonstrated by those of His effects which are known to us"; for Bonaventure, see *The Mind's Road to God* (Indianapolis: Bobbs-Merrill, 1953), chapter 2: "Of the Reflection of God in His Traces in the Sensible World."

relics,[34] the concern for visible expressions of one's piety such as processions, house blessings, devotions, veneration of the saints, and, in moral theology, a particular concern for the ways in which the human body can be seen to point toward God.[35] According to the sacramental principle, human beings find God not by leaving or denying the world, but by becoming immersed more deeply in it. This is not to say that God and the world are identical, but that God cannot be approached except *through* the world. God's mysterious and surprising presence is shot through the world, in the minute as well as the monumental, in the particular, and always in ways that escape exact classification.[36]

The sacramental principle, as already noted, is not an invention of Christianity. Human beings have always turned to the world and have developed symbols and rituals drawn from the world to express the indwelling of the sacred in their lives.[37] Karl Rahner's understanding of the "symbolic" character of human life expresses this well.[38] What distinguishes the Christian understanding of sacramentality is that it has taken historical form in the person of Jesus Christ. Sacramentality is not simply a general principle, but is itself constitutive of revelation. The traditional Catholic reliance on "natural law" as one basis for moral theology is analogous to the sacramental principle: there is not only a logic and order to creation (natural law) but a revelatory dimension to nature that goes beyond logic to an encounter with the source of life. In nature, and in historical existence, one can find God.[39]

---

34. See the work of Carolyn Walker Bynum, especially *The Resurrection of the Body in Western Christianity, 200–1336* (New York: Columbia University Press, 1995).

35. For such examples, there are more sources than can be mentioned here. See the work of Carolyn Walker Bynum (n. 34) for examples of women's piety and of veneration of relics and concern for the body; Robert Orsi's work, *Thank You, St. Jude: Women's Devotion to the Patron Saint of Hopeless Causes* (New Haven: Yale University Press, 1996); for moral theology, see Henry Davis, S.J., *Moral and Pastoral Theology,* 4 vols. (London: Sheed and Ward, 1935).

36. See, for example, Annie Dillard, *Pilgrim at Tinker Creek,* on a sense of sacred place, built on a sense of the sacredness of nature.

37. See Mircea Eliade's classic *The Sacred and the Profane: The Nature of Religion,* trans. Willard R. Trask (New York: Harcourt, Brace & World, 1957). Although Eliade's work is now considered by some in the field of the history of religions to be passé, his work has nevertheless had a powerful influence on generations of religious and theological scholars.

38. Karl Rahner, "The Theology of the Symbol," in *Theological Investigations IV,* trans. Kevin Smyth (London: Darton, Longman and Todd, 1974).

39. Here it needs to be said that an embrace of the sacramental principle without recog-

Sacramentality has at least the following three implications.[40] First, as McBrien emphasizes above, all of creation is potentially revelatory of the divine. Creation is *good*, and thus the Catholic tradition has officially condemned those movements throughout history that have looked upon material reality as intrinsically evil, as having fallen away from true spiritual reality, such as Jansenism.[41] In the early centuries of Christianity, a stress on the humanity of Christ was needed to counter those movements, like Gnosticism, which found the idea of the incarnation to be repugnant.[42] Yet, officially and unofficially, the sacramental principle has not been untouched or uninfluenced by the wider culture or by movements within the tradition itself that militate against this sacramentality. So while the tradition, on the one hand, has emphasized the goodness of creation and of the human body, it has also, on the other, ignored or countered this very principle to encourage an unhealthy asceticism and a suspicion of the body, especially the female body.[43] There has been a long thread of resistance to this sacramental principle in fear and revulsion toward the body and nature.

A number of examples suggest themselves to support this assertion: the prohibition of sexual relations before Eucharist, the valuation of celibacy over marriage, the imposition of clerical celibacy, the idea that sexual relations for pleasure alone are inherently sinful.[44] While the body and nature are good, they are not unambiguously so, and they are not under complete

---

nition of the ways in which sin has affected it raises serious questions and problems. David Tracy, relying on Paul Ricoeur, argues that manifestation (sacramentality) needs to be balanced by proclamation, which gives greater attention to the dialectical. See *The Analogical Imagination: Christian Theology and the Culture of Pluralism* (New York: Crossroad, 1982) 156ff. Or, to put it another way, as Paul Tillich described it, the "Catholic" sacramental principle needs to be balanced by the "Protestant" dialectical principle. See *The Dynamics of Faith* (New York: Harper & Row, 1957).

40. These implications are drawn from McBrien's presentation.

41. For helpful descriptions of early Christian antimaterialist movements, see Peter Brown, *The Body and Society: Men, Women and Sexual Renunciation in Early Christianity* (New York: Columbia University Press, 1988); for a sympathetic interpretation of Jansenism, see Leszek Kolakowski, *God Owes Us Nothing: A Brief Remark on Pascal's Religion and on the Spirit of Jansenism* (Chicago: University of Chicago Press, 1995).

42. See, Irenaeus, "Against Heresies."

43. See my entry, "Body," in *The New Dictionary of Catholic Spirituality*, ed. Michael Downey (Collegeville, MN: Liturgical Press, 1993) 93–100.

44. See John Mahoney, *The Making of Moral Theology: A Study of the Roman Catholic Tradition* (Oxford: Clarendon Press, 1987), especially 58ff. where he comments on the long shadow that Augustine's Manicheanism has cast on Catholic moral thinking on sexuality.

human control. We become sexually aroused despite our intentions not to; natural forces arise and erupt despite our careful planning. Nature is to be feared, and thus, controlled, so as to tame its potential to overwhelm us. In facing our embodiment, we face our vulnerability and mortality, as well as our capacity for exquisite pleasure and delight. Both an uncritical and naive glorification of creation, the body, and the cosmos, as well as fear and hatred of the sensual can overlook the ambiguity of creation, and can mask its complexity and subtlety. Illness, decay and death, as well as predatory behavior and chance occurrences, declare that the glory of creation is not always joyful, at least from a human perspective. Indeed, some theologians, like James M. Gustafson, have stressed the *theocentrism* of creation, and question whether human existence is truly central to God's plan for the cosmos.[45] In sum, the sacramental principle means that the divine is encountered in the earthly, but this encounter is always surprising, always a gift, and cannot be grasped without remainder.

Second, sacramentality is tied to the principle of *mediation* through the church.[46] That is, one's relationship to God is not purely individualistic, but is, as McBrien puts it, "corporate and communal."[47] The necessarily social dimension of human personhood is recognized in sacramentality. There are thus no "private" sacraments, since they are by definition ways in which the *community* recognizes and celebrates together how God is present in their midst, in and through the very realities with which we exist, and in and through human relationships.[48] The church's own sacramentality precedes the individual sacraments themselves as the community in which they have taken shape. Yet in practice, the corporate and communal dimension of sacramentality can assume an institutional form that overdetermines sacramentality. Sacramental practices and traditions can become detached from the ongoing and developing life of the community, as the institutional church seeks to maintain uniformity and validity and, often, control. Institutions can — and in fact do — take on lives of their own, becoming more concerned with bureaucracy and less with creative growth. In this inevitably human and sinful process, sacramentality can

---

45. See James M. Gustafson, *Ethics from a Theocentric Perspective,* 2 vols. (Chicago: University of Chicago Press, 1981–84).

46. McBrien, 733

47. Ibid., 731.

48. See, e.g., Edward Schillebeeckx's concern for "encounter" in *Christ the Sacrament of the Encounter with God,* trans. N. D. Smith (New York: Sheed and Ward, 1957) 3.

(and, in some cases, has) become more a legal than a liturgical concern. Institutionalization, while a necessary process of preservation over time, can also suck the lifeblood out of symbol and sacrament. Communities thus need to be open to the new, to the surprising, to growth, while preserving the best of the tradition, always a difficult and ambiguous process.

Third, sacramentality is tied to what Christians broadly call the "event of Jesus Christ." Not only is creation good because God created it so, but creation has a special relation to God since God has come to share fully in our humanity. As John's Gospel puts it, God has "pitched a tent" among us. God is not "up there" or "out there" but here in our very midst, knowing what it is to suffer and die. Thus the life, death, and resurrection of Jesus Christ have special significance in that Christians find the source of the sacraments in his very life, and in his actions and example. God's taking on flesh for our sake has transformed a general sense of sacrality, often expressed mythically, to a historical reality.[49] Sacraments are "saving events," rooted in the life and death of Christ. God's extravagant gift of God's self to us is at the root of all the sacraments. Yet the example of Christ can be used to validate practices and rules that may never have been imagined in the first century, as well as to support conceptions of sacrifice and atonement that have questionable scriptural roots as well as potentially harmful effects on people's lives. The words and actions of Jesus can be, and have been, taken out of their historical and narrative context to justify present-day rules and practices.[50] In the past, the issue of the Christ's "institution" of the sacraments was the way in which this problem played out; more recently, it has been the "historical example" of Christ that becomes the criterion for valid sacramental practice.[51] For

---

49. See David Power, *Unsearchable Riches: The Symbolic Nature of Liturgy* (New York: Pueblo, 1984) 94, where he emphasizes the "turn to the word."

50. As is the case with the way in which the Catholic tradition argues against the ordination of women — that the intention of Jesus was to "ordain" only men. See "Declaration on the Question of the Admission of Women to the Ministerial Priesthood," in Swidler and Swidler, ed., *Women Priests*, 37ff.

51. It is interesting to note how the "historical example" of Jesus has become one of the main criteria for the exclusion of women from ordained ministry as it is argued by the Vatican. For Aquinas, women were excluded because of their inferiority to men. In the 1976 Vatican "Declaration on the Admission of Women," the church deemed itself unable to permit the ordination of women because they lacked a "natural resemblance" to the person of Christ in his maleness. More recently, Jesus' purported "intention" to "ordain" only men has become the main reason. See "Declaration," in Swidler and Swidler, *Women Priests*, 44 (#32).

feminist theology, developing an adequate christology has been one of its most serious challenges.[52]

Thus the bases of Christian sacramentality — its rootedness in the revelatory character of creation, its communal dimension, and its connection to the life of Jesus the Christ — are not without the potential to undermine their very power. Sacramentality is an inherently *ambiguous* reality, and the dangers of overstating either its disclosive or concealing powers are great. My point is to underscore the significance of sacramentality as a fundamental principle of the Christian tradition, yet at the same time to highlight its *ambiguity*. That is, sacramentality means that created reality *both* reveals *and* conceals the presence of God.[53] Sacraments are a dimension of finite human existence and thus sacramentality is, by definition, fluid, in that the concrete reality at issue points *both* to itself *and* beyond itself. There is both an opacity and a transparency to the sacraments, as there is to human life.

Sacramentality is also related to culture and to history. Things come to be understood as revelatory of the divine not by some intrinsic characteristic of their own (although there are more and less appropriate characteristics and some limitations that may predispose some things to be symbolic more than others) but rather, largely, through their cultural and historical relation to a people and their traditions. This is why the study of history is so important for sacramental theology. Without an understanding of context, sacraments can become detached from their times, and, therefore, their root meanings. Indeed, history is not simply a context for the sacraments; the sacraments are themselves historical, emerging from particular circumstances, related to concrete events in human life.

In addition to the inherent ambiguity and historicity of the sacraments, there is also their relation to the lives of the people for whom and with whom they are celebrated. Liberation theology has been most insistent in asking how the Eucharist relates to the hunger of the world,[54] how rec-

---

52. See Mary Catherine Hilkert, "Key Religious Symbols: Christ and God," *Theological Studies* 56/2 (June 1995) 341–52.

53. See Paul Ricoeur, *The Rule of Metaphor,* trans. Robert Czerny (Toronto: University of Toronto Press, 1979).

54. See, e.g., Juan Luis Segundo, *The Sacraments Today,* trans. John Drury (Maryknoll, NY: Orbis Books, 1974); Monika Hellwig, *The Eucharist and the Hunger of the World* (New York: Paulist Press, 1976); Tissa Balasuriya, *The Eucharist and Human Liberation* (Maryknoll, NY: Orbis Books, 1979; Joseph A. Grassi, *Broken Bread and Broken Bodies: The Lord's Supper and World Hunger* (Maryknoll, NY: Orbis Books, 1985).

onciliation relates to the need for justice, how baptism incorporates one into a new community of faith. Edward Schillebeeckx's conception of the sacraments as "anticipatory signs" of the eschatological future and Juan Luis Segundo's effort to root the sacraments in the life of the Christian community are but two examples that explicitly relate the sacraments to justice.[55] Given the transformation of sacramental theology in the post–Vatican II years, from one based on a sacred/secular vision of the cosmos to a more holistic understanding, sacramentality no longer symbolizes a "higher" transcendent realm, beyond present human life, but rather the transformative possibilities for a fully human life now. The hunger of the world is for spiritual food, yes, but also a hunger for nourishing and sustaining food, for clean water, for the truth.[56]

The significance of ambiguity, the cultural/historical dimension, and the relationship of sacraments to lived experience have been underemphasized in the Christian sacramental tradition, to its detriment. Instead, sacramentality has been "fixed" in certain forms — most particularly in the seven "official" sacraments — but also in ways of thinking about the sacred that rule out its potential to be revealed in new or seemingly inappropriate places. Over the course of history, this constricted form of thinking has most often been expressed in *dualisms:* of soul/body, sacred/secular, spiritual/material, male/female. In dualistic thinking, reality is artificially divided into two related but quite distinct segments, and the distinctions between these two are held firmly, if not rigidly. Overwhelmingly, one of the dual realities is valued over the other. This has been the dominating tendency in the history of Roman Catholic sacramental theology as the sacred/sacramental comes to be valued over the secular/profane/natural. Rather than the complexity that ought to characterize the relation between the sacramental and the natural, highlighting a particular time and its relation to the life of the individual and the history of the community, the sacramental takes on a life of its own, detached from its natural and historic roots, and lacking its multivalent meanings. In Weberian terms, the sacred becomes "routinized."[57]

---

55. Edward Schillebeeckx, *Christ: The Experience of Jesus as Lord,* trans. John Bowden (New York: Seabury Press, 1979).

56. See Heather Elkins, *Worshiping Women* (n. 13, above).

57. See Max Weber, *The Sociology of Religion,* trans. Ephraim Fischoff (Boston: Beacon Press, 1964) 46–56.

Arguably, this was not the original intent of the early church, nor is it what sacramentality intends. Regis Duffy has argued that, since Augustine, the church has suffered from a difficulty in "thinking symbolically."[58] Given the tendency in Western thought to make clear distinctions, the kind of "binocular" vision required of symbolic thinking has been less valued. As Duffy defines it, "symbolic thinking is concerned more with the larger purposes of God's mystery as revealed in Christ than with the impossible task of explaining how a mystery works."[59] But from early on in the church's history, the need to explain, to distinguish, and even to exclude, often overrode the "larger purposes of God's mystery." Numerous controversies, notably those concerning the "real presence" of Christ in the Eucharist, witness to this need for clarity often at the expense of a sense of mystery; they have also served to divide the church.[60]

Symbolic thinking requires, as Duffy says above, that we take a "larger" view of the ways in which God works in human life. This "larger" view requires as well that we take account of an understanding of reality that is less sanguine about its ability to fully grasp its structures. Thus the "linguistic turn" of the postmodern world has pointed to the human inability to know absolutely. Recent sacramental theology, especially that of French theologians Louis-Marie Chauvet and Jean-Luc Marion, has explicitly rejected the metaphysical bases for sacramental theology in favor of a vision of reality that sees the sacraments as icons and as gifts, not fully comprehensible in any human way.[61]

I will argue in this book that feminist theology breaks open many of the strictures and limitations of sacramental theology, while strengthening the essential point that the sacraments are ways in which human beings, in faith, recognize God's extravagant affections for humankind and celebrate them. Drawing on the most basic of human experiences — birth, maturity,

---

58. See Regis Duffy, "The Sacraments," in *Systematic Theology: Roman Catholic Perspectives*, ed. John Galvin and Francis Schüssler Fiorenza (Minneapolis: Fortress Press, 1991) 191.

59. Ibid.

60. See, e.g., Gary Macy, *Theologies of the Eucharist in the Early Scholastic Period: A Study of the Salvific Function of the Sacrament According to the Theologians, c. 1080–c. 1220* (Oxford: Oxford University Press, 1984).

61. Although I would argue that neither Chauvet's nor Jean-Luc Marion's sacramental theologies is particularly open to feminist perspectives. For Chauvet (see n. 23, above); for Marion, see *God Without Being: Hors-Texte*, trans. Thomas Carlson (Chicago: University of Chicago Press, 1991).

spousal union, sin and reconciliation, vocation, a shared meal, and, per-haps, others — the sacraments are in turn an invitation to look to others and to the wider world for more signs of God.

"The extravagant gesture is the very stuff of creation." So too is it of re-demption. In these reflections, I draw on feminist theology to bring spark and flame to some very ancient beliefs and practices. In so doing, the rich-ness of this tradition can be released from the jars in which it is held, flowing freely to grace our lives.

CHAPTER TWO

Feminist Theology and Sacramental Theology

Yet to be faithful to ourselves and to our God, we must allow our analogies to break open and encircle us, to lead us in the dance from, into, and out of ourselves towards the riotous plenty that is God. We must risk the overmuch, trust the unfamiliar. For only here, in this precarious place, is love, and we will only know and taste it when we yield ourselves fully.

— Ann O'Hara Graff[1]

The multifaceted issue of what to call or how to approach what I name here as "feminist theology" has concerned women theologians for at least the last twenty years. The term "feminist theology," in its broadest meaning, encompasses a variety of approaches that revolve around the significance of the perspectives of women. But the issue of what to call theology from women's perspectives has become a point of contention among women theologians. For some U.S. Hispanic and African-American women theologians, as well as women theologians from non-Western countries, the term connotes a theology of and for white, middle-class women. Ada María Isasi-Díaz has coined the term *mujerista* for theology from U.S. Hispanic women's perspectives. African-American women theologians have claimed Alice Walker's term "womanist" as a name for theology rooted in the experiences of women of African descent.[2] The term "fem-

---

1. Ann O'Hara Graff, "The Struggle to Name Women's Experience," in *The Embrace of God: Feminist Approaches to Theological Anthropology* (Maryknoll, NY: Orbis Books, 1995) 85.
2. The literature on how to talk about women and theology is enormous. For some of the more important books and essays on the subject, see: Ada María Isasi-Díaz, Elena

inist" remains a problematic term: humorously referred to as "the new F word," a term that young women are reluctant to use for fear of being thought of as "man-hating," often joined with the term "radical" — one wonders why the term survives.

With some misgivings and hesitation, I choose to use the term, qualified where I think necessary. First, the term "feminist" describes the perspective that I have claimed for myself over the last twenty years. For ill or for good, the term has come to be identified with white, Western women. I cannot speak *for mujeristas* or for womanists, although I consider myself privileged as well as obligated to be in conversation with them. The issue of women's ordination in the Catholic Church has also been identified as a "white woman's issue." This is not to say that the issues I discuss in this book are relevant only for white, middle-class women (although I anticipate that this objection might be made). But many of the perspectives that I draw upon in support of my arguments are also identified as feminist. Thus I claim the term, aware of its limitations and problems, as well as the acknowledgment that "feminist" no longer connotes only one way of thinking.[3]

Second, the term is also used in international contexts (for example, the Concilium series on feminist theology), although, here again, not without some discussion and reluctance on the part of non-Western and nonwhite women.[4] The term "feminist" denotes a standpoint taken *for* women, and thus has an ideological connotation that the term "theology by women" lacks. In addition, substituting "theology by and for women"

Olazagasti-Segovia, Sandra Mangual-Rodriguez, Maria Antonietta Berriozabal, Daisy L. Machado, Lourdes Arguellas, and Raven-Anne Rivero, "*Mujeristas:* Who We Are and What We Are About," *Journal of Feminist Studies in Religion* 8/1 (spring 1992) 105–25; "Round-table Discussion: Christian Ethics and Theology in Womanist Perspective," *Journal of Feminist Studies in Religion* 5/2 (summer 1990) 83–112; Rita Nakashima Brock and Naomi Southard, "The Other Half of the Basket: Asian American Women and the Search for a Theological Home," *Journal of Feminist Studies in Religion* 3/2 (fall 1987) 135–49; Delores S. Williams, "Womanist Theology: Black Women's Voices," *Christianity and Crisis* (March 2, 1987).

3. See Susan Frank Parsons, *Feminism and Christian Ethics* (Cambridge: Cambridge University Press, 1996); *The Dictionary of Feminist Theologies,* ed. Letty Russell and Shannon Clarkson (Louisville: Westminster John Knox Press, 1996); for some helpful "secular" literature, see Alison Jaggar, *Feminist Politics and Human Nature* (Totowa, NJ: Rowman and Allenheld, 1983); Josephine Donovan, *Feminist Theory: The Intellectual Traditions of American Feminism* (New York: Continuum, 1985, 1992).

4. *Feminist Theology in Different Contexts,* ed. Elisabeth Schüssler Fiorenza and M. Shawn Copeland (Glenrock, NJ and Maryknoll, NY: Concilium/Orbis Books, 1996).

would limit the term's use and application to women by excluding pro-feminist men, further marginalizing feminist theology's critique of the theological endeavor as a whole. Janet Kalven has recently coined the term "women-defined theologies" as a way of encompassing a global perspective on women that is more inclusive than the terms "feminist," "womanist," or *mujerista*. While I find this term helpful, I am reluctant to add another qualifying term to the plethora of names for theologies. I intend deliberately feminism's ideological connotation and its wider impact. I do not intend my use of "feminist theology" to be all-inclusive, however. I draw on womanist and *mujerista* theologies throughout this book, as well as the experiences of women (and men) who may not consider themselves to be theologians at all, or who would not use the term feminist, but who nevertheless are concerned with feminist theology's issues.

At points like these in feminist works, it has also become customary to acknowledge one's own "social location" so as to make clear the limitations of a given perspective. My own is typical of many who call themselves "feminist" theologians: white, middle-class, well educated, married, heterosexual. This acknowledgment of my own situation may well help explain some of the choices I make or conclusions that I draw, but I do not intend by this to suggest that this book has relevance *only* for those like me, or worse, that this acknowledgment means that the situation of women of color, or of lesbian women, for example, is not relevant to my own thinking. At its best, such an acknowledgment means that the author makes no claims for universal validity. But I do mean this book to invite further conversation on these issues, among women and men concerned about the sacraments. Since sacramental theology does make universal claims about human sinfulness and grace, about communal contexts, my hope is that, while my own social location may well qualify what I have to say, my claims will be taken seriously from all persons concerned about the symbolic and ritual dimension of human existence.

As I shall use the term, feminist theology involves both a critical and a constructive perspective. Elizabeth Johnson provides a helpful summary of the tasks of feminist theology: "feminist theology engages in at least three interrelated tasks: it critically analyzes inherited oppressions, searches for alternative wisdom and suppressed history, and risks new interpretations of the tradition in conversation with women's lives."[5] In relationship to

[margin annotation: 3 Tasks of FT]

---

5. Elizabeth A. Johnson, *She Who Is: The Mystery of God in Feminist Theological Discourse* (New York: Crossroad, 1992), 29.

sacramental theology, Christian feminist theology can be said to share its basic principles: the inherent sacrality of the natural world and of humanity, the recognition of the communal dimension of human life, and the central significance of the life and death of Jesus Christ. Feminist theology's critical analysis of these basic principles, however, stresses particular dimensions: it raises up the inherent sacrality of all life, but especially of women, children, and the most vulnerable;[6] it emphasizes an understanding of human communal life as interdependent;[7] and it sees the significance of the life and death of Jesus as inclusive, destabilizing, and nonhierarchical.[8]

FEMINIST THEOLOGY AND SACRAMENTAL THEOLOGY

Feminist theology shares with the Christian tradition a reverence for the earth and for the body, with regard to the "goodness" and revelatory power of creation. All of creation is potentially revelatory of God and has intrinsic worth, not just that worth bestowed by humans. The natural bodily processes of human beings are seen to be good — especially including sexuality. One of feminist theology's most important contributions to the discipline has been its disclosure of ways in which women, the human body, and the natural world have been, at best, relegated to a lower position in relation to men and the spiritual, and at worst, seen to be inherently evil. Among feminist theologians, Rosemary Radford Ruether has

---

6. For literature touching on the body and the natural world, see Christine E. Gudorf, *Body, Sex and Pleasure: Reconstructing Christian Sexual Ethics* (Cleveland: Pilgrim Press, 1994); Paula M. Cooey, *Religious Imagination and the Body: A Feminist Analysis* (New York: Oxford University Press, 1994); Rosemary Radford Ruether, *Gaia and God: An Ecofeminist Theology of Earth Healing* (San Francisco: HarperSanFrancisco, 1992); Elizabeth A. Johnson, *Women, Earth and Creator Spirit* (New York: Paulist Press, 1993); Sallie McFague, *The Body of God* (Minneapolis: Fortress Press, 1993).

7. The work of feminist ethicists is notable here: See especially Margaret A. Farley, *Personal Commitments: Beginning, Keeping, Changing* (San Francisco: Harper & Row, 1986); Katie Cannon, *Black Womanist Ethics* (Atlanta: Scholars Press, 1988); Lisa Sowle Cahill, *Sex, Gender and Christian Ethics* (Cambridge: Cambridge University Press, 1996).

8. Notable here is Elisabeth Schüssler Fiorenza. Among her many works, see *Jesus: Miriam's Child, Sophia's Prophet: Critical Issues in Feminist Christology* (New York: Continuum, 1994) 12–18 for her understanding of "kyriarchal"; these particular terms come from Sallie McFague in *Models of God: Theology for an Ecological, Nuclear Age* (Philadelphia: Fortress Press, 1987) 48.

consistently pointed out the interrelationship of multiple forms of oppression, and has linked a fear and suspicion of women with similar attitudes toward, for example, people of color, Jews, and the earth. A positive regard for the material dimensions of reality has been a point that feminist theology takes pains to emphasize.[9]

On the other hand, there are certain points at which feminist theology is critical of the sacramental principle, especially as it has been developed in the Christian tradition. The Roman Catholic tradition in particular has tended to see certain dimensions of human life, especially sexuality, as bearing an enormous amount of metaphysical and moral weight. The "complementarity" of women and men, a term adopted by the Roman Catholic magisterium to describe how the different qualities of being male or female enhance the other sex, feminist theologians argue, is too often understood apart from the socio-historical dimensions of gender. Further, for the magisterium, in matters of sexuality there is "no small matter," which forecloses the pluralism of morality allowed for such other moral issues as war and economic justice.[10] In this case the point of feminist theology is to locate sacramentality in the lived context of human life, and not in an idealized and otherworldly reality. Thus any understanding of "experience" in feminist theology needs to be especially careful to acknowledge economic and social location.[11]

The goodness of the body means especially a valuing of those who are the most vulnerable, the least able to "separate" themselves from the concrete circumstances of their lives — children, the poor, the ill. Hence a reverence for creation means a revaluation of what the body is and means. Here, James Nelson's ways of thinking about the body are helpful:

---

9. See *Embodied Love: Sensuality and Relationship as Feminist Values,* ed. Paula M. Cooey, Sharon Farmer, and Mary Ellen Ross (San Francisco: Harper & Row, 1987); see also Margaret Farley, "Feminist Theology and Bioethics," in *A Reader in Feminist Ethics,* ed. Lois M. Daly (Louisville: Westminster John Knox, 1994). See also María Pilar Aquino, *Our Cry for Life: Feminist Theology from Latin America* (Maryknoll, NY: Orbis Books, 1993).

10. See Christine E. Gudorf, "If You Want a Seamless Garment, Use a Single Piece of Cloth: The Abortion Debate," in *The Public Vocation of Christian Ethics,* ed. Beverly W. Harrison and Robert L. Stivers (New York: Pilgrim Press, 1986); William P. George, "War and Other Issues," Core Nine Lecture, St. Joseph College, Rensselaer, IN, March 1994.

11. See Ada María Isasi-Díaz, "Experiences," *The Dictionary of Feminist Theologies,* ed. Letty M. Russell and Shannon Clarkson (Louisville: Westminster John Knox, 1996); Ann O'Hara Graff, "The Struggle to Name."

> Body theology starts with the fleshy experience of life — with our hungers
> and our passions, our bodily aliveness and deadness, with the smell of coffee,
> with the homeless and the hungry we see on our streets, with the warm
> touch of a friend, with bodies violated and torn apart in war, with the scent
> of honeysuckle or the soft sting of autumn air on the cheek, with bodies
> tortured and raped, with the bodyself making love with the beloved and
> lovemaking with the earth.[12]

The ecofeminist perspective contributes to this understanding by pointing out the human body needs to be seen in its *wider context* — both
natural and social, with an eye to what it takes for all human bodies to
flourish. So there is in feminist theology a profound valuation of the body,
but also a sober and realistic view of what we mean when we talk about
the body and the ecology of human life.[13] Womanist and *mujerista* theologians are especially concerned that any celebration of the body not be a
romanticization of privileged white bodies.

Second, feminist theology shares a concern for the communal dimension of human personhood and knowledge. As noted above, sacraments
make sense only in a communal context and are ultimately related to the
church as fundamental sacrament. God's presence, we recall, is always *mediated* through the community. Feminist theology's contribution here is a
revised emphasis on the sacraments' relationship to the community. Like
all ritual actions, sacraments arise out of a community's shared memory.
But memory can be selective. And in the Christian tradition, the memory
of women's contributions has nearly been erased. Women's discipleship
has been (mis)translated and (mis)interpreted so as to render it invisible.
The massive effort of feminist biblical scholarship over the last thirty
years has begun to address these contributions, and to recall, in the title of
Elisabeth Schüssler Fiorenza's work, that the gospel is to be preached "in

---

12. James E. Nelson, *Body Theology* (Louisville: Westminster John Knox Press, 1992) 42–
43; I quote here Patricia Beattie Jung on the positive nature of defecation: "I view it as
wondrous...an incredible filtration system, which in Asia becomes part of the fertilizer
used in rice fields — I think of it more like menstruation (truly ambiguous) than illness
(really negative) — I suppose it comes down to how we were toilet trained!" (personal
correspondence).

13. Note here the critical comments made by women of color to white women's focus on
ecology without regard to social situation. See "Ecology is a Sistah's Issue Too: The Politics
of Emergent Afrocentric Ecowomanism," in *Ecofeminism and the Sacred*, ed. Carol J. Adams
(New York: Continuum, 1993).

memory of her" — the nameless woman who anointed the head of Jesus.[14] Such a recollection also brings to mind the countless unnamed and invisible women who have baked communion bread, sewn and embroidered vestments, taught children. Their prayers encouraged reconciliation among families and communities, nursed the ill, mourned the dead. Feminist theology recalls that women are intrinsic to community, that women are community leaders and builders. Community is especially central in the lives of womanist and *mujerista* theologians, who have taken great pains to point out that all too frequently, feminist theologians have implicitly assumed an individualist understanding of the self, apart from family and community. Indeed, sacramental practice in Hispanic communities is not conceivable apart from the family, and particularly apart from women.[15]

How community is defined and understood is also crucial. In *Lumen Gentium*, Vatican II's dogmatic constitution on the church, the church is defined both as the "people of God" and as a hierarchical institution. The laity of the church have taken this former understanding quite seriously, and have transformed their roles from passivity to activity at increasing levels of the church. Yet the hierarchal bias of the church remains strong and seems to have taken priority over other models of church. For women, all of whom are lay, including religious women, participation in the church is active, but is constricted by institutional theories of gender complementarity.[16] This means that women's sacramental relationships are, officially, mediated through clerical men. Conceptions of the church which stress hierarchical power structures — in Elisabeth Schüssler Fiorenza's term, "kyriarchy" — are suspect from a feminist perspective, since such structures almost always privilege men over women, rich over poor, and are, in turn, mistrustful of the knowledge of the community.[17]

Feminist conceptions of self and community challenge the hierarchical model of relationships that tend to characterize the magisterial Catholic

---

14. Elisabeth Schüssler Fiorenza, *In Memory of Her: A Feminist Theological Reconstruction of Christian Origins* (New York: Crossroad, 1983).

15. See Ada María Isasi-Díaz, *Mujerista Theology: A Theology for the Twenty-First Century* (Maryknoll, NY: Orbis Books, 1996).

16. While women religious are technically "lay," they are sometimes treated as if they were clergy in disciplinary matters. See Margaret A. Farley, "Power and Powerlessness: A Case in Point," *Proceedings of the Catholic Theological Society of America* 37 (1982) 116–19; see Anne E. Patrick's discussion of this case in *Liberating Conscience: Feminist Explorations in Catholic Moral Theology* (New York: Continuum, 1996) 45–48.

17. Schüssler Fiorenza, *Miriam's Child*, 12–18.

understanding of church as community. In contrast, the feminist principle of *mutuality* suggests an egalitarian model for community.[18] This principle also demands that human beings not see themselves in isolation from each other, but rather in positions of mutual responsibility. Inspired by Jesus' disdain for traditional authority structures and his privileging of the lowest, along with a critical understanding of ideas of equality that attempt to overcome individualism, feminist theologians argue that mutuality is both more in line with the structures of the early Christian community and more adequate to a contemporary sense of the interdependent self. This means that feminist theology is committed to struggle against all forms of domination. But it is also necessary that feminist theology take a realistic and critical view of relationship and connection, being careful not to romanticize the relational.[19]

Third, feminist theologians have criticized the ways in which the life and death of Jesus Christ have been interpreted as meaningful for the Christian community. As noted above, Sallie McFague has described the ministry of Jesus as destabilizing, inclusive, and nonhierarchical.[20] By challenging rules and regulations, by including the rich as well as the marginalized in his table fellowship, and by debunking forms of hierarchical authority, Jesus set an example for his followers. Elisabeth Schüssler Fiorenza has similarly argued that Jesus was opposed to all forms of "kyriarchal" power. Traditional ideas of atonement that glorify selflessness and suffering have also been challenged by numerous feminist and womanist theologians.[21] Thus the life, death, and resurrection of Jesus have been reinterpreted: while not dismissing the doctrines of salvation, grace, and atonement, feminist (as well as other contemporary) theologians have placed Jesus' life into its historical and social context, as much as is

---

18. See Anne Patrick's development of a feminist-egalitarian model for church in *Liberating Conscience.*

19. Especially helpful on this point is Karen Lebacqz's essay, "Love Your Enemy: Sex, Power and Christian Ethics," in Daly, ed. *Feminist Theological Ethics,* 244–61.

20. See McFague, *Models of God,* 48.

21. Much as the cross and the role of suffering have been criticized by feminist theologians, there is a movement to pay renewed attention to these central symbols. See, e.g., Cynthia S. W. Crysdale, "Feminist Theology: Ideology, Authenticity, and the Cross," *Église et Théologie* 28 (1997) 245–63; M. Shawn Copeland, "'Wading Through Many Sorrows': Toward a Theology of Suffering in Womanist Perspective," in *A Troubling in My Soul: Womanist Perspectives on Evil and Suffering* (Maryknoll, NY: Orbis Books, 1993) 109–29; Sally B. Purvis, *The Power of the Cross: Foundations for a Christian Feminist Ethic of Community* (Nashville: Abingdon Press, 1993).

possible.[22] Salvation is no longer seen as otherworldly redemption, grace becomes deobjectified and reinterpreted in dynamic and relational terms, and atonement is no longer seen as the appeasement of an angry God.[23] Indeed, the very terms "salvation," "grace," and "atonement" are subject to critical scrutiny. The meaning of sacraments as "saving events" is not dismissed by feminist theologians, then, but rather redefined. In particular, understandings of Eucharist as sacrifice have come under scrutiny as problematic historically, psychologically, and theologically. Women's sacramental celebrations of God's work in human life are celebrations not only of sacrifice but also of struggle, resistance, and partial victories.

In sum, feminist theology supports and underscores the basic principles of sacramentality in the Christian tradition, but raises fundamental questions about many of the ways in which sacramentality is expressed and developed. It includes a concern for the integrity and goodness of the physical with significant implications for natural law and moral theology.[24] It also affirms a continuing need to uncover the body-denying history of the tradition.[25] Feminist theology affirms the principle of mediation, but asks crucial questions about the nature of community, and of the relation of sacraments to the community's life and concerns.

Finally, feminist theology draws on biblical scholarship to understand more deeply what it is that is significant about the life of Jesus, and what, historically, marks his significance — what his life, death, and resurrection were all about. And in all these dimensions, feminist theology stresses the *ambiguity* of sacramentality: its complexity, and fluidity, its relation to the particular event it commemorates, its relevance for communal life. Uncomfortable with fixed and absolute categories, feminist theology seeks a sacramentality that is grounded both in the lived experiences of women and men, and in the example of Jesus.

---

22. See Marcus J. Borg, *Meeting Jesus Again for the First Time: The Historical Jesus and the Heart of Faith* (San Francisco: HarperSanFrancisco, 1994); John Dominic Crossan, *Jesus: A Revolutionary Biography* (San Francisco: HarperSanFrancisco, 1994); Richard Horsley, *Sociology and the Jesus Movement* (New York: Crossroad, 1989).

23. See Delores S. Williams' critique of atonement theology in "Black Women's Surrogacy Experience and the Christian Notion of Redemption," in *After Patriarchy: Feminist Transformations of the World Religions*, ed. Paula M. Cooey, William Eakin, and Jay B. McDaniel (Maryknoll, NY: Orbis Books, 1991) 1–14.

24. See Cahill, *Sex, Gender*; Cristina L. H. Traina, *Undoing Anathemas* (Washington, D.C.: Georgetown University Press, forthcoming).

25. Gudorf, *Body, Sex and Pleasure.*

I have deliberately begun these reflections *within* the context of Christian sacramentality, rather than from an explicit standpoint of "women's ritual experiences." I can imagine some readers to be critical of this approach, since it seems to place the feminist sacramental question within a "malestream" context. Why not, one might argue, begin with a consideration of women's experiences as they themselves develop rituals and traditions of their own? Ought not a feminist sacramental theology begin with woman-defined and woman-developed symbols, not with the inherited structure of the tradition? I have reflected, discussed, and agonized over this methodological decision. But I maintain it here for these reasons. First, it is naive, I think, to argue that one can find a category of "women's experiences" that constitutes a separate place of its own, outside any connection to "malestream" literature or sacramental life. The complexity of life lived in community, among men, children, institutions, traditions, and the natural world, suggest that "women's experiences" are always in relation to that wider context. Second, I intend this book to be a contribution to Christian theology, defined as inclusively as possible. The problematic of a feminist sacramental theology arises both within the tradition and as an issue of its own. That is, how do women worship in the present official sacramental context? How do women represent the divine? My own sense is that the "problem" of a feminist sacramental theology arises precisely because it is located *within* an existing worshiping tradition. Thus my intent in locating the issue "within" the tradition is to begin where the "problem" arises.

Third, the conversations that I have had with women involved in sacramental ministries in parish contexts have brought home to me the importance of "meeting people where they are," as these women so often reflected. That is, I believe it to be essential not only to "preach to the choir," which in this case would be the community of feminist, *mujerista,* and womanist theologians, but also to those engaged in the day-to-day sacramental ministry of parishes, to those who administer dioceses, and to all those involved in sacramental theology. Sacramental practice, which is constantly mediating the presence of God through events, rituals, and symbols, is both ancient and ongoing. My challenge is to address the situations that arise in the context of day-to-day sacramental life, and to draw from these situations a clearer and richer way of understanding and experiencing the sacraments.

Uneasy as feminist theology is with absolutes, it is not without some foundations of its own, as the preceding makes clear. Underlying its concern for the body, for a more communal understanding of the self, and for a relation to justice, is feminist theology's opposition to any form of discrimination based on sex, and indeed, to social structures that privilege some over others, especially patriarchy.[26] If there is a "foundational principle" in feminist theology, it would be a rejection of patriarchy and a suspicion of hierarchical structures in human society. This foundational principle, coupled with a postmodern awareness of the historicity of human life, supports feminist's theology's suspicion and critique of all structures of domination.

Out of these methodological considerations, I propose four criteria for an adequate sacramental theology attentive to the lives of women. They are, first, a redefining of a context for sacraments that is tolerant, if not appreciative, of ambiguity. Second, sacramental theology needs to include a critical consideration of body and gender. To the extent that sacramental theology is related to the body, it cannot prescind from theories of gender, and must be explicit about its understanding of gender.[27] Third, sacramental theology must be explicit in its understanding of symbolic representation and how symbols are related to the community. And, fourth, sacramental theology is meaningless unless it is tied to a concern for justice in the communities in which sacraments are celebrated, and in the wider world. Part of the "dysfunction" that sacramental theologian David Power sees as the current situation of the Eucharist is tied to the sacrament's isolation from the concrete concerns of suffering human life.[28]

I deliberately "frame" these issues with, on the one hand, the appeal to openness and multivalency suggested by ambiguity and, on the other, the concern for normative principles suggested by the criterion of justice. Both are necessary, I will argue, for an adequate feminist sacramental theology. There is need for greater openness to ambiguity on the grounds not only of feminist theology but also of contemporary understandings of the nature of the world and cosmos. An initial openness to ambiguity suggests a range of possibilities (and problems) that will be significant in sorting

---

26. See Farley, "Feminist Theology and Bioethics"; see also Rosemary Ruether, *New Woman, New Earth: Sexist Ideologies and Human Liberation* (New York: Seabury, 1975), which explores the interrelationship of multiple forms of oppression, including racism, sexism, anti-Semitism, and attitudes toward the earth.

27. See, e.g., *Liturgy and the Body,* ed. Louis-Marie Chauvet and François Kabasele Lumbala, *Concilium* 1995/2 (London and Maryknoll, NY: SCM Press and Orbis Books, 1995).

28. See David Power, *The Eucharistic Mystery: Revitalizing the Tradition* (New York: Crossroad, 1992).

out the concerns of justice. In the section that follows, I will develop these points briefly in terms of their implications for the book as a whole. They will be expanded in the chapters that follow.

CRITERIA FOR A FEMINIST SACRAMENTAL THEOLOGY

1. *An adequate sacramental theology has a tolerance and appreciation for ambiguity.*

I have chosen the term "ambiguity" as a general term to refer to a nondualistic approach to reality. Other terms, such as multiplicity or polyvalence, might also serve my purpose; yet the term "ambiguity" suggests a "dark" side that I do not want to evade. Feminist theorists have long criticized what popular writers have referred to as the "male world view," in which reality is made up of clear and distinct realities, with well-defined boundaries and distinctions.[29] Some of the roots of this "worldview" lie in the persistence of dualistic forms of thought in Western civilization, which sees material reality as "fallen" from the higher realm of the spiritual.

Let me be clear about what I mean by "dualistic." I do not mean to dismiss what structuralist theorists refer to as the "dual" structures of human consciousness (for example, Levy-Strauss), or the "bicameral" mind, or the seemingly obvious dual nature of human sexuality.[30] The issue at hand is how these structures (if indeed they are so) are interpreted. Dualism poses these dual realities over and against each other; it resists complex and fluid relations between dual realities, and defends instead clear and distinct boundaries. Qualities belonging to one by definition do not belong to the other, and the two are often hierarchically related: one is superior to the other, or one has jurisdictional power over the other.

While much has been written about dualistic forms of thinking, my particular focus here is on the way in which dualistic thought has affected sacramentality, and, more particularly, the sacraments themselves. There are at least three points worth noting. One is that sacramental theology, over the centuries, has become closely linked with legal thinking, espe-

---

29. See Anne Wilson Schaef, *Women's Reality: An Emerging Female System in the White Male Society* (Minneapolis: Winston Press, 1981).

30. See Claude Levi-Strauss, *Structural Anthropology*, trans. Elaine Jacobsen and Brooke Grundfest Schoepf (New York: Basic Books, 1963); Judith Lorber, *Paradoxes of Gender* (New Haven: Yale University Press, 1994).

cially to canon law. Thus, categories of "validity" in the sacraments have taken on great importance, often to the detriment of other, equally if not more important, factors. The emphasis on "validity" is not entirely negative, it must be said. The importance of emphasizing the validity of a sacrament notwithstanding the piety of the minister was a crucial historical and theological development.[31] But a dualistic emphasis on validity risks turning sacramental theology and practice into legalism, and ignores important pastoral dimensions. There is a "right" way and a "wrong" way; a "valid" and "invalid" way. When such legalism rules sacramental theology and practice, not only is a sense of sacredness lost, but pastoral opportunities for reaching those hungry for healing, nurture, reconciliation, and union are also endangered.[32]

A second point is the division between the "real" and the "symbolic," which became a problem particularly in the history of eucharistic theology. Controversies regarding "real presence" involved, on the one hand, stressing the physicality of the body of Christ in the Eucharist (often to vivid extremes), and, on the other, emphasizing the "figurative" quality of the representation of Christ (often to making the presence of Christ a mere memory).[33] Again here, an either/or situation — either Christ was "really, physically" present, or he was "only symbolically" (and, thus, not "really") present — resulted in a lack of a sense of the ambiguity of symbolic representation. The result was that symbols were reduced to the category of mere sign (which bears a one-to-one relationship to its signifier) and the multivalent possibilities for symbolic representation were lost. The fact that symbols *disclose as they conceal* was, and often still is, forgotten.[34] The "tensive" quality of symbols, and thus sacraments, has

---

31. For a brief discussion of Donatism, see Peter Brown, *Augustine of Hippo: A Biography* (Berkeley: University of California Press, 1967) 212–25.

32. My point is not to argue for a sacramental "antinomianism," but rather for a balance between the personal, pastoral, and legal dimensions of sacraments. It is not that this is entirely absent, and has been given more attention since Vatican II, but the message that continually comes from Rome is adherence to canonical norms. Note, for example, the controversy stirred over President Clinton's reception of communion during his April 1998 trip to Africa. See *National Catholic Reporter* 34/23 (April 10, 1998) 8.

33. See, e.g., Gary Macy, *The Theologies of the Eucharist in the Early Scholastic Period: A Study of the Salvific Function of the Sacraments according to the Theologians, c. 1080–1220* (Oxford: Oxford University Press, 1984).

34. See Paul Ricoeur, *The Symbolism of Evil*, trans. Emerson Buchanan (Boston: Beacon Press, 1967).

been too often overlooked in favor of a more "certain" and decidedly unambiguous quality.[35]

A third point is the distinction between clergy and lay people. Here are involved issues of power, and not so much of charism. The way in which the clergy/lay hierarchy operates (at least in Roman Catholicism) is that clergy have jurisdictional, theological, and pastoral power, which the laity lack. This results in a lack of dynamic models of power in the institutional church, and, often, this power is exercised in dominating ways. For example, when a priest is "laicized," he is *reduced* to the lay state.[36] Feminist psychologist Jessica Benjamin argues that a lack of tolerance for ambiguity — a stress on dualism and either/or categories — can lead to violence.[37] A dualistic view of the clergy/lay distinction will continue to insist on clear and unambiguous modes of power (for example, bishops do not learn but rather teach) that are inattentive to dialogical possibilities.[38]

What a "tolerance and appreciation for ambiguity" involves in sacramental theology is an awareness of its metaphysical, expressive, and moral dimensions.[39] Metaphysically, ambiguity involves an understanding of God and the world in dynamic relation. Ambiguity in metaphysical terms implies an understanding of God as dynamically related to the created world and tends to criticize understandings of God as all-powerful and omniscient that are not balanced by God's all-encompassing mystery and responsiveness to creation. Thus the metaphysical dimensions of ambiguity work against hierarchical/kyriarchical power relations. Ambiguity as expressive relates to the multiple ways in which deeper realities can be conveyed. So an appreciation of ambiguity will work against too great an emphasis on neat and clear distinctions in the expressive possibilities of the

---

35. For a discussion of the "tensive" dimension of symbols, see Philip Wheelwright, *Metaphor and Reality* (Bloomington: Indiana University Press, 1962); idem., *The Burning Fountain: A Study in the Language of Symbolism* (Bloomington: Indiana University Press, 1968).

36. See *The Code of Canon Law: A Text and Commentary,* ed. Canon Law Society of America, ed. James A. Coriden, Thomas J. Green, and Donald E. Heintschel (New York and Mahwah, NJ: Paulist Press, 1985) 230–32, which deals with canons 290 and 291, on the "loss of the clerical state."

37. Jessica Benjamin, *The Bonds of Love: Psychoanalysis, Feminism, and the Problem of Domination* (New York: Pantheon Books, 1988).

38. As I write this, there is increasing discussion in church circles about the meaning of the new Vatican directives on making sharp distinctions between clergy and laity.

39. These points are more fully developed in chapter 3.

symbolic. Further, the moral dimension of ambiguity involves a recognition of the inevitably finite character of all our actions and expressions, and their potentially tragic character as participating in the metaphysical ambiguity of the cosmos. A greater appreciation of moral ambiguity will work against the arrogance that absolute power encourages, and will be ever more attentive to the consequences of any use of power.

Lastly, and perhaps more importantly, a tolerance and appreciation for ambiguity reflects the experiences of women who are themselves engaged in sacramental ministry or who find themselves in a tradition that has both nurtured and alienated them. They do not choose to reject the tradition entirely, yet they search for a more adequate way to express their own sense of sacramentality. A tolerance and appreciation for ambiguity does not mean that one remains mired in indecision, forever wavering between positions. It rather cautions against premature decisions, allows for the diversity of issues at stake, and resists premature closure. Ambiguity is not so much a substantive issue as it is a methodological principle, always open to the richness and complexity of life.

2. *An adequate sacramental theology must include a critical consideration of theories of body and gender.*

This may seem to repeat an obvious point, but sacramental theology has proven to be remarkably untouched by feminist criticism. Perhaps the main contribution of feminist thought over the last thirty years has been to raise awareness of gender as a social construction. Simone de Beauvoir's famous comment, "One is not born, but rather becomes, a woman," sums this up.[40] Frequently the distinction is made that biological sex is a given, but gender is a social construction. Yet even the understanding of biological sex as dual has been challenged by recent postmodern thinkers who question the existence of "two sexes."[41] While some of these issues will be developed at greater length in chapter 4, here I want simply to touch on some of the crucial considerations regarding body and gender that need to be taken into account by sacramental theology.

---

40. See Simone de Beauvoir, *The Second Sex*, trans. and ed. H. M Parshley (New York: Vintage, 1974 [1949]), 301.

41. See, e.g., Judith Butler, *Bodies that Matter: On the Discursive Limits of Sex* (New York and London: Routledge, 1993); idem., *Gender Trouble: Feminism and the Subversion of Identity* (New York and London: Routledge, 1990); Judith Lorber, *Paradoxes of Gender* (New Haven: Yale University Press, 1994).

First, sacramental theology, especially in the immediate post–Vatican II years, drew heavily on cultural-anthropological studies. Scholars of sacraments and liturgy, inspired in part by the pre–Vatican II liturgical movement, turned to works by Mircea Eliade, Mary Douglas, Victor Turner, and others, finding that at the root of the sacraments lay an "anthropological substructure," which supported human symbolic and ritual life.[42] But most of this anthropological work was done without consideration of gender. Indeed, as Rita Gross and Carol Christ have pointed out, there is an androcentric bias in much of what cultural anthropology and the history of religions has to offer the study of comparative religions.[43] The assumption that the data derived from (largely male) observations of (largely male) culture provided adequate material for drawing conclusions about human ritual life is sharply challenged by both Christ and Gross.

Second, the *theological* anthropology of sacramental theology deserves much closer scrutiny than it has received until recently. Not only are generalizations about "man the symbol-maker" in need of greater scrutiny, but also understandings of "complementarity" that have reigned in more recent theologies, especially of orders, but also of marriage.[44] Conceptions of what it means to be male or female are often based in metaphysical conceptions of human sexuality that have little if any reference to social-scientific data, much less feminist scholarship. Many feminist scholars dismiss theories of complementarity, often with good reason.[45] Not only are such

----

42. See Bernard Bro, "Man and the Sacraments: The Anthropological Substructure of the Christian Sacraments," trans. John Drury, in *The Sacraments in General, Concilium* vol. 31, ed. Edward Schillebeeckx and Boniface Willems (New York and Mahwah, NJ: Paulist Press, 1967).

43. Carol P. Christ, "Mircea Eliade and the Feminist Paradigm Shift," *Journal of Feminist Studies in Religion* 7/2 (fall 1991) 75–94; for an early discussion of this issue, see Rita Gross, "Issues and non-issues in the study of women in world religions," *Anima* 2 (fall 1975) 34–39.

44. The work of John Paul II has stressed this metaphysical complementarity; see his *Love and Responsibility,* trans. H. T. Willetts (New York: Farrar, Straus and Giroux, 1991). But see also Sara Butler, MSBT, "The Priest as Sacrament of Christ the Bridegroom," *Worship* 66 (November 1992) 498–517; idem, "Priestly Identity: 'Sacrament' of Christ the Head," *Worship* 70 (July 1996) 291–306.

45. See, e.g., Anne E. Carr, *Transforming Grace: Christian Tradition and Women's Experience* (San Francisco: Harper & Row, 1988); Rosemary Radford Ruether, *Sexism and God-Talk: Towards a Feminist Theology* (Boston: Beacon Press, 1983). But see Mary Aquin O'Neill, "The Mystery of Being Human Together," in *Freeing Theology: The Essentials of Theology in Feminist Perspective,* ed. Catherine M. LaCugna (San Francisco: HarperSanFrancisco, 1993) for a more appreciative approach to complementarity.

theories grounded in highly questionable understandings of human biology and sociology; they also perpetuate a psychology of women as
"receptive" and men as "active" that has tremendously destructive consequences for relationships between the sexes.[46] One must question the
extent to which such conceptions of human nature have contributed, minimally, to the lack of self-development among women, and, more seriously,
to both the threats and reality of domestic violence.[47]

Third, theories of "difference" among feminist scholars deserve close
scrutiny as well. Some of the "difference" theories, for example, of Carol
Gilligan, Sara Ruddick, the French feminists, and others, have been
criticized for not taking sufficiently into account socio-economic components.[48] Here the work of Joan Tronto is very helpful in sorting out some
of these complex issues, and revealing how issues of race and class may
figure in as well.[49] Yet I would want to argue that there are some givens
and limitations that argue against a *complete* dismissal of theories of gender "difference."[50] Women's capacity for biological motherhood cannot be
completely ignored. How serious attention to embodiment can be linked
with a critical sense of history is important here. What is necessary in a
critical consideration of gender is an awareness of the context of such theories, and their relation to race, class, and other factors; a careful use of
physical and social scientific research.

3. *An adequate sacramental theology will include a critical understanding
of theories of symbolic representation.*

---

46. See Margaret Farley, "New Patterns of Relationship," *Theological Studies* 36 (1975)
627–46, at 635.

47. See *Violence Against Women,* ed. Elisabeth Schüssler Fiorenza and M. Shawn
Copeland, *Concilium* 1994/1 (London: SCM Press; Maryknoll, NY: Orbis Books, 1994);
Violence Against Women and Children, ed. Carol J. Adams and Marie M. Fortune (New
York: Continuum, 1995).

48. Note here: Carol Gilligan, *In a Different Voice: Psychological Theory and Women's
Development* (Cambridge, MA: Harvard University Press, 1982); Sara Ruddick, *Maternal
Thinking: Towards a Politics of Peace* (Boston: Beacon Press, 1989); Julia Kristeva, *The Kristeva
Reader,* ed. Toril Moi (New York: Columbia University Press, 1986).

49. Joan M. Tronto, *Moral Boundaries: A Political Argument for an Ethic of Care* (New
York and London: Routledge, 1993); I will draw extensively on Tronto's theories in
chapter 6.

50. See here Lisa Cahill's work, and also C. Traina's work on the moral dimensions
of motherhood, "Passionate Parenting: Toward an Ethics of Appropriate Parent-Child
Intimacy," *Annual of the Society of Christian Ethics* 1998 (forthcoming).

It is difficult to separate this component entirely from a consideration of gender, since constructions of gender have great symbolic import. My purpose in giving this point separate recognition is to highlight the importance of context, to explore the richness of theories of symbol and metaphor, and to draw on theories of representation from anthropological, psychological, and psychoanalytic resources.

The importance of context cannot be overstated in any understanding of symbol and metaphor. Symbols emerge from particular social and historical circumstances that inform their meaning, and apart from which they become museum artifacts. This is not to say that one cannot understand a symbol from another culture or another time, but without an appreciation of context, one runs the risk of misinterpreting symbolic meaning. Nor does this caution mean that symbols cannot be *re*-interpreted, in new contexts, with new meaning. It is, rather, to argue that the constructive use of symbols in theology needs to be informed by a critical sense of history, and, from a feminist perspective, by a careful hermeneutics of suspicion.

The work of scholars such as Caroline Walker Bynum shows the richness of the uses of historical scholarship for the understanding of symbol.[51] Bynum has been able to demonstrate, for example, that the eucharistic piety of medieval women held deep theological import, as women embraced the bodiliness of Jesus along with the recognition of their own bodiliness. But it is also necessary to include a suspicion of the multiple meanings of a particular symbol, given the ways in which women have been symbolically represented.

An appreciation for the richness of theories of symbol and metaphor has come a long way from the times in which using the term "symbol" in relation to the sacraments rendered one suspect. Informed by the historical scholarship of the early twentieth century which contributed so much to the liturgical movement,[52] by theories of religious

---

51. See her *Holy Feast and Holy Fast: The Religious Significance of Food to Medieval Women* (Berkeley: University of California Press, 1987); *Jesus as Mother: Studies in the Spirituality of the High Middle Ages* (Berkeley: University of California Press, 1982); *Fragmentation and Redemption: Essays on Gender and the Human Body in Medieval Religion* (New York: Zone Books, 1991).

52. See, e.g., Josef Jungmann, S.J., *The Mass of the Roman Rite: Its Origin and Development*, trans. Frances Brunner; Louis Bouyer, *Eucharist: Theology and Spirituality of the Eucharistic Prayer*, trans. Charles Quinn (Notre Dame, IN: University of Notre Dame Press, 1968).

language,[53] by the theologies of Rahner and Schillebeeckx, themselves informed by the renewal of Thomistic scholarship and the phenomenological movement,[54] and by the hermeneutical theories of Gadamer and Ricoeur,[55] the interpretation of symbol and metaphor has become a rich resource for contemporary theologians, not to mention philosophers, literary critics, and other scholars. The symbol is no longer a poor substitute for reality, but a profound source of manifold meaning. Such interpretive theories offer creative ways of reinterpreting the inherited symbolic tradition as well as the possibility for new symbols and new meaning.

Finally, the work of anthropologists, psychologists, and psychoanalysts offers challenging ways of thinking of symbols, and serves as a check or caution to interpreting symbols outside their wider context. The work of Sigmund Freud is an early example of such work, which raised the question of the symbol of the Father God in relation to the helpless and dependent child.[56] Whether or not one agrees with Freud's conclusions, the great "masters of suspicion" — Marx, Freud, and Nietzsche — suggest that the uses of such symbols as God the Father, the promise of heavenly rewards, and the suffering and dying savior (to name just a few) by religious traditions have often had staggeringly destructive effects on their followers, as well as profoundly (and often surprisingly) liberating ef-

---

53. See, e.g., Ian Ramsey, *Religious Language: An Empirical Placing of Theological Phrases* (London: SCM Press, 1963); Frederick Ferre, *Language, Logic and God* (Westport, CT: Greenwood Press, 1977).

54. For Rahner, see Anne E. Carr, *The Theological Method of Karl Rahner* (Missoula, MT: Scholars Press, 1977); *A World of Grace: An Introduction to the Themes and Foundations of Karl Rahner's Theology,* ed. Leo J. O'Donovan (New York: Seabury Press, 1980); Karl-Heinz Weger, *Karl Rahner: An Introduction to his Theology,* trans. David Smith (New York: Seabury, 1980). For Schillebeeckx, see John S. Bowden, *Schillebeeckx: In Search of the Kingdom of God* (New York: Crossroad, 1983); *The Praxis of Christian Experience: An Introduction to the Theology of Edward Schillebeeckx,* ed. Robert J. Schreiter and Mary Catherine Hilkert (San Francisco: Harper & Row, 1989).

55. Hans-Georg Gadamer, *Truth and Method,* trans. edited by Garrett Barden and John Cumming from the second ed. of *Wahrheit und Methode* (New York: Seabury Press, 1975; rev. ed. Continuum, 1989); idem, *Philosophical Hermeneutics,* trans. and ed. D. E. Linge (Berkeley: University of California Press, 1976); Paul Ricoeur, *Interpretation Theory: Discourse and the Interpretation of Meaning* (Fort Worth: Texas Christian University Press, 1977); *The Rule of Metaphor,* trans. Robert Czerny with Kathleen McLaughlin and John Costello (Toronto: University of Toronto Press, 1977).

56. Sigmund Freud, *The Future of an Illusion,* trans. James Strachey (New York: Norton, 1975).

fects.[57] Feminist theorists have increased the reasons for suspicion, as they have uncovered the previously hidden role of gender in many of these critical theories.

The symbol of God the Father may indeed serve to inhibit the growth of a critical consciousness in a person, but it can also serve to repress the fear of and desire for the mother, a dynamic that I will explore in chapter 5. Psychoanalytic theory is helpful in bringing to the surface the unconscious structures of human dynamics and in drawing out the consequences of an integration of these structures.

4. *An adequate sacramental theology is ultimately judged by its struggle to overcome oppression and work for justice.*

The old Baltimore Catechism defined sacraments as "outward signs, instituted by Christ, to give grace." Within a world in which sacraments were a means of getting to the next (better) world, and in which the communal dimension of sacramentality was subordinated to the individual's relation to God, the sacraments were understood as "pipelines of grace" to the individual recipient.[58] It was to be hoped that the grace that the recipient received would enable him or her to be a "better Catholic" and, thus, would help inspire the good Catholic to perform the spiritual and corporal works of mercy. But to ask a pre–Vatican II Catholic what the sacraments had to do with justice would likely have elicited a very puzzled look, unless, perhaps, one were to ask how the condition of one's soul would be judged by divine justice.

The work of liberation theology has had a galvanizing effect on the relationship of sacraments to the conditions of the world. Theologians such as Juan Luis Segundo, in his early groundbreaking series *The Sacraments Today,* asked hard questions about the relationship of sacraments to a clerical system, of the hunger of the world to the sacramental nourishment of bread and wine, of reconciliation to a world in need of justice, of the responsibilities of members of a community to each other.[59] Other liber-

---

57. The term "Masters of Suspicion" is Ricoeur's. See his book on Freud, *Freud and Philosophy: An Essay in Interpretation,* trans. Denis Savage (New Haven: Yale University Press, 1970).

58. Schillebeeckx discusses the instrumental and mechanical understanding of sacraments in *Christ the Sacrament of the Encounter with God,* trans. N. D. Smith (New York: Sheed and Ward, 1963).

59. Segundo, *The Sacraments Today,* trans. John Drury (Maryknoll, NY: Orbis Books, 1974).

ation theologians, such as Tissa Balasuriya and Monika Hellwig, continue to ask these questions.

Feminist theology, as does liberation theology, underscores the relationship of sacraments to justice, and, with the issue of the ordination of women, asks how the institutional church can claim to be a reconciling and healing community given the structural and theological obstacles it has placed in the way of the full equality of women and men. Given these obstacles, many women and men have turned to alternative celebrations, such as those mentioned at the beginning of the first chapter, which make explicit calls for justice. Edward Schillebeeckx's understanding of sacraments as "anticipatory signs" of the eschatological future is helpful here.[60] What is celebrated in the sacraments is not an otherworldly reality, but rather what the Christian community strives for: a community in which all eat and drink together at a common table, in which justice is a reality, in which the sacramental lives of Christians reflect and inspire their lives "in the world." Both liberation and feminist theologies strive to take sacraments out of a religious context removed from the "real world," and to bring to the sacraments the issues that the world raises.

A feminist sacramental theology takes sacramentality seriously, so that the bodies of women are as revelatory of the divine as are the bodies of men. Further, the significance of the sacraments — of a reconciled and healed church, of a community that celebrates a common life where all are invited to the table, of covenant relations that are mutual and egalitarian — shows a continuity between ritual and ordinary life. That is, the two are not identical, in that rituals raise up and highlight significant moments in a community's otherwise "ordinary" life, but rather there is a dialectical relation between the two. Ordinary life raises challenges, hopes, experiences that become ritualized, which in turn reflect back on the ways that life is lived.

---

60. See Schillebeeckx, *Christ*, 836: "They are symbols of protest serving to unmask the life that is not yet reconciled in the specific dimensions of history."

CHAPTER THREE

Women, the Sacraments, and Ambiguity

Hence, instead of considering it our task to "dispose" of any ambiguity by merely disclosing the fact that it is an ambiguity, we rather consider it our task to study and clarify the *resources* of ambiguity. For in the course of this work, we shall deal with many kinds of *transformation* — and it is in the areas of ambiguity that transformations take place; in fact, without such areas, transformation would be impossible.

— Kenneth Burke[1]

Feminist theorists, like other postmodernists, should encourage us to tolerate, invite, and interpret ambivalence, ambiguity, and multiplicity, as well as to expose the roots of our needs for imposing order and structure no matter how arbitrary and oppressive these may be. If we do our work well, "reality" will appear even more unstable, complex, and disorderly than it does now. In this sense perhaps Freud was right when he declared that women are the enemies of civilization.

— Jane Flax[2]

There is no such thing as an unambiguous tradition; there are no innocent readings of the classics.

— David Tracy[3]

---

1. Kenneth Burke, *A Grammar of Motives* (Berkeley: University of California Press, 1969) xxi.
2. Jane Flax, *Thinking Fragments: Psychoanalysis, Feminism and Postmodernism in the Contemporary West* (Berkeley: University of California Press, 1990) 183.
3. David Tracy, *Plurality and Ambiguity: Hermeneutics, Religion, Hope* (San Francisco: Harper & Row, 1987) 36.

My task in this chapter is a difficult one: to write clearly about ambiguity, a condition marked by vagueness, a lack of clarity, even obscurity. Yet as the epigraphs above suggest, ambiguity can be a source of transformation and meaning. My claim in this chapter will be that the ambiguities surrounding sacramentality, as well as women's relation to the sacraments, can prove to be critical and transformative resources for sacramental theology. In order to substantiate this claim, I will need to describe the ambiguous dimensions of the sacraments themselves, the ambiguities surrounding women's relation to the sacraments, and some of the unsettled and unanswered questions that arise in this relationship. In exploring these ambiguities, I hope to uncover some basic questions and issues concerning sacramental theology that may not be evident otherwise. But before we can attend to these issues, it is necessary to sort through some of the various meanings and uses of ambiguity.

Postmodernism has come to embrace ambiguity in its rejection of sure and absolute foundations for human knowledge.[4] Awareness of the social and historical conditionedness of the human situation has led to a positive emphasis on the multiplicity of meanings and values, partly as a reaction to the "oppressive order" of certainty, as Flax notes above, and partly as a way of dealing with the explosion of knowledge in contemporary life. The academic debates on the content and value of the "canon" and the celebration of multiculturalism in the 1990s are but two examples of the toleration and appreciation of ambiguity that the postmodern situation seems to elicit. It is the perceived fluidity of conceptions of self, of society, of previously thought-of absolutes, of the lack of foundations, that suggest that ambiguity is not something to be avoided, dismissed, or even resolved, but embraced. Ambiguity, postmodernism says, is our very condition. We cannot deny its existence; we may as well learn to live with it, and even enjoy it.[5]

---

4. See, among others, Richard Rorty, *The Linguistic Turn: Recent Essays in Philosophical Method* (Chicago: University of Chicago Press, 1967); James Miller, "The Emerging Post-Modern World," in *Post-Modern Theology*, ed. Frederick Burnham (San Francisco: Harper Collins, 1989); Paul Lakeland, *Postmodernity: Christian Identity in a Fragmented Age* (Minneapolis: Fortress Press, 1997).

5. For discussion of the "playful" dimension of ambiguity, see Rebecca S. Chopp, *The Power to Speak: Feminism, Language, God* (New York: Crossroad, 1989).

THE USEFULNESS OF AMBIGUITY

Metaphysical Ambiguity

The picture of a universe of meticulous order, where the processes of the cosmos proceed with machinelike precision, has given way in recent years to a much richer, and more complex, picture. Less like a machine, the universe is more like a giant organism, and this organism is characterized by flux, unpredictability, jumps, regressions, predictable orders, and even harmony. New approaches to cosmology, like "chaos theory," suggest that the unpredictability of the cosmos is a part of its very structure. "Chaos," far from being the threat to cosmic order that the name may suggest, is in fact more descriptive of the universe than predictable order.[6]

The English theologian Ruth Page embraces ambiguity as the very condition of the cosmos itself.[7] The world in which we live is an ambiguous one, she writes. Neither "order" nor "chaos" can describe fully the human situation, nor are these terms adequate to describe "nature" — that is, if we can even speak of nature apart from the human condition, or vice versa. Order cannot account "for the continuing process of irregular change going on in the world," and chaos, Page argues, is a term used for "alien orders we dislike or cannot understand, which appear to us disorderly."[8] Indeed, to have to choose between order and chaos is "inadequate, since neither describes fully the world of experience."[9] Page draws upon examples in both natural and human history to make her point that ambiguity is unavoidable as the very condition of existence itself. She defines ambiguity as "the condition which arises from diverse action upon the changeable and changing world, continually producing new organizations, complex variety, and multiple interpretations — all of which has to integrate with or overthrow what already exists."[10]

For Page, ambiguity is a *metaphysical* reality; that is, it is a component structure of reality. The continually changing character of the world deabsolutizes any kind of human expression as inadequate to the reality it attempts to describe. "Any human attempt at order," Page asserts, "is a

---

6. See, e.g., John Haught, *Chaos, Complexity, and Theology* (Chambersburg, PA: Anima Books, 1994).

7. Ruth Page, *Ambiguity and the Presence of God* (London: SCM Press, 1985).

8. Ibid., 11.

9. Ibid.

10. Ibid., 14.

locally agreed cluster of values and interpretations involving a temporary simplification of complexity and the transient arrest of some aspects of change."[11] Ambiguity challenges human ways of knowing and acting as absolute, and it especially challenges human conceptions of God. Like other contemporary theorists, Page is suspicious of the idea that science, because of its claims to be exact and unambiguous, promises a superior knowledge to other forms of knowing, like the arts and humanities, since the latter deal with values and not facts, as science does. Quoting Carl Rogers, Page notes that "science exists only in people" and in people who exist in particular communities.[12] Indeed, it is science itself, in its theories of the physical structure of the universe as ambiguous, that grounds her argument for ambiguity in relation to God.[13]

Ambiguity has a special relevance for theology, Page writes. Building on her understanding of the ambiguous structure of the universe itself, Page probes its relevance for Christian understandings of God as prime orderer of the universe. Despite the findings of the sciences, and despite how far back "the frontiers of what God is said to have ordered" have been pushed, the belief in God's ordering remains.[14] Thus the presence of evil continues to raise problems for a conception of God who has "in some sense ordered the world," as well as to raise the challenges of historical relativity.[15] Page suggests that an understanding of God as "caring for and companioning creation as it brings about its varieties of finite order will allow religion in general and theology in particular to be much more hospitable than it has traditionally been to notions of *change and diversity*."[16]

---

11. Ibid.

12. Ibid., 74. The philosophy of science has also been an area of interest for feminist philosophers who raise critical questions about "scientific objectivity." See Evelyn Fox Keller, *Reflections on Gender and Science* (New Haven: Yale University Press, 1995); idem, *Feminism and Science* (Oxford: Oxford University Press, 1996); Ruth Hubbard, *History, Science and Gender* (Research Triangle Park, NC: National Humanities Center, 1985); Sandra Harding, *Subjectivity, Experience and Knowledge and Epistemology from/for Rainbow Coalition Politics* (Washington, D.C.: Society for Values in Higher Education, 1993).

13. See, for example, Angela Tilby, *Soul: God, Self and the New Cosmology* (New York: Doubleday, 1993); Ian Barbour, *Religion in an Age of Science* (San Francisco: Harper, 1990); W. Drees, *Beyond the Big Bang: Quantum Cosmologies and God* (New York: Open Court, 1990).

14. Page, *Ambiguity*, 86.

15. Ibid., 89.

16. Ibid., 94–95; original emphasis.

Like Burke's assertion in the opening epigraph of this chapter, Page sees ambiguity as "a necessary though not a sufficient condition for the production of the new or the different."[17] Ambiguity's connotation of flux, incompleteness, and lack of resolution provides openings for questioning why some conditions seem to be unresolved. Her qualification ("not sufficient") is important: ambiguity in and of itself has no moral valence. It is a condition or state that calls for both assessment and resolution. But without ambiguity there can be no change.

Page's conception of "metaphysical" ambiguity has at least two important implications for sacramental theology. First, the idea that the world is in a continuous process of development and change suggests that any turning to nature, or the body, as revelatory of God in some way must take into account the changing and developing character of the natural order. Serious attention to the actual workings of the natural world, in their complexity and ambiguity, is necessary in order to be as clear as possible about what it means to say that "God's will" is to be found in nature. As contemporary philosophy of science has shown, one's theory of nature may reveal far more about the theorist than the natural process itself.[18] Thus traditional theories of "natural law" may require revision in the light of new scientific knowledge, given these theories' reliance on a stable, if not even static, understanding of the world.[19] Page's point is that traditional conceptions of order in the universe, such as those espoused by some natural law positions, are out of touch not only with the structure of the universe, as it has come to be understood by contemporary science, but also out of touch with an adequate understanding of God. Thus taking ambiguity seriously as a structure of cosmic existence means revising, perhaps considerably, the ways in which humans understand God's interaction with the world, such

---

17. Ibid., 32.

18. See n. 12, above; See also Evelyn Fox Keller, *A Feeling for the Organism: The Life and Work of Barbara McClintock* (San Francisco: W. H. Freeman, 1983).

19. See, e.g., Lisa Sowle Cahill, *Sex, Gender and Christian Ethics* (Cambridge: Cambridge University Press, 1996); Susan Frank Parsons, *Feminism and Christian Ethics* (Cambridge: Cambridge University Press, 1996); Cristina L. H. Traina, "Oh Susanna: The New Absolutism and Natural Law," *Journal of the American Academy of Religion* 65 (1997) 371–402, and her forthcoming *Undoing Anathemas* (Washington, D.C.: Georgetown University Press); Pamela Hall, *Narrative and Natural Law: An Interpretation of Thomistic Ethics* (Notre Dame, IN: University of Notre Dame Press, 1994); Jean Porter, *The Recovery of Virtue: The Relevance of Aquinas for Christian Ethics* (Louisville: Westminster John Knox Press, 1990).

as God's having ultimate control over the universe, or God's knowledge of all that happens — in short, God's omnipotence and omniscience.

Some contemporary theories of natural law, especially those based on the Aristotelian-Thomistic model, have pushed toward including some features of the changing and unpredictable dimensions of "world order." Bernard Lonergan's conception of "emergent probability" is one such theory, having the potential to revise static conceptions of natural law to be more adequate to the workings of the natural and social order.[20] Some feminist theologians argue that a revised approach to natural law that takes into account the historical and social conditionedness of embodiment, of human knowledge, has the potential to ground theological assertions in both the natural and social orders.[21]

The second important implication of Page's thought, along with related theories in the sciences, has to do with ambiguity as a source for change and transformation. When a situation is marked by ambiguity, its resolution is unclear: there is more than one possible solution, more than one meaning. It is often a situation marked by tension, as competing resolutions are suggested by those involved. In between order and chaos, ambiguity demands further reflection, consideration of new and different outcomes, decisions on what issues are at stake in its resolution. Ambiguity is an *invitation* to change, not a demand for it. But such a situation means that those involved must be able to tolerate, at least for a time, a certain "lack" of order. This "disorder" allows for dimensions of the situation to reveal themselves, or to be uncovered by questioning, opening up issues and concerns that could affect the situation's resolution.

How are these two dimensions of "metaphysical" ambiguity relevant to sacramental theology, and the situation of women in relation to the sacraments? First, sacramental theology has historically turned both to the natural world and to human social institutions as providing "doors

---

20. See Bernard J. F. Lonergan, *Insight: A Study of Human Understanding* (New York: Philosophical Library, 1970 [1957]), esp. 123–28 and 209–11; Kenneth Melchin, *History, Ethics, and Emergent Probability* (Ottawa: National Library of Canada, 1985); Cynthia Crysdale, "Revisioning Natural Law: From the Classicist Paradigm to Emergent Probability," *Theological Studies* 56/3 (1995) 464–84; Michael Shute, "Emergent Probability and the Eco-feminist Critique of Hierarchy," in *Lonergan and Feminism*, ed. Cynthia S. W. Crysdale (Toronto: University of Toronto Press, 1994) 146–74; William P. George, "International Regimes, Religious Ethics, and Emergent Probability," *The Annual of the Society of Christian Ethics* 1996, 145–70.

21. See the work of Lisa Sowle Cahill and Cristina Traina (n. 19, above).

to the sacred," as one contemporary text in sacramental theology puts it.[22] In the broadest sense, the world as a whole is potentially revelatory of the divine. In Roman Catholic moral theology, this understanding of God as revealed in the order of the universe is found in theories of natural law. As it has been traditionally interpreted, natural law defines a fundamental ordering of the natural world, an order established by God in creation and one that human beings, with their rational capacities, can understand.[23] The potential problem with such traditional understandings is that this "ordering" observed in the universe takes on an "objectivity," which is then used to establish normative judgments, especially in matters relating to gender relations and sexuality. But such an assumption of fixity, of hierarchy, of clear and distinct order, may, in fact, be quite different than the kind of "order" that *does* exist, and is more changeable and in flux than most human conceptions of order may realize. Thus Page maintains a skepticism regarding natural law claims to know the "will of God," suggesting that in such claims there is potentially theological *hubris* at work.[24]

A turn to human social institutions (governance, rituals) raises similar questions. Claims that God's will is to be found in hierarchical governing systems or in the institution of marriage, for example, as it has developed socially and historically, leave themselves open to the criticism that such claims identify particular historical realities with the divine will.[25] For thousands of years, the argument was made that God had willed that some human beings could be legitimately enslaved by others.[26] On a lesser scale, the argument was also made that it was God's will that there be no interest charged on loans.[27] In both the cases of slavery and usury, theologians as well as societies came to conclude that such social constructions

---

22. See Joseph Martos, *Doors to the Sacred* (Tarrytown, NY: Triumph Books, 1991).

23. See, e.g., Thomas Aquinas, *Summa Theologiae* I–II, 94, a. 2; I–II, q. 62, a. 3; I–II, q. 91, a. 2; I–II, q. 94, a. 4.

24. *Ambiguity*, 101–4.

25. This was a criticism made by Reinhold Niebuhr of natural law theories. See *The Nature and Destiny of Man. Vol. 1: Human Nature* (New York: Scribner's, 1941, 1964) 220–21. I am grateful to William George for pointing this out to me.

26. Edward Beckett, "Listening to Our History: Inculturation and Jesuit Slaveholding," *Studies in the Spirituality of Jesuits* 28/5 (November 1996); Cyprian Davis, *The History of Black Catholics in the United States* (New York: Crossroad, 1996); John T. Noonan, "Development in Moral Doctrine," *Theological Studies* 54 (December 1993) 662–77.

27. John T. Noonan, *The Scholastic Analysis of Usury* (Cambridge, MA: Harvard University Press, 1957).

of reality were in fact not indicative of their now-changed understanding of the will of God.

Yet my point is not to reject either the natural or the social order as irrelevant for theological reflection, or as potentially indicative of the divine in some way. Their relevance, especially for sacramental theology, is very real, although their significance may not be that of the precise kind of ordering that natural law theories have usually supported. Page's theory suggests a revised perspective on natural law, one that takes into account the complex and sometimes even chaotic structures of the universe, as well as the social and historical factors that affect and interact with the physical. Her theory also suggests that human social orders share in this complexity. Because of the complexity of these "orders," such issues as sex roles and normative structures of human community need to be informed by an appreciation of the ambiguous contours of the cosmos and of human societies.[28]

Thus, "metaphysical ambiguity" sets a context for understanding natural and social order as, in some way, revelatory of God. Given the partiality of human structures of knowing and understanding (thanks to the sociology of knowledge, philosophical and theological hermeneutics, and the like), given the complexity of the most minute structures of the cosmos (thanks to contemporary physics), metaphysical ambiguity suggests a cautious approach to seeing God in the "order of the universe." Biological observations on primate sex roles, on the incidence of same-sex relations among humans and animals, to give just two examples, suggests the need for a real humility about discerning God's will in the natural order. A toleration and appreciation for metaphysical ambiguity involves a recognition that such ambiguity is a structural feature of reality; it is not an aberration from a fixed point of reference. Development and change are thus part of the structure of reality itself. Indeed, if God is immanent in the "order of the universe," as playful and chaotic as it is predictable and harmonious, then our understanding of God must also change. This, in fact, is Page's main point.

This cautious approach to "order" builds on Page's argument that there needs to be a point *between* "order" and "chaos" that can encompass the meaning of the sacraments. While sacraments are a way of "ordering" reality, they arise out of an ambiguously structured universe, and out

---

28. See Cahill, *Sex, Gender.*

of human societies that participate in this ambiguity. Postmodernism's embrace of the multivalent and ambiguous suggests, if not a total dispensing with all "traditional" structures, a recognition that all these human structures are partial, incomplete, and potentially open to change. Their fluidity, their very ambiguity, calls for an approach to natural law that takes this ambiguity into account.

Contemporary sacramental theology since Vatican II has begun to take seriously the social and historical context of the sacraments, and there have been many valuable studies that have developed these dimensions.[29] As I shall show in chapter 4, there has not yet been sufficient attention to the issue of gender in relation to the sacraments. Page's work on metaphysical ambiguity suggests that the new questions and ambiguities that have arisen in relation to the world as revelatory of God need much more careful attention than has been accorded by theologians and official church practice so far. Coupled with enhanced attention to gender, such focus may reveal a more ambiguous and more productive approach to gender than has been the case in official Catholic teachings.

Ambiguity as a potential source for change and transformation is the second important implication of Page's theory. The current ambiguous situation that women occupy in relation to the sacraments raises a number of important questions regarding the sacraments themselves, the role of ordination and leadership, and the effectiveness of sacraments. In her book, *They Call Her Pastor,* sociologist Ruth Wallace interviewed twenty-two women who are "pastoral administrators" in "priestless" parishes, mostly in rural areas in the U.S. Wallace writes, "the role of woman pastor is fraught with ambiguity that can be a constant source of strain in her daily relationships with parishioners and priests."[30] Wallace's focus on "role ambiguity" is an instructive one, as it raises issues and questions not only

---

29. The sources are too numerous to name here. For a representative sampling, see Edward Schillebeeckx, *Christ the Sacrament of the Encounter with God,* trans. N. D. Smith (New York: Sheed and Ward, 1963); Louis Bouyer, *The Eucharist* (Notre Dame, IN: University of Notre Dame Press, 1968); Josef Jungmann, *The Mass: An Historical, Theological, and Pastoral Survey,* trans. Julian Fernandes, ed. Mary Ellen Evans (Collegeville, MN: Liturgical Press, 1976); George S. Worgul, *From Magic to Metaphor: A Validation of the Christian Sacraments* (New York: Paulist, 1980); Bernard Cooke, *Sacraments and Sacramentality* (Mystic, CT: Twenty-Third Publications, 1983).

30. Ruth A. Wallace, *They Call Her Pastor: A New Role for Catholic Women* (Albany: State University of New York Press, 1992) 125.

regarding the role of the woman in a pastoral situation but also of the nature of the sacraments themselves.

The title of Wallace's book is itself indicative of an ambiguity regarding the naming of women who "lead" parishes. According to canon law, the title of pastor is "restricted, by church law, to ordained priests."[31] Yet, as the title of the book indicates, "they [parishioners] call her pastor," despite canon law.[32] Wallace discusses the importance of "naming" for these women pastors. On the one hand, these women pastors know their parishioners by name, to an extent remarked on by both their own parishioners and by visitors.[33] Yet on the other hand, the fact that there is no adequate name or title for these women is a source of dissatisfaction, if not anguish, for them. Function and title are at odds with each other.

A further point of ambiguity arises regarding the liturgical role of these women. Whether or not a woman can "preach" at a liturgy, or whether she merely "offers reflections," is indicative of the woman pastor's liturgical authority, as is also the case when it comes to the issue of liturgical garb. These women struggle as well with the implications of names and actions. Does "preaching" or wearing an alb constitute a yielding to clerical structures, of which these women are highly critical? Or do these actions give the woman pastor an authority she would lack without them? In all these situations, the woman pastor is technically in a position of authority in the parish: she is the chief administrator. Yet she is unable, because of the restriction of ordination to men, to bear the title of pastor, to administer the sacraments (although she may have sole authority in the preparation and education for the sacraments, and often brings the recipient of the sacrament up to the very moment of reception), and to be the liturgical leader for her parish. The result of such "role ambiguity" is a separation of sacramental leadership from sacramental function.

In the cases that Wallace discusses, and among the women I have interviewed who are in various pastoral roles, women's involvement in sacramental education and preparation, which I include under "sacramental function," is significant. These women are the ones who bring their

---

31. Ibid., 129. See also the November 1997 Vatican directive on titles for nonordained pastoral workers, "Some Questions Regarding Collaboration of Nonordained Faithful in Priests' Sacred Ministry," *Origins* 27/24 (November 27, 1997).

32. The insistence by the Vatican, in the November 1997 statement, that only priests can hold certain titles, such as that of pastor, underscores this point.

33. Wallace, *Pastor*, ch. 3.

parishioners to the sacraments, who teach them and model for them what the sacraments are all about: meeting God in everyday life. Since many women are instructed alongside men at many seminaries, especially those that train ordination candidates who belong to religious orders, the fact that they must part ways when it comes to ordination is a source of great pain to many women. The consequences for these women's parishioners are becoming clear: these women are doing "all but" the very moment of sacramental action — consecration, absolution — and their parishioners are increasingly wondering why their women pastors cannot "do everything." For many of the parishioners involved, "bringing in" a priest, usually not a member of the local community, seems artificial and, for some, even unnecessary, for the sacrament to accomplish its purpose in opening a "door to the sacred." Indeed, these women have helped already to open these doors.

Because the situation of women in parish leadership is regarded as a "stopgap" situation — that is, women occupy these roles, technically, and temporarily, because there are not enough ordained men to fill them — there is consequently no change in, and indeed, insufficient theological reflection on, the church's "official" position with regard to women and the sacraments. Sacramental validity remains tied to ordination. But in the experiences of those in the parishes that these women serve, and in the experiences of these women themselves, there is an ongoing transformation that is a direct result of the ambiguity surrounding their roles. "Sacramentality" has come to take on a broader meaning than one restricted to the "seven sacraments."

Indeed, in my interviews, when I have asked women in pastoral roles how they defined the sacraments, they have frequently responded, "Do you mean 'officially' or 'experientially'?" Rather than focusing on the seven "canonical" sacraments, these women often discussed the "sacramental moments" in which they were involved: in giving pastoral care to the ill, in counseling those in crisis, in baptismal, eucharistic, and marriage preparation. While cognizant of the distinction between the narrower "canonical" sense and a broader "experiential" sense of the sacraments, these women preferred to speak of the sacraments in the broadest possible sense.

While it is still in the initial stages, there is, I repeat, a real theological development, if not transformation, taking place in understanding the sacraments, one that would not be possible without the ambiguity surrounding women's new roles in relation to the sacraments. This transformation involves an extension of the "sacramental moment" beyond the moment of actual canonical reception. It involves a far lessened reliance on clergy for an understanding of what "sacramental validity" means. It also means a greater continuity between ritual and everyday life. All of these developments bring the sacramental experience closer to its theological intent and origins. They take the sacraments out of clerical control and, in so doing, work against a "magical" understanding of them. The ambiguous situation that these women occupy is seen by the official church as temporary. Yet it is the permanent condition of an increasing number of parishes, and it is providing the opportunity for a fundamental rethinking of sacramental leadership, function, and effectiveness. Thus the ambiguity of these women's situations is providing the context for change.

Expressive Ambiguity

In his book *The Flight from Ambiguity,* sociologist Donald Levine demonstrates how the modern world has grown increasingly hostile to ambiguity. This attitude has become widespread, growing in political, military, and religious contexts. But it is science, Levine argues, that has "quickened an impulse toward symbolic precision."[34] As science has gained ascendency over other forms of human knowledge, the scientific paradigm has come to be seen as the "highest grade of human knowledge." Forms of expression that are less exact are seen as less true. What concerns Levine is that "the *ambiguities of life* are systematically underrepresented, when they are not ignored altogether, by methodologies oriented to constructing facts through strictly univocal modes of representation."[35]

It is those "ambiguities of life" that demand ambiguous expression: "ambiguous modes of expression are rooted in the very nature of language and thought."[36] Levine gives examples of how many premodern cultures are dependent upon ambiguous expression, sometimes to reveal, and sometimes to conceal, both external and internal realities. Univocal expression, on the other hand, "has the properties not only of being literal, affectively neutral, and public, it is also precise. Ambiguous expressions, by

---

34. Donald Levine, *The Flight from Ambiguity: Essays in Social and Cultural Theory* (Chicago: University of Chicago Press, 1985) 2.
35. Ibid., 8. My emphasis.
36. Ibid., 20.

contrast, can be vague."[37] Ambiguity has no moral valence in and of itself; it is dependent upon its context, and ambiguity can be a way of deliberately confusing reality when clarification may be needed. But there may be times when clarification may come too quickly, and conflicts or differences resolved prematurely. In such circumstances, "the toleration of ambiguity can be productive if it is taken not as a warrant for sloppy thinking but as an invitation to deal responsibly with issues of great complexity."[38]

Levine's interest in ambiguity is as a sociologist. One of his major points is to demonstrate how traditional, premodern cultures show a greater appreciation for ambiguous forms of expression, while the culture of the modern world, and of the U.S. in particular, is characterized by a "flight from ambiguity."[39] While univocal expressions can and do serve important purposes, especially with regard to technology, their domination impoverishes society. Levine stresses that human beings in the modern world have, no less than premoderns, a need for expressivity, a need to protect privacy, a need to mediate the experience of community, and "the persisting need . . . for symbolic forms that mediate the experience of transcendent unities."[40]

Levine's comments on the positive role played by ambiguous expression are echoed, although in a different context, by Regis Duffy. In an essay entitled "The Sacraments in General," Duffy discuss the importance of "symbolic thinking" and the gradual loss of "symbolic competence" over centuries of theological reflection on the sacraments.[41] "Symbolic thinking," Duffy observes, "is concerned more with the larger purposes of God's mystery as revealed in Christ than with the impossible task of explaining how a mystery works."[42] First synthesized by Augustine, symbolic thinking on the sacraments "allowed for the complexity of God's mystery and the redemptive results that were intended."[43] Yet over the

---

37. Ibid., 35.

38. Ibid., 17.

39. Ibid., 36. It is worth noting that many premodern cultures have very strict and decidedly *un*ambiguous views on gender roles. Levine's emphasis here, however, is how conversation and negotiation are dimensions of complex relationships.

40. Ibid., 40.

41. Regis A. Duffy, "Sacraments in General," in *Systematic Theology: Roman Catholic Perspectives,* vol. 2, ed. John P. Galvin and Francis Schüssler Fiorenza, (Minneapolis: Fortress Press, 1991) 183–210.

42. Ibid., 191.

43. Ibid., 195.

centuries, especially in the medieval period, the tendency grew to turn to more "functional" questions in relation to the sacraments, particularly such questions as "how a sacrament works." More reflective of the ecclesial situation of the medieval period than of the competence of such theologians as Thomas Aquinas, instrumental approaches to the sacraments were able to explain sacramental function in a highly sophisticated way. In the process, however, they lost the communal roots of the sacramental experience, and the complexity (and, I would add, ambiguity) intrinsic to that experience.[44] Such approaches were no longer dependent on symbolic thinking, but were increasingly tied to an instrumental and legalistic approach to sacramental validity.

In the contemporary context, Duffy writes, sacramental theology has engaged in a significant process of retrieval, including the importance of the connection between praxis and theory. But unresolved issues for contemporary sacramental theology include "(1) the cultural context of evangelization and sacrament; (2) the role of the Holy Spirit and its ecumenical corollaries; and (3) symbolic competence in a postindustrial age and its corollary, the responsible reception of the sacraments."[45] Duffy defines "symbolic competence" as "the ongoing willingness to enter more deeply into that mystery [God's mystery in Christ] and appropriate its consequences." Such competence "does not bypass the larger socio-cultural situation or the individual psychological profile of communities and their individuals."[46] Duffy then calls for more interdisciplinary work in sacramental theology, mentioning in particular the work of Paul Ricoeur and Jürgen Habermas.[47]

What Duffy describes as a sacramental "loss of symbolic competence" is closely allied with what Levine refers to as a "flight from ambiguity" in our expressive language and action. The roots of this loss are complex. Duffy notes the history of this "loss" in the development of the medieval synthesis, which used Augustine's terminology "without his well-founded sense of symbol or his highly developed ecclesiology."[48] In addition, I would argue that the clericalization of the sacraments (which accompanies a predominantly hierarchical ecclesiology) as well as the concomitant

---

44. Ibid., 195–97.
45. Ibid., 205.
46. Ibid., 207.
47. Ibid.
48. Ibid., 195.

connection of sacramental theology to canon law (especially in seminary training) has intensified this development.[49]

Symbolic thinking is marked by an ability to hold together multiple ideas and meanings without collapsing them into an either/or dichotomy, and a willingness to enter into a world of meaning that is neither purely material nor utilitarian. Paul Ricoeur's famous dictum, "the symbol gives rise to thought," suggests that symbols provoke reflection, kindle the imagination, make more complicated what cannot be easily simplified.[50] The effective symbol both discloses and conceals at the same time, making something else available and yet resisting easy identification between symbol and signified. This inherent *expressive ambiguity* is intrinsic to the sacraments. Bread and wine, water and oil, sexual expression and celibacy, are all multivalent realities. When used as symbols, they provoke the one encountering them to become aware of their multiplicity of meaning.

But the "flight from ambiguity" has also played a part in the way that sacraments have been interpreted and practiced. Recall Levine's description of univocal thinking: it operates on an either/or level. If something is true, it corresponds to "scientific" reality; if it does not, it is untrue.[51] In scientific/technological thinking, things have one meaning. Such thinking can also be found in relation to the sacraments. The dualistic categories of sacred/secular, male/female, clergy/lay, spirit/body, all see reality as divided, not as multivalent. These divisions also tend to be mutually exclusive. The concern to separate, to draw clear boundaries between areas of reality, may help to illustrate how the flight from ambiguity is operative in relation to the sacraments and ecclesial life, especially when gender relations are involved.

---

49. See Rosemary Radford Ruether on this point: "The church creates a sacramental materialism when it teaches people that only the actions of the validly ordained can cause the power of God to be present, and this by simply performing the ritual acts without either the minister or the people appropriating their meaning. The communication of grace, in other words, can happen magically; that is, without real experience of meaning or conviction on either side" (*Women-Church: Theology and Practice* [San Francisco: Harper & Row, 1985], 32).

50. Paul Ricoeur, *The Symbolism of Evil*, trans. Emerson Buchanan (Boston: Beacon Press, 1967) 347ff.

51. In my view, it might be more helpful for Levine to have labeled what he terms "scientific" thinking as "technological" thinking. Science has become more aware than ever before of its own conditionedness, but technology, which is derived from science, is a certain way of thinking that is based on measurable results, on/off, either/or kinds of thinking. See, e.g., the works mentioned above in nn. 12 and 13.

Two examples may help illustrate this tendency. In recent years, seminaries have been directed increasingly to restrict the contact that those men pursuing ordination have with lay men and particularly with women, who constitute the overwhelming majority of those pursuing careers in lay ministry.[52] This practice serves to emphasize the differences between clergy and laity, not what their ministries have in common. Or, second, consider the point that women may not be spiritual directors for seminarians, at least officially. This is not so much because of the temptations involved in this kind of relationship (although this is surely one factor), but, since women lack the experience of priestly ministry, they are not suitable advisors for those who will later hold this office.[53] This difference in experience is seen to constitute an obstacle for the optimal training of ordinands, and women's "different" experience is seen not to make a meaningful contribution to seminary education. Any blurring of the line between clergy and laity endangers the "essential difference" between the hierarchical and the common (baptismal) priesthood.[54]

It is not only the blurring of the relationship between clergy and laity that is the object of concern, but also any challenge to power that is involved in these relationships. Theologically, the understanding of priesthood that has been emphasized by the Vatican in recent years has tended to stress its cultic dimension and the unique power granted to the priest in ordination.[55] While this cultic understanding has served some important purposes over the centuries, it has never shed its concern for ritual purity, which has always involved the exclusion of women.[56] And consider how questions of legitimacy and of clerical power have come to dominate the concern to separate clearly what is a "real" Eucharist from what is "merely" a communion service in "priestless" parishes or a woman-led

---

52. See John Paul II, "Pastores Dabo Vobis," *Origins* 21/45 (April 16, 1992) #60–62.

53. John Paul II, "Instrumentum Laboris," no. 49: "each candidate ought to have a spiritual director chosen from the priests approved by the bishop, and is to meet with him regularly."

54. See John Paul II, "Do Laity Share in the Priest's Pastoral Ministry?" *Origins* (May 1994) 42. In the same document, John Paul II refers to the understanding of priesthood as "headship" and thus the exclusion of the laity, and notably women, from this office. It is important to note the stress on hierarchy in John Paul II's understanding of the priesthood.

55. See David Power, *The Sacrifice We Offer: Tridentine Dogma and its Reinterpretation* (New York: Crossroad, 1987); Pope John Paul II, "Pastores Dabo Vobis," n. 52, above.

56. See Power, *The Sacrifice We Offer* and also *The Eucharistic Mystery: Revitalizing the Tradition* (New York: Crossroad, 1992).

"Eucharist," or the question of the "correct time" for a child to receive first reconciliation. Here, as elsewhere, questions of legitimacy and power have taken on an urgency in official church discussions. These examples all share a concern to establish *clear distinctions* between sacred and secular, clergy and laity, validity and invalidity, male and female. Ambiguous expression and practice, so characteristic of the ways in which symbols operate, pose a danger to the clerical power over the sacraments. While there are surely advantages in making clear distinctions at times, problems arise when these distinctions seem to become the *only* important issues.

The current situation in the church makes these boundaries even more questionable and permeable, with fewer priests in positions to maintain them. This is not to say that all priests are in favor of rigid understandings of priesthood and of sacramental life. In my experience, many priests are eager for change. But the fundamental dynamic of sacramental reality is that while such clear distinctions can be and often are made, they are human inventions, or, more likely, attempts to control reality. In the lived experience of life in the presence of God, sacramental presence cannot be legislated. For very real and practical purposes, it is appropriate that there be some institutional structures to govern the practice of the sacraments. But when these structures begin to act as barriers to participation by the faithful, sacramental life will grow and flourish outside them.

Levine's appreciation for ambiguity focuses largely, although not exclusively, on its expressive possibilities. While ambiguity is an inevitable factor in human life, we have learned, he says, to value the univocal over the multivalent, to prize "plain speech" over the rhetorical excesses of our Victorian forebears, to look for the clearest and briefest explanation. My concern is not to rule out any distinctions whatsoever nor to eschew "plain speech" in theology. It is, rather, to suggest that the most appropriate response to a complex situation is to take time to consider and even appreciate the many dimensions of its complexity, not to resort too quickly to legislative solutions. Further, the multiple possibilities of sacramental representation ought to be enhanced and not reduced.

Roman Catholic sacramental theology has long struggled with ambiguity and has frequently resorted to legalistic solutions. Debates over the nature of the "real presence" in the Eucharist, dating back to the later part of the first millennium and continuing into the present, are the most obvious example that comes to mind.[57] The theological concern was that Christ's presence was "real," that it was not an imaginative or a merely memorial presence. In the present context, the issue that most raises the value of expressive ambiguity has to do with the significance of Christ's maleness for ordination.

According to the Vatican's understanding, the historical actions of Jesus in choosing only men to be his apostles, and the subsequent decisions of the early church to call only men to community leadership have a normative status.[58] Yet historical precedent is insufficient to ground the argument for an exclusively male priesthood. The additional argument is that the priest stands "in the person of Christ" (*in persona Christi*), and since Christ was and remains a male, only men can be priests. Thus there can be *no ambiguity* in recognizing Christ in the ordained presbyter, as there would be (the Vatican argues) with a woman standing in this position.[59]

In a 1994 *Theological Studies* article, Dennis Michael Ferrara took issue with this understanding of the phrase *in persona Christi,* and in particular with the way in which this phrase has come to be understood representationally — that is, the priest as a *physical* "representation" of Christ.[60] Ferrara argued that the intent of Thomas Aquinas was that the priest points not to himself as representative of Christ, but away from himself, to Christ. Thus the priest's role is a more *instrumental* one, not a strictly representational one. In relying only on a representational understanding, Ferrara observed, the Vatican in fact relies on Aquinas's view that women are inferior to men. That is, the representational approach to *in persona Christi* is itself grounded in a subordinationist conception of women's human nature in relation to men's.[61] The instrumental role of

---

57. See Gary Macy, *The Theology of the Eucharist in the Early Scholastic Period* (New York: Clarendon Press, 1984); Joseph M. Powers, *Eucharistic Theology* (New York: Seabury, 1967).

58. See the Vatican "Declaration on the Admission of Women," in Swidler and Swidler, *Women Priests,* #10.

59. "The Christian priesthood is therefore of a sacramental nature: the priest is a sign, the supernatural effectiveness of which comes from the ordination received, but a sign that must be perceptible, and which the faithful must be able to recognize with ease" (#27); "And therefore, unless one is to disregard the importance of this symbolism for the economy of Revelation, it must be admitted that, in actions which demand the character of ordination and in which Christ himself ... is represented ... his role (this is the original sense of the word *persona*) must be taken by a man" (#30); "Vatican Declaration."

60. Dennis Michael Ferrara, "Representation or Self-Effacement? The Axiom *In Persona Christi* in St. Thomas and the Magisterium," *Theological Studies* 55 (June 1994) 195–224.

61. Ferrara, "Representation."

the priest is somewhat ambiguous: there is not a need for a one-to-one correspondence, particularly with regard to gender. The point is that the priest points not to himself (herself?), but to Christ.

Rather than simply eliminating the whole idea of representation, it might be possible to construe representation more broadly than either the Vatican and its defenders, or Ferrara, suggest. Having representation tied to gender alone is a very narrow way of construing the representative role of the presider. More fruitful, perhaps, is a closer connection to the priest as both *in persona Christi* and *in persona ecclesiae,* as representing the resurrected Christ to the community and as representing the people in their celebration.[62]

Some defenders of the Vatican position have argued that it is most appropriate that only men be ordained because, as representatives of Christ, they also represent the kind of challenge to traditional "macho," or power-oriented patriarchal masculinity that Jesus also opposed. In other words, Jesus did not rely on power, or male privilege, but took the role of a servant, and did not use the power that he could have.[63] But this again suggests that only men have power and are able to give it up. The broader, and more expressive, possibilities of the human condition are restricted in gender-based understandings of representation.

Ferrara's article is a complex one, and has led to some spirited exchanges with Sara Butler, another defender of the Vatican's position.[64] My point in briefly summarizing Ferrara's position is that his defense of an "instrumental" rather than "representational" interpretation of *in persona Christi* is, I believe, one that ironically has the potential to do more justice to the symbolic, and thus to expressive ambiguity, than does the representational approach taken by the Vatican. Ferrara's point, at least as I understand him, is that an instrumental understanding of *in persona Christi* better maintains the tension between what the symbol is and what it represents

---

62. See David N. Power, "Representing Christ in Community and Sacrament," in *Being a Priest Today,* ed. Donald J. Goergen, O.P. (Collegeville, MN: Liturgical Press, 1992) 97–123.

63. See, e.g., Francis Martin's discussion of "kenosis" in his understanding of christology in *The Feminist Question: Feminist Theology in Light of Christian Tradition* (Grand Rapids: Eerdmans, 1994) 288ff.

64. Dennis Michael Ferrara, "The Ordination of Women: Tradition and Meaning," *Theological Studies* 55/4 (1994) 706–19; Sara Butler, MSBT, "*In Persona Christi:* A Response to Dennis Ferrara," and Dennis Michael Ferrara, "A Reply to Sara Butler," *Theological Studies* 56/1 (1995) 61–91; Dennis Michael Ferrara, "*In Persona Christi:* Towards a Second Naiveté," *Theological Studies* 57/1 (1996) 65–88.

than does a more representational approach. The latter approach tends to "literalize" the symbolic, closing off expressive possibilities (in this case, of women standing "in the person of Christ") as inappropriate.

One of the main threats to symbolic thinking, and to expressive ambiguity, is a tendency to literalization, to identify the symbol with the symbolized, out of fear that the "true" meaning of the symbol may be lost. Such a tendency is unable to live with the necessary tension that symbols inevitably involve. Levine's and Duffy's calls for expressive ambiguity and a sense of symbolic complexity are both ways of suggesting that symbols be understood in their capacity to *open* new ways of seeing reality, not so much to close them, to restrict possible meanings.

Moral Ambiguity

The third sense of ambiguity that I want to explore I am terming "moral": that is, a sense of the complex *consequences* of a tradition's history. In his book *Plurality and Ambiguity,* David Tracy explores the ambiguity of the heritage of the French Revolution as a model for the importance of interpreting a mixed and complex history. He uses this as a model for discussing the complexity of interpreting religion. Despite whatever good intentions, he writes, "no classic text comes to us without the plural and ambiguous history of effects of its own production and all its former receptions."[65] To understand Christian theology in an unambiguous way is to fail to do justice to the myriad ways in which various events, persons, texts, and doctrinal formulations have come to represent a distortion of what they may have originally intended to communicate, or, more significantly, what they may be able to communicate in ways not even envisioned earlier. For example, to stress the "servanthood" of Christ as a model for human beings to follow, as Paul does in his letters, can serve an important purpose for those in positions of power. But to argue for a servant model for women, and especially for women who have been coerced into servanthood, as generations of African-American women have been, is to overlook the moral ambiguity in such a model.[66]

---

65. David Tracy, *Plurality and Ambiguity: Hermeneutics, Religion, Hope* (San Francisco: Harper, 1987) 69.

66. See, e.g., Delores S. Williams, *Sisters in the Wilderness: The Challenge of Womanist God-Talk* (Maryknoll, NY: Orbis Books, 1993); idem, "Black Women's Surrogacy Experience and the Christian Notion of Redemption," *After Patriarchy: Feminist Transformations of the*

Sacramentality is, as we noted in chapter 1, essential to the Catholic tradition. It is grounded in the conviction that God's presence can be traced, is immanent in, persons, events, rituals, objects. This sense of presence pervades all creation, but can be found especially in the sacraments themselves, and among these, primarily in the Eucharist. Thus, participation in the sacraments themselves is a grace-filled event. The ancient doctrine of *ex opere operato* is meant to convey the intrinsic sacrality and effectiveness of the sacraments themselves: that they are not dependent upon the piety of the minister, nor necessarily on the conscious awareness of the recipient. Such an understanding of sacramentality stresses the representational character of the sacraments, the continuities of the sacraments with the events and persons they symbolize, their analogous relationship of nature, humanity, and God.

But, as anyone familiar with the Catholic tradition knows, this is an ambiguous tradition as well. And a sacramentality that is unaware of its own potential and real ambiguities will find itself threatened by a too-easy familiarity with the divine, a casual approach to sin, a lack of appreciation of the power of the sacraments, and a superstitious and magical attitude toward sacramental effectiveness. In other words, sacramentality is always in danger of pushing the analogy too far into literalism, especially if there is insufficient awareness of the need for a dialectical, or self-critical approach.

Paul Tillich observed in his classic text, *The Dynamics of Faith,* that "the general criticism of the Roman Church by all Protestant groups was the exclusion of the prophetic self-criticism by the authoritarian system of the Church and the growth of the sacramental elements of faith over the moral-personal ones." The Protestant Reformation sought to overcome these problems, but "in this way it lost not only the large number of ritual traditions in the Catholic churches but also a full understanding of the presence of the holy in sacramental and mystical experiences."[67] Tillich concludes his discussion on "Types of Faith" by commenting that "only if Christianity is able to regain in real experience this unity of the divergent types of faith can it express its claim to answer the questions and to fulfill the dynamics of the history of faith in past and future."[68]

World Religions, ed. Paula M. Cooey, William Eakin and Jay B. McDaniel (Maryknoll, NY: Orbis Books, 1991) 1–14; Jacqueline Grant, *White Women's Christ and Black Women's Jesus* (Atlanta: Scholars Press, 1989).

67. Paul Tillich, *The Dynamics of Faith* (New York: Harper, 1957) 72.

68. Ibid., 73.

The complexity of the Christian tradition is revealed in its very mixed history. As Tracy puts it, "historical ambiguity means that a once seemingly clear historical narrative of progressive Western enlightenment and emancipation has now become a montage of classics and newspeak, of startling beauty and revolting cruelty, of partial emancipation and ever-subtler forms of entrapment."[69] But because this complex history is embedded in the "classic" that we have come to know as the Christian tradition, we are obligated to risk genuine conversation with this tradition: facing up to its complexity and responding to it.

This sense of moral ambiguity that Tracy describes — the fact that the classics "stir one's conscience with their demands for nobility of thought and action...[while] at the same time, they also force us to resist their half-concealed tragic flaws"[70] — describes the tradition that feminist theologians have come to know all too well. The moral ambiguity of the sacramental tradition is one that needs further exploration. Like their colleagues in biblical, historical, systematic, and moral theology, feminist sacramental theologians are confronted with a tradition that both draws and repels, invites and excludes. A few examples help to illustrate.

In 1978, Elisabeth Schüssler Fiorenza wrote about her decision to baptize her daughter in the Roman Catholic Church, despite the objections of many of her students and colleagues. Highly aware of the sexism of the tradition, they were surprised and dismayed that she would consent to initiate her daughter into a community of patriarchy. Yet Schüssler Fiorenza, while agreeing that Catholicism is in serious need of transformation, observed that within it there exist practices and traditions that are nevertheless supportive of and inspirational to women. The message of Jesus as one of liberation, rejection of hierarchy, and inclusivity remains alive despite the tradition's institutionalization and patriarchalization, she argued. Further, the veneration given to Mary sends the message that on an "emotional, imaginative, [and] experiential level...the Catholic tradition gives us thus the opportunity to *experience* the divine reality in the figure of a woman."[71] Moreover, the tradition of the saints in Catholicism teaches women that "women, like men, have to follow their vocation from

69. Tracy, *Plurality and Ambiguity*, 70.

70. Ibid., 68.

71. Elisabeth Schüssler Fiorenza, "Feminist Spirituality, Christian Identity, and Catholic Vision," in *Womanspirit Rising: A Feminist Reader in Religion*, ed. Carol Christ and Judith Plaskow (New York: Harper, 1979) 138–39.

God even if this means they have to go frontally against the ingrained cultural mores and images of women. Women, as well as men, are not wholly defined by their biology and reproductive capabilities but by the call to discipleship and sainthood."[72] The message of Jesus, the significance of Mary, and the tradition of the communion of saints, all signaled to Schüssler Fiorenza that this patriarchal tradition was both more and less than it appeared to be.

The sacramental traditions, Schüssler Fiorenza further observes, are those most reluctant to ordain women. "The sacraments, as rituals of birthing and nurturing, appear to imitate the female power of giving birth and of nurturing the growth of life. One would think that, therefore, women would be the ideal administrators of the sacrament."[73] Yet because of a fear of female power on the part of men, and a tendency to take a magical approach to the sacraments, sacraments come to represent "male power over the spiritual life of Christians."[74] In rejecting a clericalist understanding of the sacraments, Schüssler Fiorenza affirmed a critical awareness of the tradition's social and historical conditioning. In bringing her daughter into the sacramental tradition, Schüssler Fiorenza acknowledged its ambiguity as both oppressive and liberating. Certainly baptism can be interpreted as a ritual "co-opting" the power that women have to give birth. Yet Schüssler Fiorenza recognized that it is more than this, that the tradition carries with it more than it even explicitly acknowledges. Baptizing her daughter into the Christian tradition, in the particular form of Catholicism, is an act of confidence that the tradition itself is larger than it seems, and a conscious act of redefinition. It involves facing the tradition's ambiguity head-on.

A second example: in her resource book *Women-Church: Theology and Practice*, Rosemary Radford Ruether also acknowledges the ambiguity of the Jewish and Christian traditions. She observes that women who are committed to the transformation of these traditions stand in a marginal and ambiguous position. "Women-church embraces a liminal religiosity. ...It stands on two thresholds, looking backward to options in biblical and prebiblical faiths that were hinted at but probably never devel-

---

72. Ibid, 140; see also Elizabeth A. Johnson, *Friends of God and Prophets: A Feminist Theological Reading of the Communion of Saints* (New York: Continuum, 1998).

73. Schüssler Fiorenza, *Womanspirit*, 144.

74. Ibid., 145.

oped, and looking forward to new possibilities whose shape is unclear."[75] Women-church, as the gathering of women (and men) who are committed to transforming the church into an egalitarian community, is a way of living in a dialectical relationship that is sensitive to both the charismatic and the institutional dimensions of ecclesial life. Ruether notes that although a few women may prefer to live in women-only conditions of "ideological separatism," such an existence is largely impractical, and fails to acknowledge its dependence on structures that long preexist women-only communities. The more practical and realistic option is maintaining a foothold in both the present institutional structure and in a nurturing community that allows women "to articulate their own experience and communicate it with each other."[76] Ruether observes, "it is my view that the feminist option will be able to develop much more powerfully at the present time if it secures footholds in existing Christian churches and uses them to communicate its option to far larger groups of people than it could possibly do if it had to manufacture these institutional resources on its own."[77]

Ruether also discusses the sacraments themselves. She notes that the ways in which the sacraments have developed historically and have come to be understood theologically have severed them from their roots in "natural" experiences, such as giving birth, eating, reconciling, and marrying. For example, "baptism should symbolize the overcoming of alienating and oppressive modes of human relationship, and the reunion with one's authentic potential for human life by entering into a community that represents redemptive human relationality."[78] Traditionally, however, baptism has been seen as a way of overcoming the sinful origins of human life in the sexual experience of one's parents. Similarly, "Eucharist should be the symbol of our nurture, growth, and participation in the authentic human life of mutual empowerment."[79] But Eucharist, Ruether argues, has become a symbol for the preservation of clerical power; indeed, the Eucharist "has been most radically alienated from the people and transformed into a clerical power tool."[80] Nevertheless, Ruether herself, and many other women

---

75. Ruether, *Women-Church*, 4.
76. Ibid., 59
77. Ibid., 39.
78. Ibid., 77.
79. Ibid.
80. Ibid., 78.

and men continue to find in the Eucharist a place of fractured unity: never perfect, but always anticipating a greater wholeness.

For Ruether, the sacraments have become alienated from their biblical roots and communal origins, yet they are still central to the meaning of the Christian tradition. Although they have been co-opted into clerical structures, they still retain their significance. Thus women's experiences within the institutional churches, especially in sacramental rituals, are ambiguous and ambivalent ones. This ambiguity and ambivalence surrounding women and the sacraments is illustrated in an anecdote related by Mary Collins. At a meeting attended by a group of Roman Catholic men and women, the suggestion was made that there be a closing eucharistic celebration. What followed was a liturgy that "was full of compromises for everyone," yet one that involved "giving thanks together in Christ's name," even if few were "particularly satisfied with what they had done together."[81] While the Eucharist is the sacrament of unity, in the present context, where "eucharistic power" is reserved to the clergy, it has also become a symbol of the "kyriarchal" divisions that persist in Christianity.[82]

Neither Schüssler Fiorenza nor Ruether rejects the centrality or the significance of the sacraments for the Catholic tradition. Both acknowledge the need for symbolic actions that nurture and inspire individuals and communities. But the participation of women in the sacraments is an ambiguous one, involving the struggle with clericalism, the persistence of ancient symbols and rituals, the recognition that the sacraments can both nurture and exclude.

A third example of the moral ambiguity surrounding women and the sacraments is taken from a lecture given by Mary Collins to the National Assembly of the Leadership Council of Women Religious in August 1991. The title of her lecture, "Women in Relation to the Institutional Church," was, she argued, a euphemism for the crisis that in actuality surrounds women in relation to the Eucharist. Especially for women in religious congregations, whose constitutions mandate a "eucharistic center" (daily Mass), the clerical power that is exercised over women through the

---

81. Mary Collins, "Principles of Feminist Liturgy," in *Women at Worship: Interpretations of North American Diversity*, ed. Marjorie Procter-Smith and Janet Walton (Louisville: Westminster John Knox Press, 1993) 10.

82. "Kyriarchy" is Elisabeth Schüssler Fiorenza's term for unjust structures of power. See *Jesus: Miriam's Child, Sophia's Prophet* (New York: Continuum, 1994) 12–18.

sacraments is a symptom of a "symbolic reductionism" that affects both clergy and women. Collins's point in her lecture is that defining the eucharist solely in relation to gender roles and power relations, "enter[ing] into eucharistic liturgy...with controlling ideological commitments is reductionist, no matter which ideology prevails."[83]

The solution that has been taken up by many women, illustrated in the opening anecdote to the first chapter of this book, is to reject the Eucharist, to see institutional religious ritual as "poisonous,"[84] as too infected with clericalism to be worth the effort at retaining it. This stance is rejected by Collins. To equate the Eucharist and the sacramental life of the church with gender issues and power struggles is to "reduce" the sacraments to ideology and power. Collins forcefully argues that "when we make maintaining or dethroning gender-marked pretensions of spiritual power the only operative meaning in eucharistic liturgy," we are missing the fundamental meaning of the Eucharist, but it is a meaning that cannot be controlled or clearly explained.[85] She continues: "The strong sign of the assembly of outcasts and strangers — people so unlike that they would never choose one another's company — being invited to welcome and to forgive one another in Jesus' name, to be at peace, to sin no more — is suppressed *when we reject ambiguity and demand clarity and coherence* in our ecclesial relationships before we can celebrate eucharist."[86]

While the contemporary "disillusionment" and "disappointment" of women toward the church is a "grace offered to women and through women to the whole church," Collins argues strongly that the Eucharist cannot be reduced to a neoclerical power struggle, nor to an issue of gender ideology.[87] It is a much larger reality than either of these reductionist meanings, and the examples of Bartolomé de las Casas and of fourteenth-century Beguine women, both of whom struggled with the significance of

---

83. Mary Collins, "Women in Relation," Ms., 8.

84. Ruether, *Women-Church*, 5.

85. Collins, Ms., 8.

86. Collins, ibid., emphasis added. Such an appreciation for the ambiguity of the Eucharist is illustrated in Sheila Durkin Dierks, *WomenEucharist* (Boulder, CO: WovenWord Press, 1997), which describes women's gathering to celebrate Eucharist among themselves. Interestingly, many of these women, including the author, continue to maintain traditional parish memberships. Moreover, diocesan authorities are aware of this practice and seem to tolerate, at least in the present, an ambiguity regarding these rituals. See the *Chicago Tribune*, February 15, 1998, "Womannews," 1.

87. Collins, "Women," 9.

the Eucharist in the midst of their particular situations, are instructive. Neopagan "rites of empowerment for women" as well as neoclericalism Collins dismisses as "fool's gold." She concludes that the Eucharist as an ambiguous reality is far greater in its potential richness than many feminist critics will allow.[88]

These examples of Roman Catholic women's attitudes toward the sacraments suggest that the historical reality of eucharistic tradition is a morally ambiguous one: the sacraments have become symbols of exclusion, of the superiority of the spiritual to the physical, of the power of clerics over the laity, yet the radically inclusive and mysterious power of the Eucharist remains. All three of these prominent theologians argue that it is necessary to hold on to that moral ambiguity, remembering both the inclusion and exclusion of the Eucharist, and of the other sacraments.

WOMEN AND AMBIGUITY

My point so far in this chapter has been to expand upon and illustrate the potential of ambiguity for a sacramental theology that takes seriously the experiences of women. From one perspective, ambiguity is both natural and inevitable for the sacramental tradition. It is natural in that sacraments, as symbols conveying God's continued presence among us, participate in the ebb and flow, clarity and obscurity, of the universe itself. It is inevitable in that sacraments are part of a historical tradition, one that changes in time and significance.

Yet from another perspective, ambiguity is a threat. As part of an institution that struggles to maintain a common faith amid both the relativism and fundamentalism of the present time, sacraments stand for the permanence of the tradition: we do what others have done, for centuries upon centuries before us. To emphasize the ambiguity of the sacraments challenges their ability to hold together the faith of the people, to be a source of unity in worship amid diversity of experience.

Especially for a feminist approach to sacramental theology, however, ambiguity is unavoidable. From its beginnings, feminist thought has resisted dichotomies, finding in them the continual temptation to as-

---

88. Ibid., 11. It should be noted that Collins's remarks were not unanimously applauded by her audience, and that some were uncomfortable with her labeling of women's rituals as "fool's gold."

sert one side over and against the other. Male/female, rational/spiritual, mind/body, are all too easily extended to superior/inferior, white/black, Christian/Jew, humanity/nature, where in each pair the former term dominates and is superior to the latter.[89] Feminists also resist "complementary" dualisms, where the two terms are understood to complete each other, and together, to comprise a totality. Complementarity disguises stereotypical conceptions of reality — for example, where women's "receptive" nature responds to and "completes" men's "active" nature. Feminist thinkers argue that an approach emphasizing difference rather than dualism, multiplicity rather than duality, ambiguity rather than certainty, is more reflective of the complexity of human interactions.[90]

Women's lives are filled with ambiguities: cultural, linguistic, bodily. From a cultural perspective, women are both affirmed as fully human and yet often excluded from the status of adulthood or full citizenship. Ada María Isasi-Díaz emphasizes the importance of ambiguity in relation to cultural and ethnic differences. She notes that, "in *mujerista* theology, we posit embracing differences as a moral option."[91] A deliberate attention to differences involves interaction and challenging boundaries: "All of this requires embracing ambiguity, something those of us who live at the margins know much about."[92] From a linguistic perspective, women are both included in the so-called generic male and yet often excluded in normative conceptions of "man." And in relation to the body, women's experiences of menstruation, pregnancy, and lactation offer a sense of the ambiguity of the body, and work against cultural conceptions that humans are fully in control of their bodies. Pregnancy offers the experience of being both one and two at the same time. Without arguing for a biological determinism in which all women share the identical experience of embodiment, since embodied experience is always culturally mediated, or a totalizing interpretation of all women's cultural experiences, my point is to raise up ways in which the physical, psychological, and social experiences of women offer a nondichotomous approach to the sacraments.

---

89. For an especially perceptive treatment of this point, see Rosemary Ruether, *New Woman/New Earth: Sexist Ideologies and Human Liberation* (New York: Seabury, 1975).

90. See especially Rebecca Chopp, *The Power to Speak.*

91. Ada María Isasi-Díaz, *Mujerista Theology: A Theology for the Twenty-First Century* (Maryknoll, NY: Orbis Books, 1997) 80.

92. Isasi-Díaz, *Mujerista,* 81.

Women's pastoral experiences in sacramental ministry are already helping to open up dimensions of the sacraments that have tended to be
muted, or overshadowed, by clerical domination, a domination that has
interpreted the sacraments in dichotomous ways: valid/invalid, sacrament/
sacramental, real/symbolic. While the determination of these distinctions
has frequently been, in their original historic context, important theologically, the perpetuation of such distinctions in the present to the near
exclusion of other pastoral concerns — for example, the availability of the
Eucharist — has been detrimental to the theology and practice of the sacraments. The participation of women in the multiple facets of sacramental
ministry — preparation, education, pastoral care, as well as liturgical presiding — has, in fact, blurred the traditional dichotomous distinctions
between ordained and lay, sacrament and "sacramental," real and symbolic.
The consequence of this blurring is an enhanced sense of real presence as
located in the community, a greater awareness of the role of the community in initiation processes, the significance of relationships in the
sacraments of vocation and of reconciliation, and the importance of pastoral care for sacramental life. This is not to say that such "senses" I have
mentioned are absent in the historic tradition. On the contrary, they are
there, and they are ripe for retrieval and reinterpretation. The grace of
the present moment is that the participation of women has made these
dimensions more visible and more accessible to the community.

Thus the "lack" of clarity regarding women's roles in ministry and
in relation to the sacraments has made possible another look at the significance of the sacraments. When a woman presides at a "communion
service," proclaiming and preaching the word, and distributing the Eucharist, one might ask: Is the real presence of Christ less available in this
situation than at a traditional Eucharist? When a woman visits a parish-
ioner who is seriously ill, prays with that person, anoints that person, and
asks for God's loving forgiveness, is the healing power of reconciliation
less available than it would be through the official administration of the
sacrament of the sick? When a woman pastoral associate leads a group of
catechumens through the educational and preparatory process of the rite
of Christian initiation, stands with them as they are received into the community, and continues the process of mystagogy with them afterwards, are
we to say that the sacrament is administered only in the official liturgy and
not in the process? In all these processes, the role of the woman minister
is "technically" auxiliary to the "real" reception of the sacrament, which
is defined by its clerical administration or witness. But the question is in-

creasingly asked whether this participation is truly auxiliary or accidental to the real reception of the sacrament, or whether sacramentality itself needs to be broadened considerably beyond its canonical limitations.

Women's ambiguous roles lead to pressing questions concerning community participation, the relationship between clergy and laity, the limitation of sacramentality to canonical definition, and God's own way of being present in the unpredictable and unexpected. Ambiguity serves to break open necessary questions about the sacraments, questions that raise critical issues about how God is present to the community.

In chapter 7, I will return to the ambiguity of women's roles in liturgical contexts. In the meantime, my suggestion is that the ambiguity of women and the sacraments deserves careful attention, as we sort through the ways in which it can open deeper questions. Taking ambiguity seriously, in its metaphysical, expressive, and moral dimensions, has the potential to transform the theology and practice of the sacraments. For the present, taking ambiguity seriously means that the exclusion of women from sacramental ministry is an issue that deserves long and serious conversation, reflection, and prayer, drawing on women's own experiences, as well as those of the ordained. Without such considerations, the refusal of the Roman Catholic Church *even to allow conversation* on the issue challenges its openness to growth, development, and possible change, an openness it professed at the Second Vatican Council.[93] It suggests, sadly, that the jars of ointment that women's experiences bring to the tradition must be kept shut away, out of fear for what they may contain.

---

93. See *Dei Verbum*, the sacred constitution on divine revelation, *The Documents of Vatican II*, ed. Austin Flannery, O.P. (Collegeville, MN: Liturgical Press, 1975), pars. 6 and 8.

PART 2

Family as Embodied Context for Sacramentality

CHAPTER FOUR

Body and Gender in
Sacramental Theology

It follows, therefore, that through the institution of the sacraments man, consistently with his nature, is instructed through sensible things; he is humbled, through confessing that he is subject to corporeal things, seeing that he receives assistance through them; and he is even preserved from bodily hurt, by the healthy exercise of the sacraments.

— Thomas Aquinas[1]

Did the woman say . . . "This is my Body, this is my Blood?"

— Frances Croake Frank[2]

Over the last twenty years, some of the most interesting and important work in history, philosophy, and theology has concerned the role of "the body." Gendered, historical, social, postmodern — all of these perspectives on the human body have expanded human self-understanding in a number of ways: reminding us that human beings don't live from the neck up, that our social and historical contexts affect the ways we understand our embodiment, that our physical and natural contexts play important roles in maintaining social, religious, aesthetic, and intellectual life. The importance of human embodiment is a general principle in sacramental theology: the corporeal dimension of human life is the basis for all sacramental activity. This principle can be found in Aquinas's theology of the sacraments, where he comments that "it is part of man's nature to acquire knowledge of the intelligible from the sensible."[3] Moreover, post-

---

1. Thomas Aquinas, *Summa Theologiae* III, q. 61, a. 1.
2. Frances Croake Frank, unpublished poem.
3. Thomas Aquinas, *Summa Theologiae,* III, q. 60, a. 4.

Vatican II sacramental theology has focused on the inherent goodness of physical reality.[4] While its necessity had never been questioned prior to the council, the body was generally seen as flawed and affected to a greater extent by sin than was the mind.[5] A greater valuation of the "things of the world," including sexuality, accompanied the post–Vatican II attitude toward the relationship of spiritual and material.

Feminist theology, for its part, has also sought to pay close attention to human embodiment.[6] Conscious of the materiality with which women, on the whole, have been identified, feminist theologians have been critical of "disembodied" understandings of the person, of the relegation of the body to the "lower" dimensions of human personhood. Both sacramental and feminist theologians can be said to "lay claim" to the body, although what they mean by embodiment and how they construe its significance may be very different.[7] In this chapter, I will propose that situating "the body" in the context of feminist theories of the family performs at least two constructive tasks. First, such a situating maintains embodiment within a concrete situation. Second, this positioning gives adequate attention to the social construction of embodiment. By showing that the Roman Catholic magisterial understanding of embodiment lacks adequate context and that post–Vatican II sacramental theology fails to address embodiment in any but the most general sense, I will show that feminist theory and theology offer ways of situating the body that address both of these lacunae as well as adding a richer and more nuanced sense of sacramentality.

The Roman Catholic magisterium justifiably claims that it has always taken embodiment and gender seriously. The classic texts on sacramental theology — especially Thomas Aquinas, as noted above — emphasize that

---

4. See, e.g., Bernard Cooke, *Sacraments and Sacramentality* (Mystic, CT: Twenty-Third Publications, 1983) 7ff.

5. The pre–Vatican II manuals of moral theology argued that in matters of sexual sins, there was "no small matter." See, e.g., Henry Davis, S.J., *Moral and Pastoral Theology,* four volumes (London: Sheed and Ward, 1935); see John A. Gallagher, *Time Past, Time Future: An Historical Study of Catholic Moral Theology* (New York and Mahwah, NJ: Paulist Press, 1990).

6. See, e.g., *Embodied Love: Sensuality and Relationship as Feminist Values,* ed. Paula Cooey, Sharon Farmer, and Mary Ellen Ross (San Francisco: Harper & Row, 1987); Christine E. Gudorf, *Body, Sex and Pleasure: Reconstructing Christian Sexual Ethics* (Cleveland: Pilgrim Press, 1994).

7. For an early exploration of this theme, see my " 'Then Honor God in Your Body' (1 Cor. 6:20): Feminist and Sacramental Theology on the Body," *Horizons* (spring 1989) 7–27.

our knowledge is always dependent on the body. Roman Catholic magisterial theology argues that taking the body seriously means following the dictates of the natural law, which human beings can discern in the workings of the world, using their intellectual gifts. All of nature — of which human beings are a part — has a purpose that can be understood rationally. Moreover, revelation presents models of the body and of gender that draw on ancient ideas as well as expand upon "natural" models: more precisely, the models of covenant and of bridegroom and bride. Thus, the difference of sex, being both natural and revealed, has an ontological meaning, and is to be taken with utter seriousness. This difference plays a major role in sacramental theology, especially when it comes to the theology of orders, but also in the general theory of sacraments. Grounded in its interpretation of biology and revelation, the Vatican's theology of body and gender, which I will spell out below, sees men and women as "equal but different."[8]

While there are a number of theologians, including women, who strongly defend the Vatican position, the significance of gender in sacramental theology, particularly with regard to the ordination of women, is an issue that threatens to divide the church. Feminist critics challenge the Vatican position for its essentialism — that is, an ontological understanding that posits a "male" or "masculine" nature applicable to all men, and a corresponding "female" or "feminine nature" (usually related to women's capacity for motherhood), applicable to all women, apart from social or historical circumstances.[9] Feminists are also critical of the Vatican's position for having an outdated, uninformed, and overidealized understanding of women's roles, with a corresponding lack of attention to men's roles, especially as they relate to family issues.[10]

---

8. For a recent exposition of this argument, especially as it refers to the exclusion of women from ordination, see Monica Migliorino Miller, *Sexuality and Authority in the Catholic Church* (Scranton: University of Scranton Press, 1995). Miller cites "Revelation" as the main source for her position, which accords with the Vatican's (xii–xiii). There is a great deal of material defending the official Vatican position on the question of women's ordination, some of which will be discussed in this chapter.

9. For two feminist positions which argue for a modified essentialism, see Mary Aquin O'Neill, "The Mystery of Being Human Together," *Freeing Theology: The Essentials of Theology in Feminist Perspective* (San Francisco: HarperSanFrancisco, 1993) 139–60; Nancy A. Dallavalle, "Feminist Theology as Catholic Theology: The Spousal Metaphor and the Church as an Eloquent Thing," paper delivered at the 1997 American Academy of Religion Annual Meeting, San Francisco, November 1997.

10. See, e.g., the CTSA response to the first draft of the U.S. bishops' pastoral letter on women, *Proceedings of the Catholic Theological Society of America* 44 (1989) 199–205.

In the meantime, the sacramental theology of the post–Vatican II era, while stressing a "return" to the concrete context of human experience as the source for the sacraments and as the basis for an adequate sacramental theology (that is, a sacramental theology "from below" rather than "from above"), fails to attend specifically to embodiment or gender in any but the most generalized way. While embodiment is clearly a value for this theology, the lack of specificity and development of this value weakens postconciliar sacramental theology's role and influence when body and gender become contested issues.

In this chapter, I hope to convince the reader that neither an essentialist nor an "ungendered" position on the body and gender is adequate for a feminist sacramental theology. There are, however, elements of truth in both positions that cannot be ignored. While embodiment is a central value, it is not an abstract principle, but is rather specific, particular, localized — and gendered.[11] But embodiment, at least in official Roman Catholic theology, has not been adequately understood within the kind of social and historical context that it requires. Nor has it been sufficiently informed by women's experiences. This is surely the case with the official Vatican position, which fixes embodiment and gender in very specific ways that have equally specific, and often problematic, practical consequences. Nevertheless, the seriousness with which the Vatican position takes embodiment and gender is not inconsequential.

Postconciliar sacramental theology has claimed embodiment as a value, as it is understood in the broad context of human experiences as source for sacraments. But the lack of specificity with which it has understood the body and gender is also problematic. When one turns to "human experience" as the broad category from which one begins, it is very important to ask such questions as, "Whose experience are we talking about?" and "How do we define 'experience?'" For the most part, these questions have not been asked with reference to gender in postconciliar sacramental theology, but they are increasingly necessary questions. I will explore below how assumptions regarding "human experience in general" may not always be helpful ones from a feminist perspective. Nevertheless, many of the assumptions behind this "generic" conception of experience are important and serve ultimately to challenge the Vatican model of gender and body.

---

11. See Sharon Farmer, "Introduction," *Embodied Love,* 3.

Feminist thought in general, and feminist theology in particular, have stressed the importance of body and gender. In relation to the body, feminists have challenged at least three sets of interpretations: (1) those that see body and mind (or soul, or spirit) in dualistic and oppositional terms, where the body is in the inferior position. Women have been historically identified with matter and the body (and, correspondingly, nature); men, in contrast, have been identified with mind, soul, or spirit (and, correspondingly, history). The consequences for women have been overwhelmingly negative, as spirit is always interpreted as superior to matter.[12] Such an interpretation, feminists charge, while less common in the present, has characterized the understanding of body and soul, men and women, in the past, and continues to have an insidious effect on the present.

(2) Liberal understandings, which, for all practical purposes, ignore the significance of the body and emphasize the commonality and universality of the human. The problem with this position is that liberal ideas of equality cannot be achieved by women without attending to the concrete contexts in which they are to be lived.[13] Too often these positions assume the normative nature of human being to be male and thus such distinctly female experiences as menstruation, pregnancy, and lactation are seen as deviations from a norm.

(3) Essentialist understandings, which posit fixed "masculine" and "feminine" natures, applicable to all persons regardless of context.[14] Feminist thinkers are far from unanimous in their thinking on body and gender. But they agree that dualism and most forms of essentialism serve women badly, and that the particularities of women's lives (such as the fact that only women bear children) need to be included in liberal discussions of equality.[15]

---

12. Rosemary Ruether has developed this argument most extensively. See especially *New Woman/New Earth: Sexist Ideologies and Human Liberation* (New York: Seabury, 1975), which develops this point at length, and in relation to racism, classism, and anti-Semitism, which are also classified on the negative side of the dualism.

13. See Susan Frank Parsons, *Feminism and Christian Ethics* (Cambridge: Cambridge University Press, 1996), for a helpful description of liberal, social-constructionist, and naturalist paradigms in feminist thought.

14. The official position of Roman Catholicism on the nature of women represents an essentialist understanding. But essentialism is also found, in various forms, among some feminist thinkers. See, e.g., Luce Irigaray, *An Ethics of Sexual Difference*, trans. Carolyn Burke and Gillian C. Gill (Ithaca, NY: Cornell University Press, 1993).

15. See Lisa Sowle Cahill, *Sex, Gender, and Christian Ethics* (Cambridge: Cambridge University Press, 1996).

In this chapter, I will explore sacramental theology's understanding of body and gender within both a general understanding of sacramentality and with regard to particular sacramental concerns, for example, those of orders and of marriage. I will also pay attention to the metaphors and models used to describe the body. The reason for this approach is that it is in relation to the theology of ordination that discussions of gender, and to some extent, of the body as well, most often take place. But these discussions are not just about priesthood. They also involve theological anthropology (the doctrine of the person), christology, the doctrine of God, and ecclesiology. Because an exhaustive study of sacramental theology's understanding of the body is beyond the scope of this book, and would involve historical, linguistic, and liturgical studies that would take us far afield of our question, I will undertake this more limited examination of recent Vatican writings on priesthood and on women, and selected works in postconciliar sacramental theology.

THE VATICAN THEOLOGY OF BODY AND GENDER

The understandings of the body that have emerged over two thousand years of the Catholic tradition's history are complex.[16] On the one hand, the Christian tradition has affirmed the goodness of creation and, in the doctrine of the incarnation, has declared that God's very being has become inevitably connected with embodiment. The full humanity of Christ was defended repeatedly against Gnostic interpreters, who found the belief that God had taken on flesh to be an abomination. The sacramentality of marriage and the belief in the resurrection of the body are examples of the Christian tradition's affirmation that the body is good.

But on the other hand, the tradition's ambivalence toward, and sometimes even hatred of, the body is as much a part of its history as is its reverence for it. While the Christian elevation of the celibate life over marriage has complex origins,[17] there is no question that, far too often, bodily pleasures — usually food or sex — have been seen as evil, and that

---

16. For a brief review, see my entry on "Body" in the *New Dictionary of Catholic Spirituality*, ed. Michael Downey (Collegeville, MN: Liturgical Press, 1993) 93–100.

17. See Peter Brown, *The Body and Society: Men, Women and Sexual Renunciation in the Early Church* (New York: Columbia University Press, 1988), for one of the most thorough and evenhanded treatments of this complex history.

women's identification with the body has led elements in the tradition to see women as evil, or at least as potentially more evil than men.[18] The correlation of women with matter and men with form in Aquinas's theological anthropology (where form has an ontological priority),[19] of women's responsibility for original sin (see 1 Timothy 2:11–15), and of women's "naturally" greater concern with material over spiritual reality, have had profound influences on the tradition, resulting in an ambivalent attitude toward the human body, especially women's bodies, as well as attitudes of suspicion and hostility. Twentieth-century Catholic theology has increasingly recognized problematic elements in the tradition, and such major shifts as the affirmation of the "unitive" dimension of marital sexuality as equal to the "procreative" dimension, and the "turn to the world" of Vatican II, have helped to reestablish the goodness of the body as central to the tradition.

Prior to the controversies regarding the ordination of women that have arisen in the last twenty-five years, most of the Vatican discussions of gender earlier in this century took place in regard to the sacrament of marriage. *Casti Connubii,* Pius XI's 1930 response to both the women's suffrage movement and the Anglican decision to permit artificial contraception, is a foundational text for understanding the significance of "womanhood" in pre–Vatican II Roman Catholic thought.[20] Later Popes addressed what we would today call "gender issues" through treatises on Mary, the mother of Jesus, statements on marriage, and talks to midwives.[21] It is doubtful that the present pope would repeat some of the statements made by his predecessors on the "nature" of women, couched as they were in clearly subordinationist language.[22]

---

18. The strongest statement making this point can be found in the medieval *Malleus Maleficarum* (the "hammer of witches"), a selection from which is found in Elizabeth Clark and Herbert Richardson's anthology, *Women and Religion: A Feminist Sourcebook of Christian Thought* (San Francisco: Harper & Row, 1977) 116–30.

19. For a helpful discussion of the relation of matter and form in the thought of Aquinas, see Brian Davies, *The Thought of Thomas Aquinas* (Oxford: Clarendon Press, 1992) 45–49.

20. Pius XI, *Casti Connubii,* December 31, 1930.

21. See, e.g., Pius XII, *Dei Parae Virginis Mariae* (May 1, 1946); Pius XII, "Address to Midwives," 1951.

22. For example, Pius XI writes, in *Casti Connubii,* "Domestic society being confirmed, therefore, by this bond of love, there should flourish in it that 'order of love' as St. Augustine calls it. This order includes both the primacy of the husband with regard to the wife and children, the ready subjection of the wife and her willing obedience, which the Apostle

Vatican II's emphasis on the equality of women has been stressed by recent popes, and the magisterium has argued that it has promoted the equality of women throughout its history.[23] But when the question of the ordination of women arose in the 1970s, gender became an issue not only with regard to the priesthood, but also in relation to broader issues. That is, the question of the nature of priesthood provided the opportunity for the Vatican to articulate a theological anthropology, as well as a christology, ecclesiology, and a doctrine of God that drew on gendered language, and to expand one specific model of gender relations.

A few statements from Vatican II documents can help to set the context. In *Gaudium et Spes* (the pastoral constitution on the church in the modern world), the council condemned "forms of social or cultural discrimination . . . on the grounds of sex, race, color, social conditions, language or religion" and argued that they "must be curbed and eradicated as incompatible with God's design."[24] Later on in the document, in the section on "more urgent duties of Christians in regard to culture," the document states: "at present women are involved in nearly all spheres of life: they ought to be permitted to play their part fully *according to their own particular nature*. It is up to everyone to see to it that women's *specific and necessary participation* in cultural life be acknowledged and fostered."[25]

The dogmatic constitution on the church (*Lumen Gentium*), while not specifically addressing the issue of gender, uses, among its many descriptions of the church (including people, mystery, sheepfold, cultivated field, building of God, body), the ancient metaphors of "mother" and "spouse."[26] If any one model of the church is predominant in this document, however, it is that used in the title of the second chapter,

---

commands in these words: 'Let women be subject to their husbands as to the Lord because the husband is the head of the wife, and Christ is the head of the church'" (n. 26).

23. There is some basis for this point: with regard to the sacrament of marriage, the medieval church's decision to require *consent* of both partners marks an important progressive move. In addition, the roles of women in religious congregations afforded many women a kind of "equal opportunity" not possible in the secular sphere. See *Women of Spirit: Female Leadership in the Jewish and Christian Traditions,* ed. Rosemary Radford Ruether and Rosemary Keller (New York: Charles Scribner's Sons, 1979). Whether the church has truly promoted the full equality of women is another question.

24. *Gaudium et Spes,* in *Vatican II: The Conciliar and Post-Conciliar Documents,* ed. Austin Flannery, O.P. (Boston: St. Paul Editions, 1987), par. 29.

25. Ibid., par. 60, p. 965. Emphasis mine.

26. See *Lumen Gentium,* especially par. 6, p. 354, with generous citations to Ephesians 3 and 5.

"The People of God," of which both clergy and laity are an integral part. Notwithstanding this shared identity, the document insists on the "essential" difference between the common priesthood of the faithful and the hierarchical priesthood of the clergy. In general, in the documents of Vatican II, there is a concern expressed for the full equality of women — especially in the pastoral constitution — and there is a diversity of models for the church. But there is neither much explicit reference made to the details of women's "particular nature" nor a predominance given to the model of church as "spouse." Women's "nature" is largely left unexplained, and metaphors for the church draw on a variety of images.[27]

In the 1968 encyclical *Humanae Vitae,* written to address the question of the permissibility of "artificial" forms of contraception, spousal language is of course central. Most of the references in the document are to the couple in general, but one particular reference raises cautions about the dangers of "anti-conceptive practices": "It is also to be feared that the man, growing used to the employment of anti-conceptive practices, may finally lose respect for the woman and, no longer caring for her physical and psychological equilibrium, may come to the point of considering her as a mere instrument of selfish enjoyment, and no longer as his respected and beloved companion."[28] Apart from this one reference, which does not mention the potentially positive consequences of contraceptives for the woman (for example, freedom from fears of unplanned pregnancy), the letter is concerned with the couple as a unit, and not particularly with gender roles. It is worth noting at least two things here. First, the freedom from fear of an unplanned pregnancy may well be a good, but such a good could not override the intrinsic evil of contraception. Second, the implied reader is male. Marriage is defined, as it has been since Augustine, as an institution primarily for the procreation of children. But *Humanae Vitae,* like *Gaudium et Spes,* now includes mutual love as one of

---

27. See Dennis M. Doyle, "Journet, Congar and the Roots of Communio Ecclesiology," *Theological Studies* 58 (1997) 461–79.

28. See Paul VI, *Humanae Vitae* ("On the Regulation of Birth"), July 25, 1968, par. 17, in *The Gospel of Peace and Justice: Catholic Social Teaching since Pope John,* presented by Joseph Gremillion (Maryknoll, NY: Orbis Books, 1976) 436. In par. 25, addressed to "Christian husbands and wives," Paul VI mentions the "serious difficulties" couples may face in following this teaching, and quotes from Ephesians 5, although he omits references to the husband's "headship."

the *two* primary purposes of marriage: as both procreative and unitive.[29] This marked a significant development in the theology of marriage in the twentieth century.[30]

Overall, then, the language of gender is an issue neither in the conciliar documents, nor in those immediately following the council. Nor is much reference to gender found in postconciliar sacramental theology from this time. In references both to marriage and to priesthood, gendered language does not emerge as significant. This is not really surprising, since the consciousness of gender as an issue was just beginning to come to the fore in the late 1960s. But my point in emphasizing this "lack" of reference to gender is to show that "gendered" models for priesthood, for marriage, and for church became prominent when the issue of women's ordination and of women's broader participation in the church became a pressing question. Until then, the spousal model for church and for priesthood was but one among others.

The rise of the women's movement in the 1960s and early 70s brought the issue of women's ordination to the fore, and some Protestant and Jewish traditions began ordaining women during this time. The first meeting of the Women's Ordination Conference (WOC) was in November of 1975, where both women theologians and bishops addressed the question. Following upon the WOC meeting, the 1974 "irregular" ordination of eleven Episcopal women, and the subsequent 1976 vote affirming the ordination of women by that church's general convention, the Vatican in late 1976 issued *Inter Insigniores*, the "Declaration on the question of the admission of women to the ministerial priesthood."[31] The arguments against women's ordination come down basically to two. First, the "historical example" that Jesus set in calling only men to be the twelve (and the permanent value of this example). Second, the "mystery" of sacramental representation, in which the "natural resemblance" of the minister to Christ as a male is

---

29. This is an important point in and of itself, but is not of immediate importance for my purposes here. See Theodore Mackin, *What is Marriage: Marriage in the Catholic Church* (New York and Mahwah, NJ: Paulist Press, 1982); idem, *Divorce and Remarriage* (New York and Mahwah, NJ: Paulist Press, 1984); *The Marital Sacrament* (New York and Mahwah, NJ: Paulist, 1989) for a full treatment of these issues.

30. See Mackin (n. 29, above) and Lisa Sowle Cahill, "Catholic Sexual Ethics and the Dignity of the Person: A Double Message," *Theological Studies* 50 (June 1989) 120–50.

31. The text of the document and numerous responses to it can be found in *Women Priests: A Catholic Commentary on the Vatican Declaration,* ed. Arlene Swidler and Leonard Swidler (New York and Mahwah, NJ: Paulist, 1977).

normative. The document refers to the "mystery of the covenant" in its explanation and draws on the bridegroom-bride model as revealing that Jesus is the "Bridegroom and Head of the Church," and as bridegroom, is necessarily a male.[32]

The document's reference to the need for a "natural resemblance" between priest and Christ received much criticism after the document was released.[33] It is interesting that in subsequent discussions, this line of argumentation virtually disappears. But what emerges as the dominant motif, in the understanding both of priesthood and of the nature of women, is the nuptial imagery of God-humanity and Christ-church.

This is certainly the case in the theology of priesthood and of the person developed by Pope John Paul II. In his 1988 encyclical "On the dignity and vocation of women" (*Mulieris Dignitatem*), the pope describes human relationships in "spousal" terms. Grounding his point in the creation story in Genesis 1, the pope writes that human beings achieve unity in the mutual integration of "masculine" and "feminine."[34] There are distinct characteristics to each sex. In particular, a "readiness to accept life" and the "distinctiveness of her potential for motherhood" mark what it means to be a woman.[35] Much of what the pope writes draws on Mary as the model for womanhood, and also for church and laity. But what is of special importance for our purposes is the way in which the bride-bridegroom dynamics operate. Key here is the pope's description of the kind of love expressive of "spousal" love: "The bridegroom is the one who loves. The bride is loved. It is she who receives love, in order to love in return."[36]

Earlier, the pope describes the significance of the bridegroom metaphor in relationship to masculinity. It is worth quoting at length:

---

32. In Swidler and Swidler, 44–45.

33. Many of the responses in the Swidler and Swidler collection address this point; see also Catholic Theological Society of America, *Research Report: Women in Church and Society*, ed. Sara Butler, MSBT (Mahwah, NJ: Darlington Seminary, 1978); Elizabeth A. Johnson, "The Maleness of Christ," in *The Special Nature of Women?*, ed. Anne E. Carr and Elisabeth Schüssler Fiorenza, *Concilium* 1991/4 (London: SCM Press, 1991).

34. For a very perceptive treatment of the question, see Richard Viladeseau, "Could Jesus Have Ordained Women? Reflections on *Mulieris Dignitatem*," *Thought*, 67:264 (March 1992) 5–20. Viladeseau points out the strong connection between the theology of Hans Urs von Balthasar and John Paul II.

35. John Paul II, *Mulieris Dignitatem* (On the Dignity and Vocation of Women), *Origins* 18/17 (October 6, 1988) par. 18. Hereafter *MD*.

36. *MD*, par. 29.

The symbol of the bridegroom is masculine. This masculine symbol represents the human aspect of the divine love which God has for Israel, for the church and for all people. Meditating on what the Gospels say about Christ's attitude toward women, we can conclude that as a man, a son of Israel, he revealed the dignity of the "daughters of Abraham" (cf. Lk. 13:16), the dignity belonging to women from the very "beginning" on an equal footing with men. At the same time Christ emphasized the originality which distinguishes women from men, all the richness lavished upon women in the mystery of creation. Christ's attitude toward women serves as a model of what the Letter to the Ephesians expresses with the concept of "bridegroom." Precisely because Christ's divine love is the love of a bridegroom, it is the model and pattern of all human love, men's love in particular.[37]

What Pope John Paul II says here is very significant. His basic argument is that God's love, as it is understood in human terms, has been revealed in the person of Christ, who is male. Humanity, which receives this love, is therefore symbolized in feminine terms — thus the pope can say that both men *and* women are represented in feminine terms, in the role of the bride.[38] But only men can represent the essentially "male" (that is, initiatory) love of God, as it has been represented in the (male) person of Christ. Moreover, the "special nature" of women is particularly oriented to the "care of human life." Women possess, according to the pope, a "special sensitivity which is characteristic of their femininity" (par. 16); further, "woman can only find herself by giving love to others" (par. 30). Women's capacity for either biological or spiritual motherhood is thus part of the ontological "essence" of women, which finds its culmination in caring for others.

This position is further developed by Francis Martin, in a book that also argues against most of the positions taken by feminist theology.[39] Martin identifies "the feminine" as "the receptive dimension of every human being"[40] and stresses this point by stating, "women literally embody receptivity."[41] One of Martin's main points is to emphasize that such characteristics as receptivity have been wrongly denigrated in the tradi-

---

37. *MD*, par. 25

38. "From this point of view, the 'woman' is the representative and the archetype of the whole human race: she represents the humanity which belongs to all human beings, both men and women," *MD*, par. 4.

39. Francis Martin, *The Feminist Question: Feminist Theology in the Light of Christian Tradition* (Grand Rapids: Eerdmans, 1994).

40. Martin, 196.

41. Ibid., 197.

tion, and that receptivity is equal to activity in value. But his main point, as is the Vatican's, and that of other defenders of the Vatican position, is to argue that taking embodiment seriously means to argue *from* bodily characteristics *to* ontological essence. Thus women's inherent "receptivity" (which is not established, but assumed by these authors, presumably by interpreting the experience of sexual intercourse) is intrinsic to female personhood.[42] Martin and other critics of feminist theology argue that feminists assume a new form of dualism,[43] or reduce human embodiment to a collection of "body parts."[44] The priest must be male, Martin argues, because he represents "Christ as *other* in relation to the church." Females also represent Christ, Martin further points out, in that "females show forth the receptivity of Christ, a reality that characterizes him within the Trinity and is historicized in the Incarnation and continued in the Church."[45] Thus, men can share in being receptive (as members of the church) but women cannot similarly share in the active role of Christ as over and against the Church.

The "spousal" argument for ordination's reservation to men has been developed by a number of other authors, who similarly argue for the onto-logical significance of male and female sexuality as revealing, respectively, God's self-gift in Christ, and Mary's (and the church's) acceptance and response. Donald Keefe speaks for this position when he argues:

> If it be true that masculinity and femininity are thus sacramental, and that all human existence is engaged in this signing, it must follow that the *only* paradigms by which the mystery, the meaning, of masculinity and femininity may be approached are those provided by the marital relationship between Christ and his Church, between the Head and the Body, a polarity intrinsic to the New Covenant, to the New Creation, to the imaging of God.[46]

---

42. See, e.g., Paul Quay, S.J.: "The fullness of intrinsic symbolic meaning in intercourse is seen from the fact that any such description of the physical act can be read, with scarcely a change, as a description of the couple's psychic activity. The man's initiative and the woman's opening are not merely physical but also psychological. The man's dominance in penetrating and taking possession is an attitude of mind and heart, not merely bodily power." *The Christian Meaning of Sexuality* (San Francisco: Ignatius Press, 1985) 29.

43. Martin, 382: "The reflections of these theologians [e.g., Karl Rahner] show a basic agreement with feminist approaches in their attempt to subordinate the body and its inherent sexuality to an autonomous subjectivity freed of biological and material constraints."

44. Ibid., 396

45. Ibid., 404.

46. Donald J. Keefe, "Sacramental Sexuality and the Ordination of Women," *Communio* 5 (fall 1978) 228–51. My emphasis.

Thus, for these theologians, the dual nature of human embodiment is itself symbolic of the divine-human relationship.

RESPONSES TO THE VATICAN POSITION

There are significant anthropological, christological, ecclesiological, and trinitarian consequences that result from this kind of "gendering" of humanity, Christ, and God. Human persons are understood primarily in their sexual distinctness, and this distinctness is heterosexual and complementary. Christ's maleness is not a secondary characteristic of his humanity but is, rather, constitutive of its meaning.[47] The church, and more importantly, the laity, are seen as fundamentally female (that is, as receptive, and not initiatory), and most seriously, God is understood, in some essential ways, as more "male" than "female."

The difficulties of this particular approach to the relationship between Christ and church, men and women, have been discussed in a number of articles.[48] In his response to *Inter Insigniores*, biblical scholar Carroll Stuhlmueller argues that the spousal symbol is far more complex than the Vatican's use suggests, and that the intermingling of genders for God, Christ, and humanity in the biblical context work against any "single-line application" of gender imagery.[49] In his discussion of the priest's representative role, David Power comments that "it is doubtful that prevailing importance needs to be given to the sexual side of this imagery in configuring the Christ-church or Christ-humanity relationship." Such a construal "risk[s] undermining the unity that has been established between Christ

---

47. See Keefe, "Sacramental Sexuality": "Her [Mary's] affirmation is constitutive for his imaging; precisely, it is the constitution of his masculinity, which was not imposed upon her, but conceived by her in untrammeled freedom as the total expression of the perfection of her worship." (245).

48. See Carroll Stuhlmueller, "Bridegroom: A Biblical Symbol of Union, Not Separation," in Swidler and Swidler, *Women Priests*, 278–83; David Power, "Representing Christ in Community and Sacrament," in *Being a Priest Today*, ed. Donald J. Goergen (Collegeville, MN: Liturgical Press, 1992) 97–123, esp. 112–21. Sara Butler, MSBT, has defended this model in a number of articles. See "The Priest as Sacrament of Christ the Bridegroom," *Worship* 66 (November 1992) 498–517, in which she argues against the position taken by Power in his chapter; also, idem, "Priestly Identity: 'Sacrament' of Christ the Head," *Worship* 70/4 (July 1996) 290–306.

49. Stuhlmueller, 283.

and the Church through the work of reconciliation."[50] Power's point is that emphasizing sexual difference serves to separate the role of priest and community; he argues, rather, that the two ought to be seen in "intimate unity."[51] The priest as head brings the community together and ought not to be defined in opposition to it.[52]

My point is not to argue that the use of spousal imagery to understand the relation between God and humanity, Christ and church, priest and laity, ought to be entirely discarded. Clearly, this is very ancient symbolism; it draws on prebiblical traditions, medieval mystical theology, and has a long history in biblical and theological writings. Below I will argue for its significance, although within a different interpretive context. But its use in the present raises a number of serious questions. First, the relationship of bridegroom and bride is not an egalitarian relationship. In fact, this metaphor was used precisely because men and women were not equal. This is made clear by John Paul II, and the other defenders of this position, in at least two ways. First, the love between bridegroom and bride is initiated by the Bridegroom; the bride's role is responsive. Further, the bride (as symbolic of humanity in relation to God) includes both male and female; the bridegroom includes only the male. This means that not only do male and female have unequal roles (that is, brides cannot initiate),[53] but females cannot truly image God, since women are "receptive" where God is active and generative.

This leads to the second issue: that is, that God is best understood in male terms. Although the pope acknowledges that God is described in both "masculine" and "feminine" terms in the Bible, and that " 'generating' has neither 'masculine' nor 'feminine' qualities,"[54] nevertheless God's revelation takes place in the person of a male, thereby representing "the human aspect of the divine love which God has for Israel, for the church, and for all people."[55] Christ's maleness is not, as Power (and others) would argue,

---

50. Power, "Representing Christ," 120.

51. Ibid.

52. A similar point is made by Edward Kilmartin in his article, "Apostolic Office: Sacrament of Christ," *Theological Studies* 36:2 (March 1975) 243–64. Keefe's article is in large part a response to Kilmartin's article. See Keefe, "Sacramental Sexuality," 235ff.

53. See, e.g., Hans Urs von Balthasar, "Theology and Sanctity," in *Word and Redemption*, trans. A. V. Littledale (New York: Herder and Herder, 1965) 76–78, where he emphasizes the "feminine" and thus the completely "receptive" dimension of humanity.

54. *MD*, par. 8.

55. *MD*, par. 25.

the "submission of the divine Word and Wisdom to the limiting conditions of human enfleshment,"[56] but is rather, as Sara Butler argues in defense of the papal position, "a question of *fact*" and "is symbolically linked to the whole of biblical revelation and to its core mystery, the covenant."[57] Notwithstanding this somewhat circular reasoning (Christ is male because he symbolizes God as bridegroom in the metaphor of the covenant relation), the net result is that men are more appropriate symbols for God's love for humanity than are women. This is not inequality, the Vatican seems to say, but part of the "mystery" of revelation.

Another defender of the Vatican position, Monica Migliorino Miller, goes even further than the pope in arguing that "feminine images of God are aberrations that serve a particular crisis moment."[58] If human equality before God and God's transcendence of gender are basic to the Christian revelation, as John Paul II himself argues, such a heavy reliance on spousal symbolism works against such equality. Appeals to "covenant mystery" raise more problems than they solve, as I will argue shortly. In short, given the fundamental principle of human equality before God, and of all human beings created in the image of God, the use of this symbolism in these ways raises serious theological and anthropological problems. While some of these authors go to great pains to establish how "receptivity" is just as positive as "activity," and that therefore women's roles need to be "better understood" or "expanded," the conclusion that women are inevitably secondary is inescapable.[59] Further, women's "natural receptivity" is never established, or argued, but simply asserted.

There are at least two additional problems, already hinted at, with the use of this model. The first of these involves the consequences for christology. If the spousal model is the best model for understanding the person and work of Christ, then his maleness, and not socio-cultural limitation, or finitude, is the most important aspect of his humanity. As the Vatican and its defenders would argue, Christ's maleness is not accidental but a deliberate choice on the part of God. Indeed, in *Mulieris Dignitatem,* the

56. Power, "Representing Christ," 116.

57. Butler, "The Priest as Sacrament," 506.

58. Miller, *Sexuality and Authority,* 83.

59. Martin in fact argues that Karl Barth's theology offers positive possibilities. Note Barth's famous argument that man is A and woman is B. See Karl Barth, "The Doctrine of Creation," *Church Dogmatics,* vol. 3, sec. 4, ed. G. W. Bromiley and T. F. Torrance (Edinburgh: T. and T. Clark, 1961).

pope, in speaking of Mary as mother of God, writes that "the daughters of this chosen people...could hope that one of their number would one day become the mother of the Messiah."[60] The assumption that the messiah would be male makes sense in terms of the historical context. But what is emphasized is the permanent significance of this maleness, even beyond the resurrection. Butler argues that Power's interpretation of the risen Christ as "the renewed *human*, in which from one point of view, male and female together constitute the one, and in which from another 'there is neither male nor female,'"[61] effectively eliminates "any need for gender symbolism, replacing this with the vision of 'one person' who is the whole Christ, head and members."[62]

The point, however, that Power makes, is that Christ brings all humanity together in his redeeming work, without distinctions of gender. It is not so much that "there is no need for gender symbolism," but rather that this particular gender symbolism, when applied as the fundamental model for Christ's relationship to humanity, perpetuates a separation of male and female. Indeed, Power asks which takes precedence: Christ's redemptive work for all of humanity, regardless of gender, race, or class (Galatians 3:28), or a particular model of human-divine relationship, rooted in ancient cultural assumptions regarding the roles of men and women in marriage?[63]

Finally, the exclusive use of this model has serious ecclesiological implications. As long as the spousal symbol is described as an active-receptive relationship in which Christ (or the priest, or the hierarchy) always initiates and the church (or the laity) always responds, then the basic equality of the people of God, and their sharing in the common priesthood of Christ, will be undercut. While the spousal relationship is now described in terms of self-gift and mutuality, there is still a power imbalance in this relationship. My point here is that maintaining the primacy of the spousal model serves to support a hierarchical conception of church that works against the very equality and mutuality that the Vatican says is basic to its anthropology. A hierarchical spousal relationship serves as the model for clergy-lay relationships as well.[64]

---

60. *MD*, par. 3.

61. Power, 115; quoted in Butler, 509.

62. Butler, 509.

63. Power, "Representing Christ," 115.

64. See my "The Bride of Christ and the Body Politic: Body and Gender in Pre-Vatican II Marriage Theology," *Journal of Religion* 71/3 (July 1991) 345–61, which develops this point

From a number of perspectives, then, the gendered symbolism of bridegroom-bride is seriously problematic. It assumes that women possess an essentially "maternal" or "receptive" nature and that relations between men and women are to be understood as asymmetrically complementary (asymmetrically, in that God/Christ/men initiate, and that Mary/church/women respond). Men are, "by nature," possessed of an "active" personhood, while women's is "actively receptive." Thus, there is an ordering to gender relationships in which men are always primary and women secondary. Women and men can both symbolize expectant and receptive humanity, as male and female, while only men can symbolize God, as God is revealed in Christ as male. This conclusion is derived from a reliance on biblical typologies and their development within a tradition which has also maintained, until very recently, women's inferiority and "natural subjection" (Thomas Aquinas), the unsuitedness of women for political life (*Casti Connubii*), and the inherent inequality in the marital relationship (also *Casti Connubii*).[65]

In short, while spousal symbolism has a long and complex history, it is intertwined with the tradition's sexism, low regard for the (especially female) body, and hierarchical conception of marriage. Unless the church is willing to admit its complicity in sexist structures, a conclusion that even critics of feminist scholarship will acknowledge,[66] its use of gendered symbols without critique is disingenuous. Given the historical oppression of women, a hermeneutics of suspicion with regard to spousal symbolism is not only appropriate, but even necessary.

Does this brief critique mean, then, that spousal/nuptial imagery ought to be discarded? Both Stuhlmueller and Power argue that there are potentially positive implications of this symbol. The first is that marital symbolism conveys *intimacy*, and both scholars claim that such intimacy is the primary purpose of the symbol, not sexual differentiation. The signifi-

---

in reference to conflicting ideas of marriage in the years 1930–60. Martin is puzzled that feminists cannot see how hierarchy and equality can co-exist; see 401 ff.

65. On the "natural subjection" of women, see Thomas Aquinas, *Summa Theologiae*, III, Supp., q. 39; for inequality in marriage, see Pius XI, *Casti Connubii*, #26; for unsuitability for political life, CC, #74.

66. See Robin Darling Young's largely negative review of Elizabeth A. Johnson's *She Who Is: The Mystery of God in Feminist Theological Discourse* (New York: Crossroad, 1992) in *The Thomist* 58 (April 1994) 323–33, in which she writes: "It is incontestable that women have been oppressed and continue to be, in almost all human social arrangements, including institutional expressions of Catholic Christianity" (325).

cance of this intimacy is the close relationship between God and Israel, and between priest and faithful, as it is also found in the relationship between husband and wife. Another positive implication is that the symbol draws on the embodied human experience of physical union. In this, the Vatican position takes embodiment seriously, and draws upon it as a metaphor for the divine-human relationship. Further, the idea that human beings are not complete except in relationship, both to others and to God, underscores the theme of interdependence in this metaphor. But intimacy, embodiment, and interdependence are all cast within a larger picture that portrays men and women in fundamentally asymmetrical ways. While the Vatican presents nuptial imagery as intimate, it uses this imagery to argue not for intimacy but for the *differences* between men and women. This union and interdependence take place in prescribed ways ("active" and "receptive") that follow along strict lines of gender.[67]

Thus, Vatican theology is unable to disentangle itself from the stereotypical gender imagery of the active man and the passive woman. These stereotypes serve, however, to maintain not only strict gender roles, but also gendered ecclesiological roles — of active clergy and passive laity. Without a consideration of the negative effects of sexist stereotypes — a position the Vatican appears to be unwilling to take — such stereotypes will continue to reinforce the sexism that the Vatican rightly condemns. But the seriousness with which this position takes embodiment ought not to be dismissed without further thought. There is, in my view, some basis to the charges made here that some feminist theologies unwittingly promote a "new dualism," in which one's embodiment is extrinsic to one's identity as a person. An adequate feminist approach to body and gender will take physicality seriously, while at the same time giving equally serious consideration to the ways in which body and gender have been understood historically.

Post-Vatican II Sacramental Theology

The sacramental theology that emerged after Vatican II saw itself in contrast to an older theology rooted in an instrumental, and cer-

---

67. While it is not my specific concern here, the implications of this view for men and women in same-sex relations are at least as severe as they are for women in heterosexual relationships. See Patricia Beattie Jung and Ralph F. Smith, *Heterosexism: An Ethical Challenge* (Albany: State University of New York Press, 1993).

tainly legalistic, conception of both body and sacrament. This theology understood sacramental action in terms defined by Aristotelian-Thomist understandings of causality. In an article surveying sacramental theology in 1983, Kevin Irwin summarized Matthew O'Connell's 1967 characterization of the newer sacramental theology as representing

> a shift away from the traditionally expressed synthesis of *de sacramentis in genere* to a new theology of the sacraments framed in terms of personalist and existential philosophies and centering on Christ as the primary and fundamental sign (sacrament) of God's love as experienced in the life of the Church (also itself a sacrament of the presence of God). In this new theology the language of ontology generally yielded to that of encounter and union.[68]

Edward Schillebeeckx was one of the first to express this contrast in his own work. In his influential *Christ the Sacrament of the Encounter with God,* based on his 1953 doctoral dissertation, Schillebeeckx criticized older theologies that stressed a "mechanical" approach to the sacraments, the person, and sacramental grace.[69] Schillebeeckx's and Karl Rahner's approaches to the sacraments, while rooted in Thomas Aquinas, interpreted this perennial thinker anew and emphasized the importance of personal encounter (Schillebeeckx) and the symbolic character of human knowledge and experience (Rahner). It became more and more important to acknowledge the personal, communal, and embodied context of the sacraments. The flood of literature on sacramental theology that emerged in the late 1960s and throughout the 1970s gives priority to the "human context" of the sacraments.[70]

This emphasis continues in the present. Recent (that is, late 1980s) texts in sacramental and liturgical theology stress this embodied context. In a 1990 article, Kevin Irwin writes, "We live as enfleshed human persons whose very humanity has been forever graced by the God we encounter in the sacraments.... The medium for this communication is our

---

68. The quotation is Kevin Irwin's, describing O'Connell's 1967 article "New Perspectives in Sacramental Theology," *Worship* 41 (1967) 196–206; Irwin, "Recent Sacramental Theology: A Review Discussion," *The Thomist* 47 (October 1983) 592–608, at 593.

69. *Christ the Sacrament of the Encounter with God,* 3.

70. Kevin Irwin's three survey articles on sacramental theology in *The Thomist* can provide one reliable entree into this literature. See "Recent Sacramental Theology: A Review Discussion," *The Thomist* 47 (October 1983) 592–608; "Recent Sacramental Theology," *The Thomist* 52 (January 1988) 124–47; "Recent Sacramental Theology III," *The Thomist* 53 (1989) 281–313.

human bodies."[71] Similarly, Edward Kilmartin (in 1988) emphasizes that the human being must be described as *"embodied spirit."*[72]

This shift in sacramental theology was part of a larger shift that affected all the theological disciplines, and can be characterized as one in which theology no longer saw itself in isolation from other disciplines and in which the world was seen as the place of encounter with God. Strongly influenced as well by Karl Rahner's theology of grace, sacramental theologians turned to embodied and social human experience as the arena for their reflections. Thus scholars in sacramental theology incorporated the work of anthropologists and social scientists, recognizing that sacramental thinking and practice was rooted in the human condition, and had many important parallels with human ritual life in other cultures.

Much of the writing of post–Vatican II sacramental theologians reflects this shift in method.[73] In general, the more phenomenological and existential approaches begin by turning to human experience, focusing on those experiences that are implicitly sacramental (giving birth, healing, reconciling, marrying) and exploring ways in which they can be and are signs of salvation. These were understood in less otherworldly terms than in preconciliar theology. One finds in this theology an explicit valuation of the human and a genuine focus on the experiential basis of sacramental praxis. For example, George Worgul turns to the scholarship of the social sciences, arguing that "ritualization" is intrinsic to human growth and development, and therefore grounds sacramental practice.[74] Regis Duffy turns to research in "life cycle" and "faith stages," developed by social scientists and psychologists of religion.[75] Bernard Cooke turns to the human experience of friendship as the basis for the sacraments.[76] And Tad Guzie's

71. Kevin Irwin, "Sacramental Theology: A Methodological Proposal," *The Thomist* 54/2 (April 1990) 325.

72. Edward Kilmartin, S.J., *Christian Liturgy: Theology and Practice. I: Systematic Theology of Liturgy* (Kansas City: Sheed and Ward, 1988) 19. Emphasis in the original.

73. See Kevin Irwin (n. 70, above)'s series of three articles reviewing recent sacramental theology in *The Thomist* (1983, 1988, and 1989) and his "Sacramental Theology: A Methodological Proposal" *The Thomist* (n. 71, above).

74. George S. Worgul, *From Magic to Metaphor: A Validation of the Christian Sacraments* (New York and Mahwah, NJ: Paulist, 1980).

75. Regis Duffy, *Real Presence: Worship, Sacraments and Commitment* (San Francisco: Harper & Row, 1982).

76. Bernard Cooke, *Sacraments and Sacramentality* (Mystic, CT: Twenty-Third Publications, 1983).

focus on the "human dimension" of sacraments further confirms this general trend.[77]

Yet in this literature, there is surprisingly little on the body or on nature, and almost nothing explicitly on the issue of gender, except in discussions of ordination, where the issue is treated as an issue of justice. When human experience is invoked (friendship, human growth and development), it is done in broad terms and does not reveal the awareness of gender issues that has become so significant in scholarship especially throughout the 1980s. The importance of embodied experience is stressed, but not in terms that include gender. The question then becomes how to interpret this lack of attention to body and the almost complete absence of any mention of gender.

One possible reason for the absence of reference to the body might be a reluctance, on the part of these writers, to draw on the older "natural law" approach to sacraments. It has been argued that the "personalist" approach, which came to the fore prior to and during the council, tended to stress personhood, freedom, and historical development in contrast to the older, more static categories that relied on one's "place" in nature.[78] Certainly these postconciliar sacramental theologies reflect this personalist strain. And the significance of the Vatican reliance on such categories in its prohibition of "artificial" forms of contraception during this time cannot be discounted.

But my belief is that there are other dynamics at work here as well. First, sacraments come to be seen, in this literature, as *human* actions, grounded in the community. Given the Rahnerian focus on grace as "always, already" in the context of the human, this focus on the human means that the "vertical" dimension of the sacraments is downplayed, or even reinterpreted on a more "horizontal" level. This horizontal focus emphasizes the commonality and the unity of the human experience more than its diversity. Second, the communal dimension is, like the horizontal dimension, a reaction to the older hierarchical model of sacramental thinking and practice, in which the community "received" the sacraments from their dispensers, the clergy. Postconciliar sacramental theology relied heavily on Vatican II's stress on the church as the people of God, and on the common priesthood of all the faithful. Indeed, the language

---

77. Tad Guzie, *The Book of Sacramental Basics* (New York: Paulist, 1981).

78. William C. French, "Subject-Centered and Creation-Centered Paradigms in Recent Catholic Thought," *Journal of Religion* 70/1 (January 1990) 48–72.

of priesthood is used far less often, in this literature, than the language of "ministry" which is shared by the entire community.[79] Thus, there is a reluctance to make strong distinctions between human and divine, and clergy and laity, since such distinctions are most often seen in hierarchical terms. Gendered distinctions are, as we have already seen, also susceptible to this same tendency.

Yet feminist scholars have learned to be suspicious of the "generic human" when it is used to designate human experience as a whole. Valerie Saiving's classic article "Human Experience: A Feminine View" raised the question whether conceptions of sin and grace developed by male theologians Reinhold Niebuhr and Paul Tillich were adequate to women's experiences.[80] In general, feminist scholars have argued that conceptions of human experience *not* informed by a critical understanding of gender — and increasingly, also of race and class — are almost inevitably androcentric, reflecting the experiences of the (usually male) writers and our androcentric language and culture.

A similar point is made by thealogian Carol Christ, who in a 1991 article questioned the ways in which the historian of religion Mircea Eliade's ideas had influenced theoretical conceptions of religion. Picking up a thread similar to Saiving's and Plaskow's, Christ argued that "androcentric assumptions are deeply structured into Eliade's conceptions of the nature and origin of religion."[81] "These biases," she argued, "make it virtually impossible for him to recognize the importance of women and Goddesses in the history of religion."[82] Among these "androcentric assumptions," Christ identified three: (1) " 'the sacred' as standing in opposition to the chaotic and dangerous flux of things"; (2) a focus on " 'religious ideas' that are 'later valorized,' " ignoring power politics; (3) an emphasis on hunting symbols, including projectile weapons, blood sacrifice, and communion "as among the basic structures of religious consciousness that manifest them-

---

79. See Bernard Cooke, *Ministry to Word and Sacrament: History and Theology* (Philadelphia: Fortress Press, 1976).

80. Valerie Saiving, "Human Experience: A Feminine View," *Journal of Religion* 40 (January 1960), reprinted in *Womanspirit Rising: A Feminist Reader in Religion* ed. Carol P. Christ and Judith Plaskow (New York: Harper, 1979); see also Judith Plaskow's *Sex, Sin and Grace: Women's Experience and the Theologies of Reinhold Niebuhr and Paul Tillich* (Washington, D.C.: University Press of America, 1980).

81. Carol P. Christ, "Mircea Eliade and the Feminist Paradigm Shift," *Journal of Feminist Studies in Religion* 7/2 (fall 1991) 79.

82. Ibid.

selves again and again in the history of religion."[83] After surveying Eliade's work, Christ concludes that "the history of religion which Eliade tells is distorted by dualism, Idealism, and a false universalization of male experience." She argues that scholars of religion need to attend carefully to their own (perhaps unconscious) patriarchal assumptions.[84]

Christ offers some very important cautions in this article. It is not uncommon to find in sacramental theology references to the "historical" Jewish and Christian traditions as superior to the more "mythic" and "cyclical" "pagan" traditions.[85] The meaning of the Eucharist as an atoning sacrifice is another issue to which Christ's concerns ought to alert feminist readers.[86] Both these interpretations are intertwined not only with assumptions regarding nature and gender, but also with complex historical and theological issues. While I am not suggesting that all sacramental theology has had an uncritical reliance on the theories of Eliade, or that its "ungendered" assumptions are of necessity androcentric, these cautions are helpful. They suggest that statements about "human experience" (or, in earlier writings, "man's experience"), descriptions and conceptions of the sacred, and the meaning of religious symbols all need to undergo critical scrutiny by all scholars who cannot simply assume that all human understandings of the sacred are free from the insidious influence of sexism. Since most of the postconciliar sacramental theology under exploration here does not attend to gender difference, it is tempting to assume that its understanding of experience is inevitably androcentric. Yet such a conclusion may be premature.

ASSESSMENT OF POSTCONCILIAR SACRAMENTAL THEOLOGY

One of the main emphases of postconciliar sacramental theology has been the role of the community in sacramental celebration. Over and

---

83. Ibid., 81.

84. Ibid., 94.

85. Donald Keefe's article, "Sacramental Sexuality," makes this point strongly and argues that "cosmic religions" can be seen as inferior to the "worship of the Lord of history," 228–31. In *Unsearchable Riches: The Symbolic Nature of Liturgy* (New York: Pueblo, 1984) 94, David Power makes a distinction between cosmic and historical religion, but his is less pointed than Keefe's.

86. See Delores S. Williams, *Sisters in the Wilderness: The Challenge of Womanist God-Talk* (Maryknoll, NY: Orbis Books, 1993) and Rita Nakashima Brock, *Journeys by Heart: A Christology of Erotic Power* (New York: Crossroad, 1988) for their criticisms of this model.

over in these texts, the dominant role of the priest has been criticized, and older ideas of the community's (passive) "observation" of the sacraments (as opposed to its newer, and more active "participation") have been discarded, largely relying on the conciliar documents on the liturgy and on the church. New models for the people have been developed stressing their participation and activity — indeed, the *obligation* on the part of the people to be engaged, and not to be mere observers.[87] The result of much of this emphasis on experience, on the need for greater involvement on the part of the community, and on the need for sacraments to go beyond their church boundaries has been a "leveling" of the roles of clergy and laity, with a more holistic focus on the context of the sacramental experience. Now while much of this emphasis is, to be sure, not sufficiently informed by critical theories of body and gender, it nevertheless has been crucial in redefining the roles of clergy and laity in sacramental theology and practice. Thus, this unitary, even "ungendered" (and "unraced" and "unethnic") idea of the Christian community — all one, with differing gifts and ministries — has, at least in theory, invited the greater involvement of women in the sacraments, and, at least in some theologies, has left the door open to the question of women's ordination. It is also one of the main reasons, I would argue, why spousal/nuptial imagery is not used by these theologians.

Borrowing a term from secular feminist and political theory, we can characterize the understanding of body and gender in postconciliar sacramental theology as representing a kind of "liberal" approach to the human. Liberal perspectives tend to focus on such principles as the basic equality of all human beings, a respect for human dignity, and an emphasis on reason.[88] As Rosemary Ruether defines it, "liberalism rejects the classical tradition that identified nature or the order of creation with patriarchy.

---

87. See, e.g., Edward Schillebeeckx, *Ministry: Leadership in the Community of Jesus Christ,* trans. John Bowden (New York: Crossroad, 1981); idem, *The Church With a Human Face,* trans. John Bowden (New York: Crossroad, 1985); *Church: The Human Story of God,* trans. John Bowden (New York: Crossroad, 1988); Leonardo Boff, *Church, Charism and Power: Liberation Theology and the Institutional Church,* trans. John W. Diercksmeier (New York: Crossroad, 1985).

88. Susan Frank Parsons' description of the liberal, social-constructivist, and natural paradigms in her *Feminism and Christian Ethics* (Cambridge: Cambridge University Press, 1996) has been very helpful for this section. For other descriptions of paradigms in feminist thought, see also Alison Jaggar, *Feminist Politics and Human Nature* (Totowa, NJ: Rowman and Allenheld, 1983).

Instead it identifies nature or order of creation with the original un-fallen *imago dei* and affirms the equivalence of all human beings in this creation."[89] In addition, liberal theories include reform of institutions as one necessary means of expressing the full equality of women and men.[90] Liberal positions on gender equality tend to regard the "natural" dif-ferences between men and women as "purely contingent ones"[91] and to assume the possibility that *all* can participate equally in religious and political structures.

There is a great deal to be esteemed in liberal theories, both politi-cal and religious. Susan Frank Parsons argues that "it is in affirmation of this fundamental humanness that the liberal model excels. Such common humanness is also affirmed under God, whose creative power is believed to have formed, and to continue to uphold, the conditions which make and keep human life human."[92] This is, ultimately, what the sacraments celebrate: our common humanity, under God, in Christ. *All* humans, regardless of gender, race, or culture, seek to express, aesthetically and religiously, their experiences of community, of union with God, of com-mitment, of life transitions. Thus postconciliar sacramental theologies stress the unity and commonality of human experience, the universality of the human need to ritualize, and the imperative to connect ritual and ethical life. This latter emphasis also underscores the liberal concern for the ethical, for human rights. No longer belonging to an otherworldly realm of the sacred over and against the secular, sacraments serve to ex-press the intrinsic unity of the spiritual and material, sacred and secular. The political dimension of liberalism, which emphasizes equality and jus-tice, is implicitly present in postconciliar sacramental theology in that the sacraments are open to all and are an invitation to the entire Christian community to enact socially its sacramentality. I would not want to argue for an exact "fit" between the liberal model and postconciliar sacramen-tal theology — the more individualist focus of liberalism jars against the stress on community found in postconciliar sacramental theology — but it

---

89. Ruether, *Sexism and God-Talk: Toward a Feminist Theology* (Boston: Beacon Press, 1982) 102.

90. Ibid., 104.

91. See Parsons, 29, and Ruether, *Sexism,* 111: "Maleness and femaleness exist as reproduc-tive role specialization. There is no necessary (biological) connection between reproductive complementarity and either psychological or social role differentiation."

92. Parsons, 36–37.

does seem that the optimism of liberalism, its emphasis on equality and institutional reform, finds an echo in postconciliar sacramental theology.

But there are liabilities as well with the liberal model. Parsons mentions two problems that the presence of women poses to the liberal paradigm. One is that the understanding of human life that the liberal model presupposes, which emphasizes human freedom and transcendence, is often, unwittingly, in opposition to the concrete situation of many women. By *failing* to attend to the specific situations of women's lives, the liberal model can be implicitly dependent on an androcentric model of human experience. The second problem is, in Parsons' words, "the failure of this paradigm to attend to structural aspects of human life."[93] In other words, the complexities of power and politics are often overlooked in liberalism. In relation to postconciliar sacramental theology, both of these liabilities are worth at least a brief examination.

In the first case, the particularities of women's lives are seldom addressed in postconciliar sacramental theology. The models proposed — friendship, ritualization, life passages — are not inherently problematic, but reflect a picture of life that is largely informed by the experiences of men. Even the "passages" conception of human life stages, it is readily admitted, has suffered from too little attention to the ways in which women's life journeys do not always correspond to the standard, usually male, model.[94] Second, the more complex issues of power that are suggested by Parsons' reference to the "structural aspects of human life" are also seldom addressed. In terms of feminist theories, the actual structuring of human life and the need for ritual, as well as the political issues that lie behind liturgical innovations, are not always relevant to women's lives. The need to "join" together aspects of human life that have been "separated" may reveal more about what needs to be joined in men's lives than in women's. For example, the need to "return" to and "reclaim" the body so emphasized in the 1970s and 80s may well be more representative of what men need to do than women.[95]

---

93. Ibid., 47.

94. Daniel Levinson's *Seasons of a Man's Life* (New York: Knopf, 1978) was criticized for its reliance on male experience. See also Gail Sheehy, *Passages: Predictable Crises of Adult Life* (New York: Dutton, 1976); Carol Gilligan's *In a Different Voice: Psychological Theory and Women's Development* (Cambridge, MA: Harvard University Press, 1983) represents one of the most well-known approaches to the uniqueness of women's experiences.

95. In February 1992, I gave a lecture, "The Embodied Priest and the Sacraments: A Feminist Critique," at a national conference for diocesan priests (the National Organization

My point here is simply to raise the question that the assumptions of the commonality of human experience, the "universal" need for ritualization, and the developmental processes that are so much a part of postconciliar sacramental theology have not, on the whole, been attentive to the experiences of women as a whole, nor, for that matter, of those of racial-ethnic women and men. The cautions of Saiving, Plaskow, Christ, and Parsons help to suggest that before importing these theories wholesale, one ought to take a closer look at what they imply.

The "ungendered" conception of the human in postconciliar sacramental theology relies on broad conceptions of human experience and the commonality of that experience as the basis for the sacraments. The human need for ritualization, the universality of "life passages" which all experience, and the like, assume both too much and too little. On the one hand, in turning to psychologists, anthropologists, and sociologists, sacramental theologians assume too much in that these accounts of human experience inadequately incorporate women's experiences and draw on androcentric conceptions of human development (for example, Erikson's). On the other hand, in remaining with the seven-sacrament model and assuming its continuing relevance, theologians failed to explore other areas of experience (for example, women's bodily experiences) that had potential sacramental relevance, and thus assumed too little about human experience. An account of sacramental theology that fails to deal critically with body and gender, especially as they are inherited from the past tradition, will unwittingly perpetuate androcentric accounts of experience and fail to attend to the particularities of women's lives. Such a model risks failing to capitalize on the potential fullness of symbolism by relying on a liberal transformation of the past tradition.

Yet there are many positive dimensions to the postconciliar model of sacramental theology. Its communal orientation, its horizontal model of sacramental activity, and its concern for the ethical dimensions of the sacraments all point to a more egalitarian conception of human life, and a closer relation between sacraments and human activity. Ungendered models of the human-divine relationship have the potential to open up

---

for Continuing Education of Roman Catholic Clergy, in New Orleans) on the need to "reclaim" the body. I suggested that what men (especially celibate men) needed to do and what women needed to do to "reclaim the body" might not be the same things. See "Sacraments and Women's Experience," *Listening* 28/1 (winter 1993) 52–64 for a slightly revised version of this address.

greater imaginative possibilities. Perhaps most importantly, the conception of priesthood that emerges from postconciliar sacramental theology is rooted in a broader conception of the ministry of all the baptized, relies more strongly on scriptural models of ministry, and contributes to an understanding of the church that is informed by a historical sensitivity to complexity and development. But what remains is the need to integrate embodiment and gender with these categories.

FEMINIST THEORIES OF BODY AND GENDER

The models of body and gender that emerge from the Vatican and post-conciliar sacramental theologies might lead a feminist to exclaim, "a pox on both your houses!" With relation to the Vatican's position, the understanding of women as essentially maternal, receptive, and nurturing plays into stereotypical conceptions of women's nature as belonging to the realm of the private, personal, and emotional, and thus having little impact in the public arena. In addition, there are class-based, and potentially race-based, assumptions about the "nature" of women that are seriously problematic. That is, that women need to stay home to take care of children; that women will lose their "distinctive" nature by becoming "masculine" — which we can assume means active — that one cannot be active and maternal at the same time. All these assumptions play out best in a middle-class home where the man is the primary wage-earner. But if the Vatican model presents a picture of womanhood that feminists reject, the postconciliar model presents a picture of humanity in which women fail to appear in any distinct way. The understanding of human experience that emerges from this literature does not acknowledge the presence of women explicitly; perhaps even more problematically, it does not explore the possibility that a feminist perspective on sacraments might even define them differently. If feminism makes a difference at all for postconciliar sacramental theology, it is that one can "add women and stir" without upsetting the basic mix. Clearly neither of these approaches to gender, and by extension, to the body, is adequate.

One of the main criticisms that conservative theologians have made of feminist interpretations of embodiment is that they neglect to take the symbolism of embodiment seriously. Rosemary Ruether's comment that "maleness and femaleness exist as reproductive role specialization"[96]

---

96. Ruether, *Sexism and God-Talk,* 111.

has been singled out by these critics for perpetuating a dualistic under-standing of embodiment.[97] Others argue that if embodiment is to be understood sacramentally, then nuptial imagery provides the "only para-digms by which the mystery, the meaning, of masculinity and femininity may be approached."[98] Thus, if embodiment is to be understood as hav-ing symbolic significance, is there a way of construing it so that it is neither essentialist nor dualist? Is it possible to construe embodiment so that its historical and social shaping are also acknowledged? Fur-ther, are there examples within the Christian tradition that can provide such models?

Debates among feminists about the significance of gender differences and the role of the body have been heated and complex, and have not resulted in any unanimity. Various ways of sorting through these views have been proposed.[99] Susan Parsons' recent work, *Feminism and Christian Ethics,* uses the three broad categories of liberal, social-constructivist, and natural. The liberal position, we have already seen, sees sexual difference as incidental to one's shared human nature. The naturalist position is, in essence, the Vatican's position, which sees sexual difference as intrinsic to human nature, not only in terms of physiology, but also in terms of one's emotional and, indeed, one's spiritual make-up. The social-constructivist position, in which one will find various forms of postmodernism, argues against any "natural" construal of gender, or even of sex difference. Such concepts as "male" and "female," these authors argue, are the result of social conditioning and are potentially transcendable. Judith Butler, for example, argues that human selfhood is "performative," in that we enact ourselves in relationships to others, and that it is not something that is "given."[100] The postmodern take on the body, which emphasizes its end-less "play" of possibilities, its lack of stability and natural situatedness, is questionable for some students of the body. The feminist philosopher Susan Bordo asks:

---

97. Francis Martin quotes Ruether on this point; see *The Feminist Question,* 378.

98. Keefe, 250.

99. See Rosemary Ruether, *Sexism and God-Talk;* Alison Jaggar, *Feminist Politics and Human Nature* (see n. 86); Anne E. Carr, *Transforming Grace: Christian Tradition and Women's Experience* (San Francisco: Harper & Row, 1988).

100. Judith Butler, *Bodies That Matter: The Discursive Limits of Sex* (New York: Routledge, 1990); idem, *Gender Trouble: Feminism and the Subversion of Identity* (New York: Routledge, 1990).

> What sort of body is it that is free to change its shape and location at will, that can become anyone and travel anywhere? If the body is a metaphor for our locatedness in space and time and thus for the finitude of human perception and knowledge, then the postmodern body is no body at all.[101]

Yet while the endlessly changing and self-constructed body may raise questions for some theorists — here, I think, is where the Generation-X fascination with tattoos, body-piercing and the Hollywood/rich dependence on plastic surgery can be understood best with the help of some postmodern ideas — its lessons regarding the historical and cultural influences on the way in which we come to understand our embodiment are nevertheless valuable.

Thus liberalism is at fault for its failure to deal with embodiment in a serious way (for example, in its inability to account for reproductive differences), naturalism is problematic for its tendency to equate anatomy with destiny, and social-constructionism is deficient in its disconnection from stable categories. Yet each of these positions has valuable insights that help to correct the excesses or failures of the others. Is there some sort of "common ground" that can draw upon the helpful insights of all three positions?

FAMILY AS EMBODIED CONTEXT FOR SACRAMENTALITY

I propose that there is, indeed, a way to make the connection between embodiment, the tradition, and feminist concerns for historical and social context, as well as to offer ways in which to relate meaning to embodied reality (my point here is symbolism). This can be done by grounding the meaning of embodiment, not in spousal terms, but in the context of the family, specifically the family as developed by feminist theorists. Drawing on Lisa Sowle Cahill's recent work, as well as the work of *mujerista* theologian Ada María Isasi-Díaz, and womanist theologian Delores Williams, I will develop an understanding of *family as embodied context for sacramentality*. In her book, *Sex, Gender and Christian Ethics*, Cahill argues for an understanding of the family as "a biologically based, cross-cultural

---

101. Susan Bordo, *Unbearable Weight: Feminism, Western Culture, and the Body* (Berkeley: University of California Press, 1993) 229.

phenomenon, which may, nonetheless, vary widely in form, especially as to the flexibility of its boundaries and as to the intimacy and equality of its internal relations."[102] Her point is to make the case for a moral theology that is rooted in an understanding of objective reality and to counter postmodern and social-constructivist views of gender and sexuality that question the very existence of "male," "female," and gender as "unnatural."[103] As Cahill puts it, "the issue for contemporary feminists is whether, in a nondualist perspective, the differential embodiment of men and women must be assumed to make a difference in their way of being in the world, even if not a difference which implies hierarchy, or even very extensive or firmly demarcated role allocation."[104] By using family as a relatively stable category within which to understand sex and gender, Cahill links embodiment with its social and historical context. Such an understanding, I will argue, can prove to be fruitful as well for sacramental theology.

Another perspective on the context of embodiment comes from Ada María Isasi-Díaz, who stresses the centrality of the family (*la familia*) for Latina women.[105] Isasi-Díaz is concerned to understand the family within its social, cultural, and historical context. Women have found *la familia* to be the place where Latina women "are agents of our own history," where "we can claim a historical role within space and time."[106] The family, as she defines it, is an "amplified" one and includes "a vast network of relationships and resources in which Hispanic women play a key role."[107] This understanding of the "amplified" family is central for my concerns.

Similarly, for womanist theologians, family emerges as central. Because many African-American families have suffered from the disastrous and lingering effects of slavery, family is not a romanticized ideal, as it tends to be in so many treatments of "the family," especially by the religious right. Rather, it stands as both a source of strength and as an arena of struggle. Black mothers often found themselves forced to nurture children not their own out of economic necessity, while black fathers saw their manhood

---

102. Cahill, *Sex, Gender*, 106
103. Ibid., 4.
104. Ibid., 84.
105. Ada María Isasi-Díaz, *Mujerista Theology: A Theology for the Twenty-First Century* (Maryknoll, NY: Orbis Books, 1997) 137.
106. Ibid., 139.
107. Ibid.

perceived as a threat to white society.[108] Family, in womanist theology, is thus a reality that cannot be taken for granted: while threatened by a racist society, it still serves to ground the physical and social lives of the African-American community.[109] I want to draw on this idea of family as a goal to be struggled for, not as something taken for granted.

Like moral theology, sacramental theology relies on an understanding of the revelatory character of human existence. Both disciplines ask the question: What does embodied experience mean? An understanding of gender that is based in both an appreciation of and a critical approach to the "natural" has obvious benefits for sacramental as well as moral theology. Using the family as context for embodiment has the potential to uncover new richness of meaning in embodied human life, and to fill in gaps that the symbolism of the bride and bridegroom leave open. In what follows I sketch out some of the reasons to consider family as embodied context for sacramentality. My point is not to argue for family as sole context, nor to develop all of the possible dimensions of the family. It is, rather, to ground embodiment in a relatively stable locus, one that has both biological bases as well as social construals, one that is sensitive to the multiple dynamics of women's lives.

I am understanding family here as multigenerational, in that the family is a dynamic reality to which all human beings are connected in some way. In other words, I am not equating family solely with marriage. All human beings are familial, in that we are all daughters and sons, as well as, possibly but not necessarily, spouses or parents. My understanding is more of the "family of origin," as family systems therapists term it, than of a conception of family that classifies adults as married, parents, or single. Hence "family" is an institution that involves and affects all persons, even those not living in what might be termed a traditional family context (for example, single people).

What, then, are the advantages of placing sacramentality within a familial context? First, family is grounded in both biology and history. Like

---

108. Delores S. Williams, *Sisters in the Wilderness,* 77–80; see also Toinette M. Eugene, "African American Family Life: An Agenda for Ministry in the Catholic Church," *New Theology Review* 5 (1992) 33–47.

109. See Jualynne E. Dodson and Cheryl Townsend Gilkes, "There's Nothing Like Church Food: Food and the U.S. Afro-Christian Tradition: Re-Membering Community and Feeding the Embodied S/spirit(s)," *Journal of the American Academy of Religion* 633 (fall 1995) 519–38.

the symbol of bride and bridegroom, family is based in biological kinship relations that are extended, and even transformed, by social existence. Embodiment is experienced in a social context, and human beings come to know their embodiment, gender identity, as well as racial and ethnic identity, initially in the context that we call "family." While families have no fixed structure (that is, families can be biological, adoptive, multigenerational, extended), there is a cross-cultural and historical stability to the family that is grounded in human sexuality.[110] The distinctive reproductive capacities of women and men partially but not entirely ground the meaning of human embodiment. Not all men and women are fathers and mothers, but human beings, ideally, grow in some sort of "family" context. It is all but universally recognized that lack of such context has disastrous consequences for children and, ultimately, for social stability.[111] Human beings are linked both biologically and socially to parents, siblings and other relatives; they also affiliate with others (for example, in spousal and friend relationships). But their embodiment — their sexuality, affective relations, needs for physical and psychic nurturing — is experienced within a cultural context. Thus embodiment, in the context of family, is not limited to the sexual, but includes it. One initially experiences one's embodiment as a child, then grows into maturity, possibly as mother or father, but always as gendered, and related.

Thus for sacramentality, such a family context involves a community and interdependence. The sacraments are not signs that mediate grace only to an individual, but are as well the community's way of mediating God's grace to all, individually and socially. This is not to dispute the uniqueness that pertains to each person, but to note that human beings live in communities, and experience grace in communities.

Second, the meaning of family I intend is dynamic. In the more static symbolism of bridegroom and bride, each has a specified role, based in an interpretation of one significant, though not exclusive, sexual act. Thus the bridegroom is active (based on his "active" role in intercourse) and the

---

110. See the series, "The Family, Culture and Religion," edited by Don S. Browning and Ian S. Evison: especially *Faith Traditions and the Family*, ed. Phyllis D. Airhart and Margaret Lamberts Bedroth (Louisville: Westminster John Knox, 1996), and *Religion, Feminism and the Family*, ed. Anne E. Carr and Mary Stewart Van Leeuwen (Louisville: Westminster John Knox, 1996).

111. See, e.g., Marianne Berry, *The Family at Risk: Issues and Traditions in Family Preservation* (Columbia: University of South Carolina Press, 1997).

bride is "receptive" (again, based in her role in intercourse).[112] While one might rightly question whether this construal of male and female person-hood does justice to the complexity of sexual intercourse, it also allows little flexibility in roles. It is a remarkably limited picture of human sexual relationships, seeing all of human embodied personhood to be symboli-cally encompassed by the act of heterosexual intercourse. By contrast, the family evokes a greater complexity of roles. It can include intercourse, but it also includes maternal and paternal sexuality, embodied development in biological life passages, nurturing and caring roles, and social relations. Everyone comes from a family, of varying types; in the family, it is at times appropriate to be receptive, as in infancy, or in times of serious illness and vulnerability. But it is also appropriate that receptivity be bal-anced, in the same person, by activity, again depending on the context. A strict construal of embodiment in the limited context of intercourse does not allow for the inevitable ambiguity that human embodied existence involves. To quote Cahill:

> Ethicists, Christian and humanistic, may need to acknowledge ambiguity and a certain "incoherence" to human life as embodied. Tension among the con-stitutive components of our nature gives morality and culture the character of a *project of integration*, rather than of a *call to authenticity* to our "real" or "true" nature.[113]

Further, the sole centrality of heterosexual intercourse for human sexu-ality perpetuates an androcentric (as well as heterosexist) understanding of the meaning of sexuality. For women, and for men as well, sexual pleasure is not necessarily connected to intercourse. While intercourse cannot be excluded as a significant embodied experience, and needs to hold a central role for its part in human reproduction, the broad range of human sexual expressions — some for pleasure, some for reproduction — is not done jus-tice by a singular focus on intercourse as fully or even primarily revealing the sacramental meaning of human embodiment.

Third, the meaning of family I intend is multidimensional. In the bridegroom/bride symbol, the couple is in relation to each other and only to each other. There are no children, in-laws, friends. Such a rela-

---

112. See Margaret Farley's incisive critique of this model in "New Patterns of Relation-ship," in *Woman: New Dimensions,* ed. Walter Burghardt (New York and Mahwah, NJ: Paulist, 1977).

113. Cahill, *Sex, Gender,* 97. Emphasis in the original.

tionship seems oddly isolated for expressing both human interrelationship and the divine-human relationship. By contrast, in family, relationships are complex. This point is especially relevant to the extended family, where parenting may be taken on by a number of different family members. One's relationships to one's parents, siblings, children, and different generations shift over time. One is shaped by one's family context in relating to one's spouse, friends, children. The exclusively dyadic conception of relationality in the nuptial model does not do justice to the complexity of communal existence in which relationships are sometimes dyadic, but also triadic, quadratic, and so forth. Indeed, even one of the central symbols of the Christian tradition, the Trinity, is a communal relationship of three persons in one. The love of creator and redeemer finds its fullest expression in the reality of Spirit, which continues to enrich the trinitarian life and all creation.[114]

Fourth, the idea of gender that prevails in nuptial symbolism supports a fundamental inequality. In this model, as we have seen, women are not initiators, but essentially receivers. But this hardly does justice to the complexity of women's roles in families. As mothers, women take active roles in rearing and nurturing children, as do their partners. Women's sexuality, which encompasses far more than intercourse, involves both cooperation and activity, as well as receptivity, for example in conception, in experiencing orgasm, in lactation, in menstruation, and menopause. A more adequate way of terming the parental relationship is in terms of responsibility. This term recognizes that we come into existence in relationship, and are called to respond to those whom we encounter. This capacity to respond sometimes means taking the initiative (as with mothers and fathers who teach their children), sometimes being receptive to new knowledge, which may come from unexpected sources (for example, from parents who learn from their children). To be "responsible," suggests, as H. Richard Niebuhr put it, that one is capable of responding, engaging in dialogue, willing to be as receptive to new ideas as willing to put them forth.[115]

This understanding of relationality as responsibility also calls into question an instrumentalist understanding of sacraments as "pipelines of grace," in which human beings simply *receive* the sacraments, and the grace

---

114. See Catherine M. LaCugna, *God for Us: The Trinity and Christian Life* (San Francisco: Harper & Row, 1991).

115. See H. Richard Niebuhr, *The Responsible Self: An Essay in Christian Moral Philosophy* (New York: Harper & Row, 1963).

they confer, from the priest who administers them. Such an understanding of sacrament ignores the ways in which all human beings are potentially sacramental ministers (for example, in emergency baptisms, in marriage, where the partners confer the sacrament on each other) and thus limits sacramental participation to the simple act of reception.

Finally, this use of family can claim scriptural roots. While the nuptial relation also has scriptural grounding, primarily in the Pauline literature, the symbol of family has an equally strong basis in scripture. To be sure, not all the biblical construals of family are potentially valuable for a feminist understanding. Nor are all biblical portrayals of spousal relationships. But the understanding of family that emerges from the New Testament and in early Christianity, especially the family that goes beyond the biological family, has real potential for both symbolic meaning and moral action. Cahill suggests that "the specifically Christian contribution of the family is sublimation of kinship loyalty into identity with all those who suffer or are in need, as 'God's children' or our 'brothers and sisters in Christ.' "[116] In chapter 6, I will use this understanding of family as embodied context for sacramentality to develop its ethical implications.

It must be noted that the use of "family" as a model has real limits and many potential dangers. The limits of the model are fairly clear. The understanding of family that we inherit is largely a patriarchal one, one that has been used to maintain male control over women. The use of "family values" by the Christian right to justify a largely individualistic, capitalist, and antifeminist political agenda makes even the term "family" suspect. Families can be places of pain, dysfunction, abuse, hatred, and sorrow. Further, the (mistaken) assumption may be that the nuclear family is the ideal form of the family, and that those who are single, gay, or lesbian, or alienated from family of origin are therefore excluded. Gender roles, as first learned in families, can be very limited. In the Roman Catholic tradition, the family has been seen as an inferior context to the "higher" calling of religious life.[117]

When extended to divine-human relations, the symbol of family has problems as well. The difficulties with a parental conception of God have been extensively developed by feminist scholars, who point to an excessive reliance on images of God as Father as having seriously negative conse-

---

116. Cahill, *Sex, Gender,* 210.

117. See Margaret A. Farley, "The Church and the Family: An Ethical Task," *Horizons* 10/1 (1983) 50–71.

quences for all human beings.[118] Further, the dependence implied by the child-parent relationship has been criticized as perpetuating an unhealthy conception of self. I would want to make it clear here, though, that by turning to family I have not automatically assumed that God takes the parental role and humanity that of the child. This model suggests a fairly limited picture of family where I am trying to point out the potential for multiple relations.

The family has been, and unfortunately continues to be, a place of oppression, pain, and injustice. But human beings have not (yet) found another biological-social institution that can fulfill the functions of the family, as Cahill has identified them: intimacy, pleasure, and reproduction. The real issue, then, is the transformation of the family, not its destruction or rejection for another institution. Thus family is an ambiguous reality, like our embodiment, and like our social and indeed especially our ecclesiastical institutions.

The point in using family as a basis for a sacramental conception of embodiment is to acknowledge the "givenness" of our beginnings and the potential of this "givenness" for social and spiritual transformation. All human beings are daughters or sons, while some are mothers or fathers, sisters or brothers, aunts or uncles. What we make of this "givenness" is where our social and historical existence makes a difference. Thus there are also families "by affiliation." But ultimately, the Christian faith makes us all sisters and brothers to all human beings. The significance of "family" is that it is a *model*, not a template. It roots our physical being in a communal context, where relations with others have the potential to expand our lives and families, as well as to stunt them. But family *grounds* our being both physically and relationally. It does not exhaust the meaning of being human. Family makes it possible to understand the sacramentality of our embodied existence as enacted in a social and cultural context.

Family as embodied context for sacramentality involves human physicality but a physicality not defined only by gender. To the extent that family also includes culture, race, and class, the complexity of embodiment is heightened by its grounding in family. This use of family also suggests that it is not a static reality, but one that grows and changes over time. Motherhood can be, for a time, a central way of understanding who one is, as the Vatican would argue, but as children and adults grow, it comes

---

118. See Ruether, *Sexism and God-Talk;* Rita Nakashima Brock, *Journeys by Heart.*

to be a part of a mosaic of identity, where friends as well as spouses, children, or siblings, come to be central in one's relationships. Further, in an understanding of family that is contextualized in time, internal and external family dynamics change. Family helps to locate those dimensions of one's being that are "givens" — race, gender, even personality — but does not solely define them, as one comes to see oneself not only in relation to family but to the wider society as well. Like all symbols, family is ambiguous, helping to illumine as well as to shadow.

How does such a construal of embodiment and gender as rooted in the context of family contribute to a feminist perspective on sacraments? While the following chapters will develop these points at much greater length, let me simply sketch a few suggestions. First, this construal roots sacramentality more concretely in daily, lived existence. The bride-bridegroom model, while contributing to the rich dynamics of symbolism and rooted in a long tradition, is based in an idealized conception of persons, especially women. I would argue for nuptial symbolism as one, partial, dimension of familial symbolism. As grounded in lived existence, seeing family as context for sacramentality speaks, I would hope, to the lives of women and men across cultures who are immersed in the daily life which is, as María Pilar Aquino says, "at the center of history, invading all aspects of life."[119]

Second, this daily life — of the family — is where basic values are passed on. The splitting off of family as private and domestic from the public arena perpetuates the injustices that have come to be seen as "natural." As Aquino puts it, "daily relationships become the basis and image of all social relations."[120] The point of seeing family as embodied context for sacramentality is *not* to perpetuate a false understanding of unjust family structures as "natural" and thus sacramental — which is how they have been construed in the magisterial tradition. It is, rather, to raise up the structure of *all* biological and social relationships as revelatory of the body of Christ and of the reign of God. The radical relativizing of family ties that is expressed in the New Testament calls for "the family [to be] a place, and a way of life, in which we can share a hope for, but also the fruits of, justice."[121]

---

119. María Pilar Aquino, *Our Cry for Life: Feminist Theology from Latin America* (Maryknoll, NY: Orbis Books, 1993) 39.
120. Aquino, 40.
121. Farley, "Church and Family," 71.

Third, the imperfections of family life also contribute to a richer, more complex, indeed, more ambiguous understanding of sacramentality. Conflict, anger, hurt, injustice, but also reconciliation, shared joy, compassion, and understanding are part and parcel of life in a family. Without frank acknowledgment of problems, families run the risk of failing to face serious issues that have destructive potential. Families are a school for realism, in which the givenness of our biological heritage provides the material for our psychological, social, and cultural context to shape and transform.

CHAPTER FIVE

Women, Sacraments, and the Symbolic

> The death or absence of the mother sorrowfully but fortunately makes possible the construction of language and of culture.
>
> — Margaret Homans[1]

> We, [Eve's] daughters, have kept silent for so long that now we have forgotten that knowledge from and about the body is also knowledge about the world.
>
> — Madeleine R. Grumet[2]

In this chapter, I want again to focus our attention on the family, but this time using a different set of lenses — those of psychoanalytic and feminist psycholinguistic theories. These theories are helpful in at least two ways. First, they use the dynamics of familial structure to forge a connection between embodied experience and language. Second, they suggest how gender is a crucial factor in the construction of the symbolic. I will develop the critical implications of these theories for sacramental theology, showing how the dynamics of family and gender have affected the theological and social construction of the sacraments.

These theories also suggest constructive ways of thinking about women and the sacraments. But before turning immediately to these theories, we need first to set the context for the symbolic within the general "turn to language" that has been a major part of late twentieth-century thought.

---

1. Margaret Homans, *Bearing the Word: Language and Female Experience in Nineteenth Century Women's Writing* (Chicago: University of Chicago Press, 1986) 2.

2. Madeleine R. Grumet, *Bitter Milk: Women and Teaching* (Amherst, MA: University of Massachusetts Press, 1988) 3.

THE SYMBOL

In a letter to a Protestant friend, the Catholic novelist Flannery O'Connor wrote: "If Christ actually teaches through many forms then for fifteen centuries he taught that the Eucharist was his actual body and blood and thereafter he taught part of his people that it was only a symbol."[3] Her comment on Protestant teaching on the Eucharist — "that it was only a symbol," and therefore not real — is representative of much of the modern, especially pre–Vatican II Catholic, understanding of the meaning of symbol, especially in relation to the sacraments, which goes something like this. A symbol is something that stands for something else, something more real than itself. Like a metaphor, it is decorative, perhaps even profoundly beautiful, but it is no replacement for the real. For a pre–Vatican II Catholic — and Flannery O'Connor wrote those words in 1959 — to say that the Eucharist was a symbol of Christ's presence was to utter heresy: it was, in effect, to say that there was no "*real* presence." Given this reductive understanding of the symbolic, it is no wonder that O'Connor was so dismissive of any idea that the Eucharist was "only" a symbol. That Christ was really present, and that this presence was symbolic, was a contradiction that was impossible for Catholics to sustain.[4]

Although we might well be critical of O'Connor's dismissive attitude toward symbolic thinking, her quite legitimate concern was that the *reality* of the presence of Christ not be explained away in abstractions. This real presence was, for her, more real than anything else. Her concern for the concreteness of the sacraments, that they were intended to help human beings follow the two great commandments, is instructive.[5] I want to keep

---

3. Flannery O'Connor, *The Habit of Being*, ed. Sally Fitzgerald (New York: Farrar, Straus, Giroux, 1979) 341.

4. Ibid.

5. Ibid., 346: "You [Dr. T. R. Spivey, the addressee of her letter] speak of the Eucharist as if it were not important, as if it could wait until you are better able to practice the two great commandments. Christ gave us the sacraments in order that we might better keep the two great commandments. You will learn about Catholic belief by studying the sacramental life of the Church. The center of this is the Eucharist." O'Connor's remarks invite speculation as to how she would have responded to Vatican II and its aftermath. She abhorred intellectual laziness and, I think, would have welcomed the better-educated laity of the post–Vatican II church. But her conviction that the Roman Catholic Church was the (certainly flawed but nonetheless) real presence of Christ on earth would have, I suspect, led her to some impatience with the reforms of the post–Vatican II church. She was especially suspicious of emotion in relation to faith. See *The Habit of Being*, 100ff. and 346ff.

this concern for the real, the concrete, for living flesh and blood, in mind as we sort through how thinking about the symbol has shifted over the last fifty years.

This suspicion about symbols and their dubious relationship to the real and true can also be seen as the corollary of an attitude that understands truth as something "graspable," something to which human beings have more or less assured access, especially through church doctrines. In this view, symbols are not intrinsically related to what they represent, but are rather (inferior) substitutions for the real. But it is precisely this attitude that has come under scrutiny in the late twentieth century: the idea that one *can* grasp reality, and, consequently, that representations of reality can be severed from what they represent. Such an attitude presupposes that the conceptual is superior to the representational, that the philosophical is superior to the aesthetic (Kant and Hegel), and, theologically, that the doctrinal is superior to the symbolic.

The shift in thinking that has come to be known as postmodernism, with its focus on the "linguistic turn," has challenged this confidence in the human ability to know, to manipulate language, and to grasp the "real." The "linguistic turn" both challenges the optimism and confidence of modern thinking's ability to know (and thus it constitutes an episte-mological challenge) as well as intensifies the significance of the ways in which we do come to know (in language, symbols, cultures).[6] In short, what is meant by the "linguistic turn" is that human knowing takes place *in language,* not prior to or outside it. The idea that we can know reality outside language is an illusion. Bound to the "plurality and ambiguity" of history, to language and the symbolic, our claim to sure knowledge is questionable.[7] We dwell in language — as Heidegger has said, "language is the house of being" — so the potentialities of linguistic and symbolic expression, as well as their shortcomings, are the potentialities and shortcomings of human knowledge and expression.[8]

––––––––––

6. The literature of the importance of language and symbols in twentieth-century thought is vast and complex. For some helpful discussions, see Anne E. Patrick, *Liberating Conscience: Feminist Explorations in Catholic Moral Theology* (New York: Continuum, 1996) 48–53; David Tracy, *Plurality and Ambiguity: Hermeneutics, Religion, Hope* (San Francisco: Harper & Row, 1987); see also Thomas Guarino, "Postmodernity and Five Fundamental Theological Issues," *Theological Studies* 57/4 (December 1996) 654–89.

7. See Tracy, *Plurality and Ambiguity.*

8. Martin Heidegger, *Being and Time* (New York: Harper, 1962) 145.

Although not verbal, symbols do in fact constitute a language, in that they are vehicles of expression, rooted in the body, culture, and history. Symbols themselves participate in a world of meaning, dependent upon cultural and historical context, as does language. For what the linguistic turn is all about is that human beings have no *unmediated* knowledge. *All* our knowledge is symbolic. All of it is mediated through our bodies: through sound, vision, touch, hearing, taste. Like the Enlightenment "turn to the subject," which challenged the existence of supernatural knowledge by placing the human person at the center, the turn to language further unsettles our certainty in knowing the truth by challenging the ability of human constructions to transcend their linguistic, symbolic, cultural, and historical limitations. One cannot do an "end run" around language or the symbolic to attain the truth. One finds the truth *in language,* in the symbolic.

The "linguistic turn" has had a profound influence on sacramental theology. Catholic theologians such as Karl Rahner (who was influenced as well by Martin Heidegger), Edward Schillebeeckx, and the Protestant theologian Paul Tillich have made significant contributions to theology in their claims about how human beings come to know reality and God — through language, symbols, cultures.[9] These thinkers stress the point that human beings do not use language and symbols as tools, as if we first had "pure" ideas and then formulated them into words. Our use of language is as much a being "shaped by" as it is a means of shaping. Similarly, sacraments are not simply substitutions for another spiritual reality, or instruments for manipulating spiritual reality. They are, rather, the very ways in which God has chosen to reveal who God is to humanity and how humanity, in return, expresses its relationship to God. In other words, sacraments are the language of the church, expressive in symbolic form of what, in verbal form, the scriptures reveal. In their linguistic and symbolic forms, word and sacrament are *mediating.* That is, they are not direct, transparent, or self-evident. They conceal as much as they reveal. The scriptures possess a sacramentality in that the word of God conveys who God is, but only partially. They are privileged in that the church has, over the centuries, designated certain texts as revelatory, as the sacraments are his-

---

9. See, e.g., Edward Schillebeeckx, *Christ the Sacrament of the Encounter with God,* trans. N. D. Smith (New York: Sheed and Ward, 1957); Karl Rahner, "The Theology of the Symbol," in *Theological Investigations,* vol. 4, trans. Kevin Smyth (London: Darton, Longman and Todd, 1974); Paul Tillich, *The Dynamics of Faith* (New York: Harper & Row, 1957).

torically privileged places of encounter with God, rooted in the human experience of the Christian Gospel.[10] As we cannot make an "end run" around language, neither can we do so with word or sacrament. Word and sacrament, for the Christian traditions, are the very expressions of who God is to human beings, the very places of encounter with God.

In chapter 4, we saw how an instrumental understanding of sacraments gave way to a more personal and existential approach in the years surrounding Vatican II. This newer approach understands symbols, then, not as substitutions for reality, but rather — in the more ancient sense in which symbol was originally intended — as the *means* by which we come to understand reality.[11] That is to say, the symbol bears within itself what it is that it communicates; it is not a mere vessel for an extrinsic message. Hence an understanding of Jesus as primordial sacrament of God. In his humanity, Jesus makes present who God is, as unconditional love, as fellow sufferer, as united in our vulnerability. Hence an understanding of the church as sacrament of Jesus the Christ's continuing presence among us: as, in our diversity and complexity, making present the body of Christ, as God's presence among us. The sacraments, then, to use Scholastic language, "effect what they signify" — they *do* what they mean.[12]

But even more importantly, the sacraments, in an understanding informed by the linguistic turn, are not simply "remedies" for human sinfulness or a somewhat inferior way of encountering God, due to the frailty of human embodiment and its sinfulness.[13] Rather, the sacraments, as physical realities, are the very medium of our encounter with God. They are not expressive of another, deeper, encounter with God, possible in some ideal world without physical mediation. Such a longing for

---

10. For the Bible as revelatory, see Sandra M. Schneiders, *The Revelatory Text: Interpreting the New Testament as Sacred Scripture* (San Francisco: Harper San Francisco, 1991). For sacraments as revelatory, see Karl Rahner, "Theology of the Symbol"; Edward Schillebeeckx, *Christ the Sacrament.*

11. See Duffy's comments on the symbolic in Regis Duffy, "Sacramental Theology," in *Systematic Theology: Roman Catholic Perspectives*, vol. 2, ed. Francis Schüssler Fiorenza and John Galvin (Minneapolis: Fortress Press, 1991) 181–210.

12. See Thomas Aquinas, *Summa Theologiae*, III, q. 62, aa. 1, 4.

13. See, e.g., Thomas Aquinas, *Summa Theologiae*, III, q. 61, a. 2; see also Hugh of St. Victor, *On the Sacraments of the Christian Faith*, trans. Roy J. Deferrari (Cambridge, MA: Medieval Academy of America, 1951) for an understanding of sacraments as "remedies for sin."

an unmediated encounter with God is representative of the strand within Western thinking that seeks absolute certainty.[14] It is also reminiscent, some contemporary thinkers argue, of the human desire to merge (again) in wordless unity with the (m)other. Both are desires that are humanly impossible to fulfill.

PSYCHOANALYSIS AND SYMBOL

Such language linking the desire for union with God and one's parent may strike the reader as odd, perhaps even blasphemous. Sigmund Freud, the architect of modern suspicion toward religion, is an unlikely ally for an understanding that strives to bring together sacramental theology and feminist theory. Freud was sympathetic neither toward religion nor to women. But twentieth-century interpreters of Freud, including Jacques Lacan, Julia Kristeva, and object relations theorists, have suggested ways of understanding human psychosexual dynamics that can prove helpful for sorting through the complexities of human desire, the role of language, and the significance of parent-child relationships. These, I will suggest, can help in formulating both a critical and a constructive approach to women's relationship with the sacraments through an understanding of the role of the symbolic. In addition, these theories are rooted in the family context, and thus will prove helpful for our purposes in developing the model of family as embodied context for the sacramental. Moreover, this context will prove to be an ambiguous one, having both positive and negative consequences for women, but nevertheless expressive of its muddy and messy reality.

Let us return to the idea of language as the shaper of human thought (and not the reverse) and its involvement in human development. In the Lacanian paradigm of human psychosexual development, with Freud's theory as a starting point, infants see the entire world, including their mothers, as extensions of themselves. This "primary narcissism" is a seamless world, where infantile demands — for food and warmth, for example, are (ideally, at any rate) readily met. But with physical and psychological

---

14. Louis Marie Chauvet labels this strand of thinking "onto-theology." See his *Symbol and Sacrament: A Sacramental Reinterpretation of Christian Existence,* trans. Patrick Madigan, SJ, and Madeleine Beaumont (Collegeville, MN: Liturgical Press, 1995 [1987]), especially chapter 2, "Overcoming Onto-Theology?" 46ff.

growth, and especially the development of language, a gap emerges between the child and the child's needs and desires. The mother is no longer
instantly available to meet the child's desires, and the child comes to the
"shattering" realization that there is another who enjoys the love of the
mother — the father. The "difference" that the father represents comes to
be symbolized by the phallus, "which stands for both the terrifying sense
of 'absence' (of the imagined union with the mother) *and* the possibility
of its one day being overcome through romantic reunion."[15]

The phallus as *psychologically* (not, Lacan argues, as physically) constructed symbolizes the "Law of the Father," the symbolic/linguistic world
into which the child now enters.[16] Since the mother desires the phallus
and not only the child, the phallus comes to symbolize both the mother's
"absence," in that she is no longer there to meet the child's every need, as
well as the possible overcoming of this absence. All language, in this framework, is thus an expression of desire, a desire that can never be fully met.
Language symbolizes the "gap" between the self and the object of desire, of
which the mother is the primary symbol. For Lacan, the term "symbolic"
represents all forms of language; it is the world of representation.[17]

Now the implications of Lacanian theory for feminists are many, and
significant, and worth far more time and attention than I can give them
here.[18] While I will focus on the role of the mother below, at this point it
will suffice to say, briefly, that for Lacan, "woman" — and note here that
"woman" and "mother" are identified — is not a subject in and of herself,

---

15. Mary Frohlich, "From Mystification to Mystery: Lonergan and the Theological Significance of Sexuality," in *Lonergan and Feminism,* ed. Cynthia W. Crysdale (Toronto:
University of Toronto Press, 1994) 180. I am indebted to Mary Frohlich's analysis for
helping to illumine Lacan's thought.

16. Both Margaret Homans and Jane Flax argue that this construction is indeed a phys-
ical one, although denied by Lacan. See Homans, *Bearing the Word,* 9; Jane Flax, *Thinking
Fragments: Psychoanalysis, Feminism, and Postmodernism in the Contemporary West* (Berkeley:
University of California Press, 1990) 103–7.

17. This is true as well for Julia Kristeva, who makes a distinction between the semiotic
and the symbolic. See Julia Kristeva, *Essays in Semiotics,* ed. and trans. Josette Rey-Debove
and Donna Jean Umiker (The Hague: Mouton, 1971).

18. See Homans and Flax, n. 14, above. See also Elaine Hoffman Baruch, *She Speaks/He
Listens: Women on the French Analyst's Couch* (New York: Routledge, 1996); Elizabeth A.
Grosz, *Jacques Lacan: A Feminist Introduction* (London; New York: Routledge, 1990);
Jane Gallop, *The Daughter's Seduction: Feminism and Psychoanalysis* (Ithaca, NY: Cornell
University Press, 1982).

but becomes rather a "division in language," a "gap," an "absence," which is produced by entering into language itself.[19]

As Jane Flax, a feminist theorist, psychoanalyst, and critic of Lacan, points out in relation to his theory, "all speaking beings 'inscribe themselves' on the masculine side, no matter what their physical attributes might be. To speak one must enter into and become constituted by the realm of the symbolic: the play of signifiers and the signified and the 'universal signifier' (the phallus)."[20] In other words, Lacanian theory *assumes* a "male" positioning with regard to language: that is, we are all, so to speak, the sons who desire the mother.

Feminist theorists have found Lacan's theories problematic because of this assumption, which raises critical questions about women's relationships with the symbolic. This is an issue with which French feminist theorists especially have been concerned, and some, like Hélène Cixous and Luce Irigaray, have argued for an *écriture féminine* — literally, a feminine writing, which begins from the recognition that women's experience, especially of language, is "essentially" different from men's, is less alienated (in that women do not ever have to reject the feminine in the way that men do), and is more bodily.[21] Others, notably Julia Kristeva, provide a revised account of the Lacanian paradigm, noting that the "gap" that is the marker of "woman" provides the possibility for a new kind of language.[22]

The French theologian Louis-Marie Chauvet, in his *Symbol and Sacrament,* underscores the symbolic as the inevitable consequence of our

---

19. Here I am indebted to the work of Homans, *Bearing the Word,* and of Diane Jonte-Pace, "Situating Kristeva Differently: Psychoanalytic Readings of Woman and Religion," in *Body/Text in Julia Kristeva: Religion, Women and Psychoanalysis,* ed. David R. Crownfield (Albany: State University of New York Press, 1992).

20. Flax, *Thinking Fragments,* 99.

21. See, e.g., Hélène Cixous, *"Coming to Writing" and Other Essays* (Cambridge, MA: Harvard University Press, 1991) and Luce Irigaray, *An Ethics of Sexual Difference* (Ithaca, NY: Cornell University Press, 1993). For a helpful introduction to these issues, see Pam Morris, *Literature on Feminism: An Introduction* (Oxford, UK, and Cambridge, MA: Blackwell, 1993); *Contending with Words: Composition and Rhetoric in a Postmodern Age,* Patricia Harkin and John Schrib, eds. (New York: Modern Language Association of America, 1991).

22. See Julia Kristeva, *Language — the Unknown: An Initiation into Linguistics* trans. Anne M. Menke (New York: Columbia University Press, 1989); idem, *Polylogue* (Paris: Seuil, 1977). See also the work of Kelly Oliver, *Ethics, Politics and Difference in Julia Kristeva's Writing* (New York: Routledge, 1993); idem, *Reading Kristeva: Unraveling the Double Bind* (Bloomington: Indiana University Press, 1993).

human embodiment. In this, he also relies on the Lacanian understanding of language as a "gap." Chauvet extends this understanding to say that symbolic and bodily mediation is tragically but necessarily always involved in our subjectivity, especially in our relationship to God. We have to resign ourselves to the mediation of language and symbols; we can never leave them behind, as much as we want. As he puts it, "we must accept the death of the illusion *everything in us desperately wants to believe, that is, the illusion that we can somehow pull ourselves out of the necessary mediation of symbols,* situate ourselves outside of discourse, and apprehend reality directly, without passing though cultural tradition or the history of our own desire."[23] This emphasis on the tragic quality of mediation is rooted in his conviction that the human desire for unmediated unity is, in part, a nostalgia for that original unity with the mother. While not a reductionist, by saying that religion would be *nothing but* this nostalgia, Chauvet nevertheless accepts the basic conviction that this dynamic is operative in all human relationships. But this illusion is also indicative of an even greater illusion — that is, that we can be in immediate unity with the divine.

Chauvet argues that the Enlightenment desire to grasp the truth fully without mediation is a similar kind of nostalgia for this immediacy. He is particularly critical of Scholastic thinking on the sacraments, which, because of its dependence on metaphysical categories — categories, he argues, that are inherently opposed to the incompleteness and mediated quality of the symbolic — sees the sacraments in *instrumental* terms of cause and effect, and not in symbolic terms.[24] The sacraments, Chauvet argues, are not instruments but symbols: the very ways in which we communicate with God. Instrumentality carries with it a conception of the world which is antisymbolic.[25] In sum, postmodern psychoanalytic thinking on language, symbol, and desire links language and symbol to the desire to overcome the gap that is experienced in language itself.

It is worth raising the question here — and it will receive more attention below — whether the dynamics of desire for an unmediated relationship with the (m)other, as understood psychoanalytically and linguistically by Lacan and as interpreted sacramentally by Chauvet, represent a universal desire in human experience, or whether this desire is more characteristic of men than of women. If one's relationship with one's mother is affected by

---

23. Chauvet, *Symbol and Sacrament*, 81–2. Emphasis in the original.
24. See Chauvet, esp. chapter 2: "Overcoming Onto-theology?" 46–81.
25. Chauvet, 116.

the dynamics of gender, might this desire for the unmediated be similarly affected? Might this suggest that women's relationship to the symbolic could follow a different journey than that of men? We will return to these questions below.

From this very brief and highly condensed summary of some recent thought on symbol and language, two issues emerge for consideration from a feminist perspective. The first is the necessarily mediated quality of human knowing. That is, as we have seen above, human beings do not come to know apart from language and symbols, and, indeed, all human knowing is mediated through the body. The second is that language and symbol are inevitably intertwined with human knowledge and desire. From a psychoanalytic perspective, this desire has to do with that of the child for the mother; more broadly speaking, it has to do with the dynamics of family relations. From a religious perspective, this desire is for unity with the divine. While I am not seeking to *identify* the desire for the parent with the desire for God, I also do not want to dismiss any possible connection between the two. If we take seriously the necessarily mediated character of knowledge — that it is always through symbols, language, and culture that we come to know — then we cannot reject out of hand the ways in which our desires for love, for unity, for God, are intertwined with our familial and cultural lives. If feminist theory raises questions here, it asks whether these mediating symbols, language and culture might function differently for women than for men.

How can these issues help to open up a deeper understanding of the dynamics of symbolic representation and women's role in it? My hypothesis is that a fuller understanding of the multifaceted dynamics of human relations will enrich our understanding of sacramental theology. The desire for union with the mother needs to be understood as a dimension of the desire for God, but a desire that is later denied. Such a perspective can have a critical function in helping to demystify the sometimes uncritical and even romantic use of familial and spousal imagery (as we saw in chapter 4), as well as to explain more fully the visceral reactions that the prospect of women's ordination can evoke.[26] It can also serve a constructive use in opening up the possibilities for the use of family as embodied context for sacramentality that are, first, coherent with the dynamics of human experience and responsive to currents in contemporary thought; second, that are

---

26. "Vicar would burn women priests," *Chicago Tribune* (Monday, March 4, 1994) 9:6.

coherent with the images of relationships and family that emerge from the Christian message; and, finally, that speak to the needs of contemporary women and men in their efforts to help establish the reign of God.

FEMINIST PSYCHOANALYTIC AND OBJECT RELATIONS THEORY

Feminist psychoanalytic criticism has long been both interested in and critical of the work of Sigmund Freud. The androcentric character of his understanding of human psychosexual development is something he himself admitted; its worth for feminists continues to be debated.[27] As we saw above, the work of Jacques Lacan, whose own work is based in Freud's ideas, has been a resource for feminist critical and constructive work on both men's and women's development. Object relations theory, especially as developed by the English psychologist D. W. Winnicott, has also been important for feminists.[28]

Nancy Chodorow's 1978 book, *The Reproduction of Mothering,* has provided one relatively accessible interpretation of object relations theory that continues to influence feminist theory, far beyond the realm of psychology alone.[29] In that work, Chodorow argues that, at least in Western culture, boys' and girls' processes of coming to understand their gender identities follow different routes. Freudian theory has charted this process as the "Oedipus complex," in which the boy's desire for the mother must be suppressed in favor of identification with the father, with the process for girls concerning their desire for the father and identification with the mother.[30]

---

27. For one of the earliest feminist works on Freud, see Juliet Mitchell, *Psychoanalysis and Feminism* (New York: Pantheon Books, 1974).

28. D. W. Winnicott, *The Child, the Family and the Outside World* (Harmondsworth, UK: Penguin Books, 1964); idem, *The Family and Individual Development* (London: Tavistock, 1965).

29. Nancy Chodorow, *The Reproduction of Mothering* (Berkeley: University of California Press, 1978).

30. This is, of course, not even a complete summary of what the Freudian theory argues, since the girl's process is not a reverse of the boy's. For Freud's own work on this, see Sigmund Freud, *The Ego and the Id,* trans. Joan Riviere, revised and edited James Strachey (New York: Norton, 1962, [1960]); idem, *Collected Papers,* ed. Philip Rieff (New York: Collier Books, 1963); idem, *The Interpretation of Dreams,* trans. and ed. James Strachey (New York: Basic Books, 1956); *Freud on Women,* ed. Elisabeth Young-Bruehl (New York: W. W. Norton, 1990).

Chodorow, basing her theories on those of Winnicott and others, and, like Lacan, revising the Freudian account to focus on the significance of the *mother* for both boys and girls, turned to the pre-Oedipal phase of close bonding between child and mother, and the process of separating from her, for understanding gender identity and development. For boys, the need to assert a distinct identity, apart from the mother and all who represent her, becomes paramount. Because the presymbolic and prelinguistic bond with the mother must be abandoned for the world of the father, boys are, on the whole, more concerned with issues of *separation*, especially from the mother. Girls, because they identify with the mother, find the challenge of individuation a different process. The closeness and identification with the mother (experienced by both boys and girls in infancy) need not be entirely abandoned, since the girl is like her mother, and may also one day be a mother. Connection and identification are hallmarks for female personal identity. For girls, the need to be a self *in relationship*, rather than in individuality, becomes key. For Chodorow, the "reproduction of mothering" and the gendered dichotomies we continue to experience (especially in Western industrialized culture) will only be overcome when men and women participate equally in the task of child-rearing.[31]

Chodorow's work has had wide (and controversial) influence on feminist thought, particularly on the work of Carol Gilligan, whose work on moral development draws on Chodorow's ideas of gender identity.[32] The emphasis on relationality and connection as being more characteristic of girls than of boys has led to considerable debate within both psychology and feminist theory, as well as in feminist ethics.[33] But the influences

---

31. See also Dorothy Dinnerstein, *The Mermaid and the Minotaur: Sexual Arrangements and the Human Malaise* (New York: Harper & Row, 1976) for a similar proposal.

32. Carol Gilligan, *In a Different Voice: Psychological Theory and Women's Development* (Cambridge, MA: Harvard University Press, 1982).

33. See Cynthia S. W. Crysdale, "Women and the Social Construction of Self-Appropriation," *Lonergan and Feminism* ed. Cynthia C. W. Crysdale (Toronto: University of Toronto Press, 1994) 88–113; Seyla Benhabib, "The Generalized and the Concrete Other: The Kohlberg-Gilligan Controversy and Moral Theory," *Women and Moral Theory*, ed. Diane T. Meyers and E. F. Kittay (New York: Rowman and Littlefield, 1987) 154–77; Susan Heckman, *Moral Voices, Moral Selves: Carol Gilligan and Feminist Moral Theory* (University Park, PA: Pennsylvania State University Press, 1995); *Justice and Care: Essential Readings in Feminist Ethics*, ed. Virginia Held (Boulder, CO: Westview Press, 1995); *Approaches to Moral Development: New Research and Emerging Themes*, ed. Andrew Garrod (New York: Teachers College, 1993).

of Freud, Lacan, and the object relations theorists on feminist theory go beyond the strictly psychological dimensions of their work. My concern here is the way in which these theories can be helpful for understanding the connections between family dynamics and symbolic representation.

Margaret Homans provides one such interpretation in her book *Bearing the Word: Language and Female Experience in Nineteenth-Century Women's Writing.*[34] Homans draws on the work of both Lacan and Chodorow in developing a theory of the role of the literal and the symbolic in women's writing. She begins by making the stark observation about women, language, and culture with which I began the chapter: "the death or absence of the mother sorrowfully but fortunately makes possible the construction of language and of culture."[35] This assertion draws directly on Lacan's understanding of language and culture in which, as we have seen, "woman" represents the gap between the desiring subject and the object of desire.[36] Homans proceeds to make the case that "women are . . . identified with the literal, the absent referent in our predominant myth of language," and that "from the point of view of this myth, the literal both makes possible and endangers the figurative structure of literature."[37]

Briefly put, the "symbolic" represents a movement away from — and also a step above — the purely literal and nonlinguistic realm (that is, the presymbolic realm; for Kristeva, the "semiotic") of embodied and emotional connectedness that all humans experience (at least ideally) as infants in relation to their mothers. As we have already seen in Lacan's paradigm, children must engage in a process of separation (and, for males, alienation) from their mothers. This process is simultaneous, Lacan argues, with the awareness of gender identity and of language acquisition. What this means for language — and, I suggest, also for other symbolic constructions like sacraments — is that the symbolic becomes associated with the masculine and the literal with the feminine. Women are thus excluded from the symbolic, since they cannot participate as subjects in that which at the same time is premised on their absence. As Homans puts it:

> The differential valuations of literal and figurative originate in the way our culture constructs masculinity and femininity, for if the literal is associated with the feminine, the more highly valued figurative is associated with the

---

34. Chicago: University of Chicago Press, 1986.
35. Homans, 2.
36. See Jonte-Pace, "Situating Kristeva Differently," 1–25.
37. Homans, 4.

masculine. To take something literally is to get it wrong, while to have a figurative understanding of something is the correct intellectual stance.[38]

These "differential valuations" do not mean, however, that women are completely excluded from the realm of the symbolic. Women, Homans argues, *both* learn the "language of the Father" as well as retain the "presymbolic" and embodied awareness that is not fundamentally conceptual or symbolic (that is, the language of the mother). In fact, *both* men and women retain this awareness, yet women's and men's relationships to the "presymbolic" differ. Men, Homans suggests, are able to distinguish themselves from this presymbolic realm — in fact, they must, in order to develop language and a sense of self. It is fundamentally a process of alienation that is necessary in order for the boy to become a subject. The awareness of the presymbolic is something that must be continually (and sorrowfully, as Homans points out) rejected, if not mourned. We can note here the parallel with Chauvet's idea that human beings want "desperately" to be able to escape the symbolic.

Women also struggle to develop a sense of self as subject, while at the same time they are aware, on some level, that they also represent that which must be rejected.[39] As Kristeva observes, there is a difficulty for girls in separating from the mother in order to "accede to the order of signs as invested by the absence and separation constitutive of the paternal function."[40] There is a "doubled awareness" of being both subject and object present in women's consciousness, and especially evident, Homans shows in the rest of her book, in women's writing.[41] Women's sense of subjectiv-

---

38. Ibid., 5.

39. For some interesting work on female adolescent development, see the papers of the Stone Center, as well as some of Gilligan's recent work. Carol Gilligan, Jill McLean Taylor, and Amy Sullivan, *Between Voice and Silence: Women and Girls, Race and Relationship* (Cambridge, MA: Harvard University Press, 1995); Carol Gilligan, Nora Lyons, and Trudy Hammer, eds., *Making Connections: The Relational Worlds of Adolescent Girls at Emma Willard School* (Cambridge, MA: Harvard University Press, 1989); Carol Gilligan, Annie Rogers, and Deborah Tolman, *Women, Girls and Psychotherapy: Reframing Resistance* (New York: Haworth Press, 1991). For an introduction to the Stone Center's research, see Judith Jordan et al., *Women's Growth in Connection* (New York: Guilford Press, 1991).

40. Julia Kristeva, "Women's Time," *The Kristeva Reader,* ed. Toril Moi (New York: Columbia University Press, 1986) 210.

41. Elizabeth Fox-Genovese likens this awareness to the sense of "twoness" described by W. E. B. Du Bois. See her *Feminism Without Illusions: A Critique of Individualism* (Chapel Hill: University of North Carolina Press, 1991) 139ff.

ity is therefore profoundly *ambiguous:* as *both* subject and object, women struggle to be firmly a self in the world and as such face greater psychological and social obstacles than do most men (especially privileged men). Yet by the same token, women's "inability" or "difficulty" in separating suggests an ongoing connection to the (m)other that men "lack."

Jane Flax, a political scientist and psychotherapist, draws on some of the same psychoanalytic material in her book *Thinking Fragments: Psychoanalysis, Feminism, and Postmodernism in the Contemporary West.*[42] Relying more heavily on the work of Winnicott than of Lacan, and on her own experience as a therapist, Flax concurs that the formation of the male self occurs primarily through "acts of alienation."[43] Lacan's theories are helpful in describing this process, Flax observes, but they are seriously flawed in that they lack an awareness of the social context in which human beings come to self-consciousness. This social context does not regard gender neutrally, but invests it with particular, and asymmetric, values.[44] Further, Flax points out, the theories of Chodorow, Gilligan, and others fail to take seriously the ambivalent experiences of mothers themselves, and the ways in which mothering can also be a form of manipulation and control.

Object relations theory privileges the perspective of the child in relation to the mother, who tends to remain a static object. The perspective of the (often ambivalent) mother must be taken seriously so as to guard against what Flax sees as a kind of benevolent essentialism in which women's relationships with others become over idealized. An emphasis on women's embodiedness can become a kind of "glorification of the distinctly female aspects of our anatomy," Flax cautions, and thus can serve to hide the social construction of our gender relations.[45] What is needed is a feminist theory that takes into account the complexity of both men's and women's perspectives: the "suppressed, unarticulated" elements within men's experiences for which there is little if any cultural support, as well as the ways in which women's experiences are "partially constituted by and through their location within the web of social relations that make up any 'society.' "[46]

Feminist psychoanalytic theories thus raise the question whether there might be differences in women's and men's relations to language and the

---

42. Berkeley: University of California Press, 1990.
43. Flax, 106.
44. Ibid., 120–25.
45. Ibid., 179.
46. Ibid., 183.

symbolic. They suggest that the predominant theories of the symbolic arise out of an androcentric conception of parent-child (that is, mother-son) relationships and the desire of the son for the mother. The daughter's desire is not as fully attended to (or understood), nor is the role of the mother, who, Flax argues, is seen too often merely as the mirror of the child. Thus feminist psychoanalytic and object relations theory looks, minimally, to point out the "gender dynamics" of the symbolic. By highlighting the subjectivity of the daughter and of the mother, these theories show how the process of symbolic representation positions the subjectivity of men and women differently. A feminist perspective on sacramental theology, then, needs to take these dynamics seriously.

SACRIFICE AND GENDER

A provocative perspective on the role of gender, family relations, and sacrifice is offered by the late anthropologist Nancy Jay. Her theories have influenced the work of William Beers, who brings psychoanalytic theory to bear on the understanding of sacrifice. Jay's work is not specifically dependent upon nor related to psychoanalytic theory, but because Beers' theory is, and because of his dependence on Jay's prior work, it will be helpful to outline Jay's own thesis concerning women, men, and sacrifice.

Jay's book, *Throughout Your Generations Forever: Sacrifice, Religion, and Paternity*, argues that rituals of sacrifice are ineluctably connected with the need for men to establish patrilineal relationships with other men.[47] These relationships transcend the mortal bond with one's mother, and indeed transcend time as well, since they are eternal bonds. Jay writes:

---

47. Nancy Jay, *Throughout Your Generations Forever: Sacrifice, Religion, and Paternity* (Chicago: University of Chicago Press, 1992). The work of René Girard on sacrifice is both well known and significant, although I will not be dealing directly with his theories here. See his *Violence and the Sacred*, trans. Patrick Gregory (Baltimore: Johns Hopkins University Press, 1979); idem, *The Scapegoat*, trans. Yvonne Freccero (Baltimore: Johns Hopkins University Press, 1986). For some works relating to Girard's theories, see Gil Bailie, *Violence Unveiled: Humanity at the Crossroads* (New York: Crossroad, 1997); *Violence and Truth*, ed. Paul Dumouchel (Stanford, CA: Stanford University Press, 1988); Robert G. Hamerton-Kelly, *Sacred Violence: Paul's Hermeneutic of the Cross* (Minneapolis: Fortress Press, 1992); Andrew McKenna, *Violence and Difference* (Urbana, IL: University of Illinois Press, 1992); Raymond Schwager, S.J., *Must There Be Scapegoats?* (San Francisco: Harper & Row, 1987).

Sacrifice can expiate, get rid of, the consequences of having been born of woman (along with countless other dangers) and at the same time integrate the pure and eternal patrilineage. Sacrificially constituted descent, incorporating women's mortal children into an "eternal" (enduring through generations) kin group, in which membership is recognized by participation in sacrificial ritual, not merely by birth, enables a patrilineal group to transcend mortality in the same process in which it transcends birth. In this sense, sacrifice is doubly a remedy for having been born of woman.[48]

What are the consequences of having been born of woman? According to Jay, they are, primarily, mortality and pollution. Jay's work focuses on biblical, African, and Hawaiian accounts of sacrifice. She also interprets the Roman Catholic tradition of priesthood, based in apostolic succession, and the emphasis on the sacrificial character of the Mass as underscoring the effort to maintain an eternal father-son lineage. The ambiguity and insecurity of one's relationship to one's father are overcome in the act of blood sacrifice, which firmly (socially and culturally, not biologically) establishes the son's relationship to the father. The exclusion of women ensures the eternal nature of this relationship.

Jay notes that "having been born of woman" is something that humans share with beasts. Reproduction is thus a natural activity that must be elevated in some way so as to become human.[49] And fatherhood is equally problematic because the relation between biological father and child is so tenuous.[50] Jay comments, "social paternity and biological paternity may, and often do, coincide, but it is social paternity that determines patrilineal membership."[51]

According to this understanding, sacrifice is based in large part on the need to control the reproductive powers that women have and to put them into a carefully defined social context. William Beers agrees with Jay's conclusion but points out that the psychological grounding for this male need to exclude women needs to be more fully explained. In his book *Women and Sacrifice: Male Narcissism and the Psychology of Religion*, Beers makes the argument that the rationale behind men's need to establish this lineage comes from unresolved male anxiety and narcissism arising from

---

48. Ibid., 40.
49. Ibid., 30.
50. Ibid, 36.
51. Ibid.

separation from the mother.[52] He writes: "in sacrifice, the psychological motivation of men is to control the male-perceived power of women."[53] Later in his book, he expands this point: "The psychodynamic structure of sacrifice reflects a religious *inability* to mourn, to give up the idealized loss object through identification and internalization, because sacrifice reflects a psychodynamic tendency to acquire aspects of the idealized object that may not be internalized."[54] Because the identity of men is grounded in the imperative to separate from the mother, because this separation is deeply traumatic, and because the sense of self that develops is a fragile one, men are therefore "more likely to feel threatened by factors affecting their grandiose sense of self-esteem... because they have experienced the omnipotent maternal self-object as other, rather than experiencing themselves as subjective extensions of the self-object, as will be the case with women."[55]

In a very helpful and lucid essay on Freud, Lacan, and Kristeva, Diane Jonte-Pace takes up a similar theme. Jonte-Pace notes how Kristeva "argues that what religion represses is not a primal parricide [that is, Freud's view] but a primal abhorrence of the mother."[56] The mother, according to Kristeva, represents the fundamental absence that death is — that is, the terror of nonbeing. Recall that when the child realizes that the mother loves the father (the phallus), the difference that the father represents indicates the mother's absence. The mother is no longer "there" for the child alone. Dealing with the mother as absence is, for Kristeva, a "positive, beneficial, even miraculous image," since it prevents a "collapse into meaninglessness."[57] Without the mother, there would be nothing. The mother therefore provides a way for the human psyche (Beers would note, especially for the male psyche) to cope with its potential nonbeing.

What all these theorists are arguing, although with differing foci and details, is that separation from the mother, and particularly male separation from females, is at the root of language, symbol, and certain — albeit central — religious rituals, perhaps especially sacrifice. Psychoanalytic

---

52. William Beers, *Women and Sacrifice: Male Narcissism and the Psychology of Religion* (Detroit: Wayne State University Press, 1992).

53. Ibid., 12.

54. Ibid., 119.

55. Ibid., 138.

56. Jonte-Pace, "Situating Kristeva," 10.

57. Ibid., 20.

categories, these theories suggest, can help to uncover the unconscious motivations that lie behind the exclusion of women from rituals of blood sacrifice, as well as from the holy sacrifice of the Mass.[58] To enter into the realm of the symbolic, into the world where representation comes to have a greater value than what it represents, where symbolic rebirth is more significant than ordinary physical birth: this is, fundamentally, leaving the world of women, who represent the physical, the literal, the mortal. Beers argues that men desire children and immortality, and are thus jealous of the powers of the mother and seek to appropriate them;[59] Kristeva argues that identifying women with death "provides a protection against collapse into meaninglessness,"[60] because, without being able to project the fear of the abyss on the mother, one is left with nothing. Whatever the motivation, these analyses suggest that the concern for women's full participation in the symbolic, and in religious rituals, especially those tied to a language of sacrifice, encounter deeply entrenched psychological processes that will not lend themselves easily to rational arguments about equality.

INTERIM REFLECTION

Women's relationship to the symbolic, these theories suggest, is a complex one. Language and symbol are intricately bound up not only with history and culture, but also with the gendered dynamics of the family. If this is true with relation to women and literature, it is surely the case with women and the sacraments. These theories relating religion and psychology are a complex set of materials that raise some intriguing as well as troubling questions about the human desire for God, for the mother, the nature of language and symbol, and our confidence in what we say about religion. My point in reviewing this literature is not to make a case that postmodern psychoanalytic or object relations theory provides the best or the only explanation for what we *think* are really religious issues, but which are in reality deeply troubling psychological issues. Such a posi-

---

58. See Kelly Raab, "Nancy Jay and a Feminist Psychology of Sacrifice," *Journal of Feminist Studies in Religion* 13/1 (spring 1997) 75–89. I agree with Diane Jonte-Pace's assessment of Raab's work on women, ordination, and sacrifice. See her "New Directions in the Feminist Psychology of Religion: An Introduction," in the same volume, esp. 68–9.

59. Beers, 11.

60. Jonte-Pace, "Situating Kristeva," 20.

tion wrongly creates a chasm between the religious and the psychological. Rather, my point is to see whether the conclusions of these theorists can help to shed light on the relationship between the symbolic and what it represents, on the role of gender in relationship to the symbolic and sacramental, and on the dynamics of familial relationships. I think that they can, but this does not mean that in using these theories, we import their world views wholesale.

There are at least three tentative conclusions that we can draw from these theories. First, these theories help to explain the ways in which language and the symbolic tend to be the domain of men. Psychoanalytic and object relations theories provide a kind of "diagnosis" for understanding the ways in which women are symbolic *objects* (especially as the mother) but far less often symbolic *subjects* — that is, as speakers, as ones whose perspective the symbolic represents. These theories may help shed light on why the position of women as preachers, as liturgical presiders, as public leaders, seems to raise almost irrational fears among many men (as well as some women) — that women in such positions are literally and symbolically "out of place." The suggestion that the domination of the symbolic by men has psychological roots is not to exclude other bases for the historical exclusion of women from the public sphere, but broadens our ways of understanding and overcoming such exclusion. Psychoanalytic theories are thus suggestive, although not exhaustive.

Second, feminist theorists who have worked with the psychoanalytic perspective have made some intriguing suggestions as to how women relate to the symbolic. Homans' theory, for example, that women attain a kind of "bilingualism" helps to explain how women's writing (and for our purposes, women's symbolic and ritual expression) can maintain a grounding in *both* the preconceptual or presymbolic (in Kristeva's terms, the semiotic) and the symbolic. Kristeva's well-known "Stabat Mater" is an expression of just this very bilingualism: on the one side, the careful, well-researched documentation of the role of Mary throughout the ages; on the other, the fluid, nonlinear reflections of the mother on her maternity, bodily sensations, feelings. The perceived marginality of women's language provides a way, as Rebecca Chopp suggests, of developing a new discourse about the sacred: one that is playful, multivalent, and nonlinear.[61]

---

61. Rebecca S. Chopp, *The Power to Speak: Feminism, Language, God* (New York: Crossroad, 1989).

The point I would stress is that these perspectives do not suggest a dualistic opposition of male and female approaches to language and symbol. Rather they suggest a more ambiguous, if also ambivalent, way of understanding how it is that those who are marginalized in the dominant discourses of the religious and social order can still maintain a subjectivity, a language, a perspective on human relationships and the desire for unity with the real that can exist alongside other, more powerful, discourses. The nature of this ambiguous and ambivalent discourse will be explored below. This is, of course, not to argue that women's subjectivity *should* remain on the level of the marginal, but, rather, that women's discourse does not seek simply to reverse the traditional hierarchies. Women's symbolic capacities and discourses have served and still can serve to interrupt, to challenge, and to provide an alternative to these dominating discourses.

Third, these theories also help in understanding the role of presence and absence in both their symbolic and psychological dimensions. As Homans put it, basing her ideas in Lacan, women are the "absent" referent that makes language possible. If the speaking subject is always "male," psychically if not physically (Flax), then language and symbol are ways of attempting to breach a fundamental absence — the absence of the (m)other. Religiously, symbols are a way of making present what is absent (Chauvet). Their presence is always indicative of the (even more basic) absence of God. That is, we cannot ever fully *grasp* God — the true, the real, the ultimate — apart from God's mediated presence in symbols and language. For Chauvet, sacraments are the presence of the absence of God.[62] Women's experience as the "absent referent" in language, as absent liturgically and historically (women are constantly encountering a language and symbolic presence that excludes them) is also an absence that is, at the same time, a presence (in that women are there, silent, perhaps, but nevertheless there, despite symbolic and linguistic absence).

Given these theories, it is thus not surprising that the absence of women as representative of the divine is so important to sacramental traditions such as Roman Catholicism and Eastern Orthodoxy, since the *absence* of the mother is what makes possible the rituals and symbols themselves. Yet these theories also raise questions about presence. Homans suggests that nineteenth-century women's writing continually invokes the presence of the mother and is founded in the literal and not the symbolic. I will

---

62. Chauvet, 74: "the face of God shows itself only by erasing itself." See also chapter 13, "Symbols, Symbolic Figures of God's Effacement," 506ff.

suggest that the approach women take toward both feminist liturgy and the more traditional celebration of the sacraments is one that emphasizes presence, and not primarily absence: of women, of bodies, of children, of nature, as ways of intensifying the mediated presence of God.

Let me attempt to tie together these multiple strands of men and women, symbol and language, presence and absence, family, and God with sacramental theology, and to highlight certain threads. First, it is important to acknowledge that language and symbol are indeed tied to desire, that they represent this "gap" or "breach" between desire and fulfillment. This is true not only for men but also for women; yet the *experience* of this desire may be different for men and for women, and women experience this *as daughters* first. The role of the woman as mother is subsequent to her experience as daughter.[63] And her experience in relation to the mother marks this breach differently. While there is a gap, a breach, there is also continuity, and the ambiguous nature of this relationship means that clear boundaries between self and other do not emerge as significantly as they do in men.

The dynamics of men's experiences are well documented in the Freudian and post-Freudian literature, especially as sons. They are, perhaps, not completely understood. But the real issue here is the desire of the child for unity with the mother and the desire of the human person for unity with the other. While we seem to know quite a lot about men's experiences, we don't know as much about women's. Here, feminist scholarship can help to begin to understand what has been lacking: an understanding of the desires of women. What seems to emerge is a strong sense of *ambiguity* on the part of the female, in contrast to a greater sense of *dichotomy* on the part of the male. Women, it might be said, desire both unity and connection as well as separation and individuation with the other. The presence of the (m)other is less of a breach, a gap, for women, than it is for men, according to these theories. Thus *continuity* in sacramental theory and practice emerges as an important theme.

Family dynamics, as we saw in chapter 4, have been understood in magisterial Roman Catholicism from the perspective of the spouses. In this model, human beings are all either bride or bridegroom. I drew out some of the problems in this model as the basis for sacramentality. But if we turn to psychoanalytic theory and attempt to understand the desire for connec-

---

63. This is one of the main theories of Homans's book: that is, the writer as daughter. See Homans, *Bearing the Word*, 13–22.

tion and unity with the (m)other as a dynamic that affects both men and women, albeit in different ways, as grounding the drive to language and symbol, and even the resistance to language, we have some suggestions as to how language and symbolic expression may affect the ways in which symbols, sacraments, and gender dynamics may be interrelated.

The second theme comes not from the human sciences but from the scriptural accounts of the life and death of Jesus, and of the early Christian community. Jesus' name for God, Abba, (father, papa) is a familial one. The fact that Jesus' language for God is masculine — even patriarchal — has been very important for those who defend the traditional understanding of God as male, for Jesus' "choice" of all male disciples, and for the enduring significance of Jesus' own maleness. But what tends to be overlooked in this construal of Jesus' preferred term for God is the fact of the familial, rather than the specifically patriarchal, context in which he understood himself and his relationships with his disciples. Jesus saw himself as the child of God, and his disciples and friends as his brothers and sisters. In other words, the message of Jesus says, we are all children of God, all longing for God. The birth, ministry, death, and resurrection of Jesus Christ tell us that this longing for God will not result in God's making Godself purely and immediately present to each one of us. Rather, God has chosen to make Godself present in humanity, *in each other*, in our brother, Jesus.

Further, the familial dynamics of which Jesus speaks in the gospels are not so much "antifamily," as some have suggested, but rather a radical relativization and stretching of familial loyalties and hierarchies.[64] If the New Testament is "against the family" it is "against" an understanding of hierarchical and blood-kinship structures as fully defining family.[65] The family is not so much rejected as it is enlarged, broadened, and made more inclusive. The gospels and the literature of the early Christian communities suggest a broader understanding of family that sees all others as brothers and sisters to each other, with a rejection of dominating structures and narrow loyalties.[66]

---

64. Stanley Hauerwas has emphasized the ways in which the family in Christianity is understood differently than, for example, in Judaism. See Stanley Hauerwas, *A Community of Character: Toward a Constructive Christian Social Ethic* (Notre Dame, IN, and London: University of Notre Dame Press, 1981) 174.

65. Anne E. Carr and Mary Stewart Van Leeuwen, ed., *Religion, Feminism and the Family* (Louisville: Westminster John Knox Press, 1996).

66. See especially Peter Brown, *The Body and Society: Men, Women and Sexual Renunciation in Early Christianity* (New York: Columbia University Press, 1988).

My basis for linking psychoanalytic perspectives on parent-child relations with the scriptural material on familial language and symbols in the
life of Jesus is the sacramental principle itself: that God is revealed in the
world, not apart from it. If the family is a historical and social construct,
as well as a relatively stable biological reality, it will have the capacity
both to expose the fragile and sinful structures of our humanity as well
as potentially to transform these structures for human flourishing. Even
more, it has the capacity to reveal God's extravagant affections for humanity, in God's self-gift in the person of Jesus. With the assumption that
postmodern psychoanalytic scholarship can shed light on the dynamics of
family relationships, language, and gender, I suggest that it can also help in
both critical and constructive perspectives on women and the sacraments.

FAMILY, SYMBOL, LANGUAGE, SACRAMENT

Why focus on family as link with language and sacrament? First, to
recall from chapter 4, it is the embodied context in which human beings come into existence and develop into maturity. As Lisa Sowle Cahill
has argued, "human sexual differentiation and reproduction . . . stand as experiences which begin in humanity's primal bodily existence, and which
all cultures institutionalize (differently) as gender, marriage, and family."[67]
Cahill's point is to argue, on the one hand, against some of the more
radical forms of postmodern theory on the body that make the claim
that "there is no such thing as 'sex,' or that sex in humans has no intrinsic connection to reproductive physiology." This claim, Cahill argues,
"is more rhetorical than factual."[68] On the other hand, she is also arguing against some traditional forms of natural law theology that posit
essentialist meanings of gendered embodiment that can be "read" from
physiological processes — that is, the "natural" receptivity of women and
the corresponding "natural" initiatory activity of men. In arguing for a
revised natural law approach, Cahill is seeking to establish that sexuality
is grounded in the family, which is both a biological and a social organization. In looking to family as context for sacramentality, my point is to

---

67. Lisa Sowle Cahill, *Sex, Gender and Christian Ethics* (Cambridge: Cambridge University Press, 1996) 110.
68. Ibid., 111.

ground sacramentality in this embodied and social context, as well as to draw attention to the dynamics involved in familial life.

But with a consideration of the familial processes outlined above by psychoanalytic and object relations theories, I suggest, second, that sacramental theology has come to be understood within a particular and limited vision of the family, rooted in a culture that has separated men's and women's roles economically, politically, socially, and religiously. That is, magisterial sacramental theology is clearly rooted in one vision of patriarchal culture and speaks especially to those families that have mirrored the kind of processes of which the magisterium speaks. Such pictures of familial life (that is, dominating, active father and subordinate, receptive mother) help to illustrate the theological and social construction of the sacraments, a construction that does not define or much less exhaust the possibilities of family life. That the dynamics of gender have become so central for the sacraments, especially ordination, and that sacramental theology has proven to be so resistant to feminist insights, suggests that there are powerful dynamics at work.

While the psychoanalytic explanations suggested here are not intended to be exhaustive, they can help to illustrate how these dynamics have proven to be fruitful in other fields, and may suggest avenues of exploration here. But these portraits of the family, I want to stress, are limited ones. The psychoanalytic construction of the family, while providing a helpful analysis, reveals the problems involved in a system in which women lack voice. And the picture of spousal relationship provided by magisterial Catholicism does not speak adequately to the realities of life as experienced by different cultures nor to those struggling with the issues of the late twentieth century. The ecclesiological challenges of Vatican II, the women's movement, and the increasing diversity of family structures, are all working to provide a different, and more inclusive portrait of what it means to be family.

Third, my intent is an ethical one. As Cahill argues, in turning to the Catholic tradition's emphasis on the family, "the New Testament household churches and the metaphor of the family as 'domestic church' in patristic writings and in Roman Catholic teaching, are examples of the power of Christian commitment to *transform* body-based sympathies *without eradicating them.*"[69] This, it seems to me, is fundamentally a sacra-

---

69. Ibid., 107. My emphasis.

mental statement: as grace builds upon and perfects, but does not destroy, nature, the Christian tradition's challenge to human life, from its familial to its political structures, is to build upon and perfect that which we are given. By arguing for the embodied context of sacramentality to be in the family as a whole, and not only in the dyadic spousal relationship, nor only in the parent-child relationship as seen by the son, I am also arguing for the potential psychological and social dimensions of embodiment and relation to be understood as central to this understanding as are the physical. As I comment above, one compelling way of understanding Jesus in relationship to God and to others can be seen (but is not fully exhausted by) the image of family. My intention in focusing on family as an embodied, psychosexual, cultural, as well as scriptural, context for the sacraments is to find an image that can lend itself to multiple interpretations while also doing justice to these multiple contexts.

There are, it must be repeated, serious pitfalls in the use of family, most of which are very familiar to feminist readers, and some of which I mentioned at the end of chapter 4. The family as patriarchal institution has perpetuated unjust structures of domination that are based not only on sex but also on race, class, and sexual orientation. The family is also where one learns the language and symbols of the culture and tradition. I am not suggesting that the family provide the *limit* explanation for human life, and thus make it primary over any other structures, such as political or economic ones. Rather, I am proposing that family is central to thinking about symbols, gender, and social structures; that contemporary theories can shed light on its functions, both critical and constructive; that it can provide a grounding for personal and social transformation. No one has yet come up with an acceptable alternative to the family, in Cahill's terms, for providing a place for reproduction, intimacy, and pleasure.[70] Without a consideration of the complex dynamics of the family, the use of familial and embodied metaphors in sacramental theology serves to limit severely their revelatory potential.

Looking to the life of Jesus in relation to God and to his disciples and friends via the family also has some serious risks. A number of feminist scholars have pointed out the problem of the Father-Son relationship, especially with regard to theologies of the atonement.[71] The role of the

---

70. Ibid., 110.

71. See Rita Nakashima Brock, *Journeys by Heart: A Christology of Erotic Power* (New York: Crossroad, 1988); Delores S. Williams, "Black Women's Surrogacy Experience and

obedient Son in relation to the almighty Father provides a dangerous model, it has been suggested, for familial relationships in the world. The "holy family" has long served as a model for the family in which personal growth, especially that of women, is sacrificed for others.

Nevertheless, the family is a reality that perdures. What these psycho-analytic theories have helped to suggest is a kind of "diagnosis" for the relationship of women to sacramentality: that is, that the sacraments, es-pecially in twentieth-century magisterial theology, can be viewed as ways of overcoming the "gap" of the absence of the (m)other through linguis-tic and symbolic forms. Such forms are predicated on the absence of the woman/mother, whose visible presence is a threat to the stability of the sacramental order. But both the family and the sacraments are larger, and deeper, realities that transcend the historical, theological, and cultural lim-itations of the various forms they have taken. A feminist perspective on sacrament through the lens of psychoanalytic theory on the family not only can provide a "diagnosis" for the distortions of both theologies of sacrament and family but also can suggest some possible "prescriptions" for their transformation.

WOMEN AND THE PRACTICE OF THE SACRAMENTS

Since the Second Vatican Council, women have become involved in the church in increasingly visible ways. Women's participation has always been active and essential, yet there has been an "invisible" quality to this par-ticipation until relatively recently. As bakers of the sacramental bread, as designers, cleaners, and preparers of vestments and linens, as educators of those who receive the sacraments, and, not least, as the physical source of the people of God, women have been in the background of sacramental practice. But with the changes mandated by the council since the 1960s, women have moved into greater and greater visibility in the church: most

---

the Notion of Redemption: Coercion vs. Voluntary Surrogacy," *After Patriarchy: Feminist Transformations of the World Religions,* ed. Paula Cooey, William Eakin, and Jay B. McDaniel (Maryknoll, NY: Orbis Books, 1991) 1–14; Elizabeth A. Johnson, "Jesus and Salvation," *Catholic Theological Society of America Proceedings,* 49 (1994) 1–18; Joanne Carlson Brown and Rebecca Parker, "For God So Loved the World?" *Christianity, Patriarchy and Abuse,* ed. Joanne Carlson Brown and Carole Bohn (Cleveland: Pilgrim Press, 1989) 1–30; Mary Grey, *Feminism, Redemption and the Christian Tradition* (Mystic, CT: Twenty-Third Publications, 1990).

obviously as cantors, lectors, eucharistic ministers, but also as liturgical committee chairs, directors of religious education, and as pastoral coordinators or associates. The impact on parishes and congregations of women in these roles has been both practical and symbolic. It has been practical in that the importance of these functions has been increasingly recognized.

Simply put, if women were not there to perform these functions, they would not be done. And these functions are not peripheral to parish life, but are increasingly seen as central. The symbolic impact of women's participation is also significant. As congregations have become accustomed to seeing women in roles of pastoral and educational leadership, their own imaginations have been transformed, and the psychological barriers to women's ability to symbolize the sacred have been challenged.

In what follows I want to suggest four ways in which the theories I have used above as a kind of critical "diagnosis" for the situation of women in relation to the sacraments can also have some constructive possibilities. The first has to do with women, subjectivity, and the sacraments. Psycholinguistic theory suggests that women's subjectivity cannot be assumed. That is to say, women have tended to function, in language as well as symbols, as the objects of men's thoughts and desires. When women *do* speak and act as subjects, their subjectivity is often expressed in relational terms.[72] I will suggest how both recent theoretical work on women and ritual as well as the practice of women working in sacramental ministries in parishes illustrates this relational subjectivity.

The second has to do with the dynamics of presence and absence. The absence of the mother, in Lacanian theory, is the condition for the possibility of the movement to language and symbol. The symbol is always an invocation of the presence of the absent mother. I will suggest here that the feminist emphasis on women's bodies and the goodness of women's biological and social experiences and their importance for liturgy and ritual are ways in which women have come literally to "make their presence felt."

The third way draws on Homans' point that women "speak two languages at once" — both the preverbal and bodily "language of the mother" and the conceptual "law of the father." The ways in which women are participating in sacramental ministries indicate this "bilingual" capacity, in which the language of the church — "the law of the father," so to speak — is

---

72. See Gilligan, *In a Different Voice.*

interrupted, reinterpreted, translated, and reformulated into the "language of the mother." Because of women's involvement in sacramental education, preparation, liturgy planning, and parish administration, the practice, if not the official language, of the sacraments, is being transformed. This is not happening in opposition to the official practice; rather, women's involvement is transforming it from the inside.

Fourth, the role of family is increasingly central to sacramental practice. But a feminist understanding of family sees itself in contrast to other familial models in which there are clear hierarchies, where gender roles are carefully circumscribed, where individualism takes precedence over the concerns of the community, and where the family is isolated from the broader issues concerning the socio-political and economic situation of society. An alternative feminist vision of family, I will argue, provides a connection between sacraments and ethics.

First, then, on women's subjectivity and the sacraments. Who is the speaking, expressing subject? The difficulty for women in gaining a sense of subjectivity has received much attention in feminist literature: What does it mean to be a subject? What does it mean to speak, to have a voice? The literature examined in this chapter suggests some reasons why women's voices have not been supported or affirmed, especially by religion.

Margaret Homans' work has suggested that when women have spoken, as writers, it is as mothers and daughters, out of their familial contexts. Women's symbolic speaking and acting, I suggest, draws in large part on these familial experiences, and names and celebrates these realities in ways not restricted to canonical sacramental rubrics. The emerging literature on women's ritual activity is evidence of the attention given by women to embodiment but also to the importance of relationships. Some of this will be explored more fully in chapter 7.

But the insights from psychoanalytic and psycholinguistic criticism are especially significant because they reveal the moral dimensions of women's subjectivity. In other words, using these theories to interpret traditional sacramental theology reveals how its gendered structures and dynamics work to prevent women as women from emerging as subjects at all. Therefore, women's persistence in speaking and acting symbolically constitutes a resistance to such structures as well as the construction of a language that dares to speak of a God whose affection for humanity is so extravagant that this God takes up a home in the body of a woman. For a woman, then, to say, "this is my body; this is my blood," is to utter a profound truth: one that sees God's embodiment not only in the metaphysical structures of bread and wine but in the flesh and blood of human beings, men and women. Women's subjectivity affirms God's presence and counters women's absence.

Moreover, it has been stressed, especially in feminist ethics, that the moral person is not a person in isolation. We are all related, these ethicists remind us, and we have come to be moral persons within a family, a community, a tradition, and a society.[73] The work done by feminist scholars in ritual and liturgy also emphasizes this communal dimension. For example, Mary Collins, in her important article setting out the principles of feminist liturgy, stresses that feminist rituals are the community's own production; they are not the result of the work of ritual experts.[74] Similarly, Diane Neu observes that women's rituals arise out of women's solidarity and a sense of women's communal and shared power.[75]

My suggestion is that the observations of feminist (and nonfeminist) theorists that women's sense of self is more communal than individualist is, to some extent, illustrated in these feminist liturgists' work. This is not to say that there is something "essential" in all women that orients women more than men to relationship. Our senses of who we are are socially constructed, within the limits of our biology. But feminist ethicists and ritualists are also convinced that the individualist focus of Western society and of some of our theological tradition needs to be corrected by an emphasis on our interdependence. This has also been the case with the (eco)feminist movement, which stresses human interdependence with our natural environment. The sense of community that arises especially out of womanist and *mujerista* theologies and the women-church movement is a sense not only of shared experience but of shared *struggle*. Thus the awareness is intensified that women cannot "do it alone," that the struggle for one is the struggle for all.[76] Further, the sense of subjectivity as communal

---

73. See *Embodied Love: Sensuality and Relationship as Feminist Values*, ed. Paula Cooey, Sharon Farmer and Mary Ellen Ross (San Francisco: Harper & Row, 1987); also Margaret Farley, "Feminist Theology and Bioethics," *Theology and Bioethics: Exploring the Foundations and Frontiers*, ed. Earl Shelp (Boston: D. Reidel Publishing, 1989) 163–85.

74. Mary Collins, "Principles of Feminist Liturgy," in *Women at Worship: Interpretations of North American Diversity*, ed. Marjorie Procter-Smith and Janet Walton (Louisville: Westminster John Knox, 1993) 9–26.

75. Diane Neu, *WomenChurch Sourcebook* (Silver Spring, MD: WaterWorks Press, 1993).

76. See especially Ada María Isasi-Díaz, *En la Lucha/In the Struggle: Elaborating a Mujerista Theology* (Minneapolis: Fortress, 1993).

suggests that the understanding of God as triune, as essentially in relation, has more in common with this idea of subjectivity than do theologies that stress God's self-subsistence, impassibility, and immutability.[77] A God who is "for us," a God whose compassion for humanity has drawn this God into solidarity with suffering and embodiment, is a relational God.

Second, the dynamics of presence and absence. If one were to identify the guiding principles of feminist theology, two of them would certainly be relationality and embodiment.[78] The emphasis on embodiment in feminist theology is intended to counter the long history of the Christian tradition's aversion to the real bodies of women — in favor, some would argue, of the not-so-real immaculate body of Mary and the celibate bodies of men. This emphasis is also illustrative of the goodness of all bodies, male and female, well and ill, able-bodied and disabled, straight and gay. One of the most striking dimensions of the women-church movement has been its effort to develop rituals and liturgies that celebrate, mourn, or simply acknowledge, significant events in women's embodied lives. Rituals for a girl's menarche, for the loss of a child due to miscarriage, abortion, or neonatal death, for recovery from rape or familial sexual abuse, for menopause, for childbirth, are all ways of deliberately inserting the embodied presence of women into the liturgical life of the church. This presence is not so much the symbol of the (absent) presence of God, a way of thinking that stresses the "otherness" of God, but rather the intentional assertion of God's presence *here*, in the bodies of women. The work of many feminist liturgical theologians is intended to counter the absence of women in the sacramental invocation of God's presence. In addition, the feminist emphasis on embodiment has been to make participants more consciously aware of their own bodies, through gesture, dance, movement.

But more importantly, from a feminist perspective, the sacraments do not so much invoke the presence of the absent God (Chauvet), a presence that we long to embrace without mediation, as much as they *intensify* the ambiguous presence of God within the immediate, concrete, and particular. We encounter God not by "leaving the world" but by immersing ourselves more deeply in the world. Traditional, and even contemporary sacramental theology and practice, has emphasized how the sacraments are

---

77. For a rich exploration of this theme, see Catherine Keller, *From a Broken Web: Separation, Sexism, and Self* (Boston: Beacon Press, 1986).

78. On this point, see Margaret Farley, "Feminist Theology and Bioethics" (n. 73, above).

to be *distinguished* from life-cycle events.[79] Magisterial teaching stresses the importance of canonical validity, the "essential difference" between the hierarchical and common priesthood, the caution that communion services cannot be "substitutes" for the Eucharist. While there are, at times, important distinctions to be drawn — not everyone is called to ministry, not all communal meals share in the identity of the Eucharist — what has not received adequate emphasis is the *continuity* between the everyday and the sacramental. It is this sense of continuity, I suggest, that women have had the opportunity to develop, given the social and psychological constructions of selfhood and relationship. A feminist conception of presence is not so much an invoking of an absence as the intensification of an always already-there presence.

Third, the capacity of women to speak "two languages at once" can be seen in at least three ways: 1) in women's liturgies, which are both intended to critique patriarchal liturgies, but which are also intended to provide a means of emancipating and empowering women; 2) in the ways in which women work within the sacramental "system," educating and preparing people for the sacraments (which will be presided over by someone else), critiquing yet also participating in this system; 3) in women's involvement in pastoral administration — also working "in the system" yet transforming it even as they work within it. In all these situations, there is significant "crossover" between the official and the unofficial, the familial and the public.

Sheila Durkin Dierks's book *WomenEucharist* vividly illustrates such "bilingualism" present among women who maintain both traditional parish membership, but who at the same time commit themselves to membership in an ongoing "WomenEucharist" group, where bread and wine — or, perhaps, milk and honey, or tea and rice — are blessed and shared.[80] Those women who work as pastoral associates, religious educators, liturgy directors, are often working in two systems at the same time: one is the official system, administered largely by clerical men; the other is the more informal and more personal approach to the sacraments in which women adapt, work around, or ignore the rules, so that the sacramental life of the church may go on.

---

79. Aidan Kavanagh, "Life Cycles, Civil Ritual and the Christian," *Liturgy and the Human Passage,* ed. David Power (New York: Crossroad, 1979) 14–24.

80. Sheila Durkin Dierks, *WomenEucharist* (Boulder, CO: WovenWord Press, 1997).

Rosemary Ruether has written on the need for women to have spaces and places that can serve as refuges from the overwhelmingly patriarchal language and symbolism of the traditional ritual system. Women's worship groups, as recounted in a growing body of literature, provide ways for women to develop strategies of ritualization that can assist in highlighting new areas for special ritual attention.[81] Moreover, women's work in the sacramental system, as religious educators, volunteers in sacramental preparation, liturgical directors, and so forth, is also revealing new ways of expanding sacramentality. This work — of education, preparation, continuing education — is itself an intrinsic part of the sacrament itself and is increasingly receiving more attention, from all of those involved in sacramental ministry. And women's work in pastoral administration is, despite canon law and increased concern on the part of Vatican authorities, continuing to redefine sacramentality.[82]

Fourth, the role of family as mediating the presence of God between individual and society. The purpose of my focus on the family has been to establish an embodied context for sacramentality: in other words, to locate sacramentality in physical and social life. The traditional sacraments are based largely in family practices: bringing a new life into the family, sharing meals, reconciling, healing, maturing, marrying, dying. As I have tried to show in this chapter, the separation of these practices from the family and their ritualization into a "sacred sphere" controlled by unmarried men works to prevent the sacraments from fully affecting and indeed transforming family life into the communities envisioned by the early Christian communities. If the sacraments are meant to be mediating signs of grace to the world, transforming the most mundane and the most physical experiences into encounters with God, what better place to ground them than in the life of the family? The psychoanalytic theories I have drawn on here are helpful in illuminating certain troubling issues — the absence of women in the more sacramentally oriented traditions, the need to distinguish the sacred from the profane. But they can also be useful in suggesting how these "troubling issues," when faced fully, can yield to a deeper understanding of sacraments and gender roles. The feminist slogan "the personal is the political" underscores that family and domestic life are

---

81. See Catherine Bell, *Ritual Theory, Ritual Practice* (New York: Oxford University Press, 1992).

82. See "Some Questions Regarding Collaboration of Nonordained Faithful in Priests' Sacred Ministry," *Origins: CNS Documentary Service*, 27 (November 27, 1997) 397–407.

intricately involved in political, social, and economic life. While there is a negative dimension to these connections, as feminist analysis has revealed, there is also a positive one. Women's experiences in linking work and family, the conception of family as domestic church, have the potential to link the sacramental and the everyday in a way that traditional sacramental theology has not succeeded in doing. In the next chapter, I turn to feminist theories of the family as a way of linking sacraments and ethics.

CHAPTER SIX

Women, Sacraments, and Ethics

The world will look very different if we move care from its current peripheral location to a place near the center of human life.

—Joan C. Tronto[1]

Within the Christian story a (nonpatriarchal) family model is the lens through which persons are perceived as morally linked to one another by obligations of mutual respect, service, and support.

—Patricia Beattie Jung[2]

Feminist ethics has emerged as one of the richest areas in feminist thought, both secular and religious. Because feminism arises from the realization that women have suffered from and continue to endure injustice, *all feminist thought bears an intrinsically ethical dimension.* This is particularly true for feminist theology.[3] Some of the earliest writings in feminist theology concerned the ways in which sin and grace were understood by the mainstream theological tradition. They argued that including women's experience made a difference, for example, in developing an adequate in-

1. Joan C. Tronto, *Moral Boundaries: A Political Argument for an Ethic of Care* (New York: Routledge, 1993) 101.

2. Patricia Beattie Jung, "Abortion and Organ Donation: Christian Reflections on Bodily Life Support," in *Feminist Ethics and the Catholic Moral Tradition,* ed. Charles E. Curran, Margaret A. Farley and Richard A. McCormick (New York and Mahwah, NJ: Paulist Press, 1996) 462.

3. See Lisa Sowle Cahill, in her review of the literature: "Virtually by definition, feminist theology is 'moral' theology or ethics," in "Feminist Ethics: Notes on Moral Theology," *Theological Studies* 51, no. 1 (March 1990) 50.

terpretation of the meaning of Christian love.[4] Feminist ethical thought has gone on to challenge ethical method, normative understandings of the human person, ways of construing the relationship between the human and God, between human and nonhuman, and models of virtue, to name only a few areas.[5]

The contributions of feminist theory to ethics have now become well known. Feminist ethicists, both secular and theological, have argued that the understanding of the person that has prevailed in traditional ethics has been an androcentric one. Not only has the person been understood as normatively male, but the characteristics of the person — rationality being foremost — have tended to privilege a male-centered view of the world and of experience that implicitly and explicitly sees women as inferior moral agents.[6] Feminist ethicists have sought to develop an understanding of moral agency that is contextualized: that is, which recognizes the person in relation to developmental, historical, social, and environmental forces.

In addition, feminist ethicists question the privileging of rationality, and the consequent denigration of emotion that has emerged from Enlightenment ethics. Certainly feminist ethicists are not the only ones to do so. Ethical theories of virtue, of narrative, have made similar challenges.[7] While this point can be argued, I would suggest that the distinctiveness of feminist ethics lies in its reliance on the experiences of women, in all their

---

4. Valerie Saiving, "The Human Situation: A Feminine View," *The Journal of Religion* 40 (1960); reprinted in *Womanspirit Rising*, ed. Carol P. Christ and Judith Plaskow (San Francisco: Harper & Row, 1975); Judith Plaskow, *Sex, Sin and Grace: Women's Experience and the Theologies of Reinhold Niebuhr and Paul Tillich* (Washington, D.C.: University Press of America, 1980); Barbara Andolsen, "Agape in Feminist Ethics," *Journal of Religious Ethics* 9 (spring 1981) 69–83; *Women's Consciousness, Women's Conscience: A Reader in Feminist Ethics*, ed. Barbara Hilkert Andolsen, Christine E. Gudorf, and Mary D. Pellauer, ed. (Minneapolis: Winston, 1985).

5. There are too many works to name here. For two anthologies of important articles in feminist ethics, see *Feminist Theological Ethics: A Reader*, ed. Lois K. Daly (Louisville: Westminster John Knox Press, 1994) and *Feminist Ethics and the Catholic Moral Tradition*, ed. Charles E. Curran, Margaret Farley, and Richard McCormick (New York: Paulist Press, 1996). Recent important works in feminist ethics would include Susan Frank Parsons, *Feminism and Christian Ethics* (Cambridge: Cambridge University Press, 1996); Lisa Cahill, *Sex, Gender and Christian Ethics* (Cambridge: Cambridge University Press, 1996).

6. See, e.g., Rosemarie Tong, *Feminine and Feminist Ethics* (Belmont, CA: Wadsworth Publishing, 1993).

7. See Stanley Hauerwas, *Character and the Christian Life: A Study in Theological Ethics* (San Antonio: Trinity University Press, 1995); Alasdair MacIntyre, *After Virtue: A Study in Moral Theory* (Notre Dame, IN: University of Notre Dame Press, 1981).

diversity, but with a special focus on the embodied and relational contexts in which human beings live. Thus it seems more than appropriate to turn a feminist ethical eye to the theology and practice of the sacraments.

Most theological considerations of the ethical dimension of the sacraments have revolved around the problem of the distinction of spheres: that is, traditionally, sacraments belong properly to church life, to the realm of ritual and the sacred, whereas ethics is concerned with the concrete application of religious faith to everyday life. Ideally, of course, what we express and model in sacramental worship is what we live out in our lives, and what we live is expressed in our worship. But the sorry state of the world and, I will argue here, of the sacraments as well, shows all too clearly that this both true and untrue. That is, if we were genuinely to live out a faithful Christian sacramental vision and practice, where God is present and revealed in the midst of every action, then the issues of hunger, of the need for reconciliation, of the failures of communal living, would receive far greater attention in our lives than our budgets and calendars now show. Moreover, the inequities and failures of our lives are also reflected in our sacramental practice, where clerical domination continues to be the norm.

The ethical gap between worship and daily life has concerned the church since the earliest days of the Christian community and, indeed, goes back at least as far back as the Hebrew prophetic tradition. The words of the prophet Amos, brought into the present by Martin Luther King Jr.'s quotation of them, sum up the issue:

> I hate, I despise your feasts, and I take no delight in your solemn
> assemblies.
> Even though you offer me your burnt offerings and cereal offerings,
> I will not accept them,
> and the peace offerings of your fatted beasts I will not look upon.
> Take away from me the noise of your songs;
> To the melodies of your harps I will not listen.
> But let justice roll down like waters
> and righteousness like an ever-flowing stream.[8]

In his First Letter to the Corinthians, Paul admonishes his readers that their behavior at table is a scandal. If they were not willing to be reconciled with their neighbors, he writes, then they ought not even to approach the com-

---

8. Amos 5:21–23.

munion table.[9] More recently, the documents of Vatican II have stressed the interrelation of church and world, particularly with regard to the liturgy.[10] This perennial concern has received a great deal of attention in recent years. In what follows, I first want to review some of the ways in which contemporary theologians have addressed the "gap" between sacraments and ethics. What is the nature of this gap? How are the ethical dimensions of the sacraments and the sacramental dimensions of the moral life to be connected? The approaches I will discuss briefly have been serious ones and have contributed much to closing this gap. But, for the most part, they fail to incorporate the issue of gender justice.

Second, I will turn to feminist ethics, particularly feminist reflection on the family, as one resource for addressing — and, more properly, re-conceiving — the relation between sacraments and ethics. Given feminist ethicists' understandings of the person as embodied and relational, and their arguments for the role of the family as central to moral, political, and religious life, I will argue that the traditional conceptions of the "problem" of the relation between sacraments and ethics are fundamentally flawed, since they widen the very gap they are intended to bridge.

Third, I will develop some of the implications of considering both family and sacraments as more involved in public and ethical life than they are ordinarily understood to be. Central to this understanding is the work that women do, both in families/households and in "ancillary" sacramental activities. Finally, I will draw together the threads of Christian moral life as reflected in the love command, the role of "women's work," and the sacraments. The result will be a more adequate conception of the relation between sacraments and ethics.

ATTENDING TO THE LINK BETWEEN SACRAMENTS AND ETHICS

As I have noted, attention to the ethical dimensions of the sacraments is nothing new in Christian theology. Nor is attending to worship and ethics

---

9. 1 Corinthians 11: 17–34.

10. Sacrosanctum Concilium, the sacred constitution on the liturgy, *The Documents of Vatican II*, ed. Austin Flannery, O.P. (Collegeville, MN: Liturgical Press, 1975) par. 6: "The sacred council has set out to impart an ever-increasing vigor to the Christian life of the faithful; to adapt more closely to the needs of our age those institutions which are sub-ject to change; to foster whatever can promote union among all who believe in Christ; to strengthen whatever can help to call all mankind into the Church's fold."

a particularly Christian endeavor. What is distinctive about the Catholic approach to making this connection is its use of eucharistic models of the moral life, in seeing everyday life as a way of living out the eucharistic vision of sacrifice, plenitude, and community.[11]

In the years immediately surrounding Vatican II, sacramental theologians stressed anew the close relationship between sacraments and ethics. Edward Schillebeeckx's understanding of sacraments as "encounters" with God through others was one early expression of this, as he stressed the concrete dimensions of human existence and criticized "spiritualized" and over abstract sacramental theologies. Later, he developed the point that sacraments were "anticipatory signs" of the reign of God, expressing in symbolic and liturgical form the fullness of Christian love, how God calls human beings to transform their lives in response to the suffering of the world.[12] Much postconciliar sacramental theology has stressed the intrinsic link between human action in the world and the sacraments. Indeed, the great failing of pre–Vatican II sacramental theology, according to many of these theologians, was its tendency to emphasize the individualistic and otherworldly dimensions of the sacraments, to see them as a means of personal grace and salvation without sufficient attention to their grounding in the community or their implications for everyday life.[13] Schillebeeckx was especially critical of any conception of the sacraments that tended to regard them as "pipelines of grace," without sufficient attention to their anthropological and communal roots.[14] One need only survey briefly the many works in sacramental theology that emerged in the years following Vatican II to get a sense of the pervasiveness of this concern.[15]

---

11. See, e.g., Regis Duffy, *Real Presence: Worship, Sacraments and Commitment* (San Francisco: Harper & Row, 1982); Michael Downey, *Clothed in Christ: The Sacraments and Christian Living* (New York: Crossroad, 1987).

12. Edward Schillebeeckx, *Christ the Sacrament of the Encounter With God*, trans. N. D. Smith (New York: Sheed and Ward, 1963); also idem, *Christ: The Experience of Jesus as Lord*, trans. John Bowden (New York: Seabury Press, 1980) 810.

13. Bernard Cooke, *Christian Sacraments and Christian Personality* (New York: Holt, Rinehart and Winston, 1965).

14. Schillebeeckx, *Christ, the Sacrament.*

15. See, e.g., Odo Casel, *The Mystery of Christian Worship* (Westminster, MD: Newman Press, 1962); David Hollenbach, "A Prophetic Church and the Sacramental Imagination," in *The Faith that Does Justice*, ed. John Haughey (New York: Paulist, 1977); Aidan Kavanagh, *On Liturgical Theology* (New York: Pueblo, 1984); Karl Rahner, *The Church and the Sacraments*, trans. (New York: Herder and Herder, 1963); R. Vaillancourt, *Toward a Renewal of Sacramental Theology* (Collegeville, MN: Liturgical Press, 1979).

Liberation theologians have devoted a great deal of their attention to the moral dimensions of sacramental life. One of the first to do this was Juan Luis Segundo, in his series *A Theology for Artisans of a New Humanity*, and specifically in the fourth volume of that series, *The Sacraments Today*.[16] The problem, as Segundo saw it, echoing the words of Amos, was that sacraments were too often seen as "religious rites," relegated to the outer margins of human life. He argued, "we must . . . show that the sacraments form part of the very essence of authentic Christian existence."[17] Sri Lankan theologian Tissa Balasuriya observes that "the main problem [is] that the whole Mass is still a bulwark of social conservatism and not yet a means of human liberation."[18] Other theologians have developed these themes, noting, for example, the scandal of hunger in the world amid the celebration of the Eucharist.[19]

These are ancient themes, with no less relevance in the world today than they had thousands of years ago. But liberation theology has often failed to recognize the sinfulness of sexism as an evil as serious as racism or economic oppression. Until relatively recently, nearly all the works published as "liberation theology" were written by men and focused on economic, racial, and social injustice. A number of feminist theologians working in the area of liberation theology have taken their male colleagues to task for their lack of concern for injustice toward women.[20] Further, these women theologians have also developed new approaches to worship

---

16. Juan Luis Segundo in collaboration with the staff of the Peter Faber Center in Montevideo, Uruguay, *The Sacraments Today*, trans. John Drury, vol. 4 of *Theology for the Artisans of a New Humanity* (Maryknoll, NY: Orbis Books, 1974).

17. Segundo, 12–13.

18. Tissa Balasuriya, *The Eucharist and Human Liberation* (Maryknoll, NY: Orbis Books, 1979) 8.

19. See, e.g., Monika Hellwig, *The Eucharist and the Hunger of the World* (New York: Paulist Press, 1976); Enrique Dussel, "The Bread of Celebration, Communitarian Sign of Justice," *Concilium* 72 (1982) 236–49; Mark Searle, ed. *Liturgy and Social Justice* (Collegeville, MN: Liturgical Press, 1980).

20. See María Pilar Aquino, *Our Cry for Life* (Maryknoll, NY: Orbis Books, 1993); Ada María Isasi-Díaz, *En la Lucha/In the Struggle: Elaborating a Mujerista Theology* (Minneapolis: Fortress, 1993); idem, "*Mujerista* Liturgies and the Struggle for Liberation," *Liturgy and the Body*, ed. Louis-Marie Chauvet and François Kabasele Lumbala (London: SCM Press, 1995/ Maryknoll, NY: Orbis Books, 1995); Ada María Isasi-Díaz, Elena Olazagasti-Segovia, Sandra Mangual-Rodriguez, Maria Antonietta Berriozabal, Daisy Machado, Lourdes Aguelles, Raven-Anne Rivero, "*Mujeristas*: Who We Are and What We Are About: Roundtable Discussion," *Journal of Feminist Studies in Religion* 8 (spring 1992) 105–25.

that do not assume that the celebration of the sacraments is adequate and simply needs to be more fully lived out. Rather, they suggest that, when women's experiences are incorporated consciously into worship, they do not simply "add on" to it but also transform it. The point to be made here is that a critical focus on sacraments and justice needs to be attentive to injustice's multiple facets, particularly gender.

Liturgical approaches to sacraments and ethics also make important contributions. These recognize that liturgy is not simply invented anew every time it is celebrated. Anglican theologian Harmon L. Smith observes that ritual and liturgy "carry meaning prior to our understanding and comprehension...worship itself is a moral act which displays our deepest convictions about who we understand and intend ourselves to be."[21] Thus liturgy has a formative power. It has profound effects of which we may not always be consciously aware. Timothy Sedgwick notes that "in worship the participant is changed and formed in relation to God."[22] Regular participation in the life of a worshiping community reveals an intentionality — that is, that one claims membership in a particular community as it is communally and ritually defined. Thus it is impossible to participate fully in the sacraments without, in some way, being affected by them. Proclaiming and celebrating one's beliefs *is* a moral act, as both Smith and Sedgwick note. The ancient saying *lex orandi, lex credendi* is another way of expressing the insight that these two Anglican theologians emphasize. That is, to understand the fundamental values of a person or community, one need only look to how they pray and worship. Worship is not simply the result of one's belief or actions; rather it also shapes them.

This insight too is significant. Certainly, the moral dimensions of the acts of the worshiping community — gathering together, asking forgiveness for sins, hearing the word of God proclaimed, sharing in the eucharistic meal — are rich and cannot be ignored. And the reminder that worship is not a purely rational activity, but works upon people in powerful yet subtle affective ways is important. But feminists observe that these ancient ceremonies, even as they have been renewed, made more relevant by the use of vernacular language, and become more inclusive, still bear the stain of sexism. Even setting aside the issue of the ordination of women as a jus-

---

21. Harmon L. Smith, *Where Two or Three are Gathered: Liturgy and the Moral Life* (Cleveland: Pilgrim Press, 1995) 36.

22. Timothy Sedgwick, *Sacramental Ethics: Paschal Identity and the Christian Life* (Philadelphia: Fortress, 1987) 14–15.

tice issue, there remain the predominance in the liturgy of male language and imagery for God, a lectionary that fails to do justice to the participation of women in the tradition, prayer formulations that can perpetuate unhealthy attitudes toward oneself and others.[23] Thus many feminists have difficulty accepting the liturgy and sacramental celebrations as they are presently constituted as having an adequate moral vision.

The emerging discipline of ecofeminism has drawn on the sacramental principle as a resource for a more adequate understanding of the relation between human beings and the natural world. A sacramental view of the cosmos — that is, a vision that sees all of creation and nonhuman life as inherently sacred — is the natural and logical outcome of a sacramental faith. There are concrete moral consequences to this vision. Sallie Mc-Fague and Rosemary Radford Ruether are two prominent exponents of this approach. Both are critical of what they perceive to be an instrumental attitude toward nature: that is, one that sees the natural world as a resource to be used and even manipulated by humans for their own purposes. This attitude, ecofeminists charge, is profoundly antisacramental. The nonhuman world does not exist merely to be used by humans; rather all of life is to exist in creative interdependence; all of life has intrinsic value. McFague and Ruether both contrast a mechanistic model of the cosmos, one developed in the Enlightenment, with an organic model rooted in embodiment.[24]

McFague is critical of traditional sacramentalism for its anthropocentrism and its focus on the body as a sign of "human sin and destruction."[25] But she notes that "a form of Christian sacramentalism for an ecological era should focus not on the *use* of all earthly bodies but on our *care of them*, in the ways that the Christic paradigm suggests."[26] Sim-

---

23. See Ann Patrick Ware, "The Easter Vigil: A Theological and Liturgical Critique," and Diane L. Neu, "Women-Church Transforming Liturgy," in *Women at Worship: Interpretations of North American Diversity*, ed. Marjorie Procter-Smith and Janet R. Walton (Louisville: Westminster John Knox Press, 1993); Regina A. Boisclair, "Amnesia in the Catholic Sunday Lectionary: Women — Silenced from the Memories of Salvation History," in *Women and Theology*, ed. Mary Ann Hinsdale and Phyllis H. Kaminski (Maryknoll, NY: Orbis Books, 1995).

24. Sallie McFague, *The Body of God: An Ecological Theology* (Minneapolis: Fortress, 1993) 182–91; Rosemary Radford Ruether, *Gaia and God: An Ecofeminist Theology of Earth Healing* (San Francisco: Harper Collins, 1992) 321ff.

25. McFague, *The Body of God*, 185.

26. Ibid., 187.

ilarly, Ruether charts the loss of a sacramental vision in the development of Christianity and observes that "although the cosmos too will participate in the resurrected, immortal 'new heaven and earth,' the focus is on humans and on planetary spheres, not on other forms of earthly life."[27] Thus what is needed is a new attitude in which we no longer "seek to grasp our ego centers of being in negation of others...[but rather] we can dance gracefully with our fellow beings, spinning out our creative work in such a way as to affirm theirs and they ours as well."[28] Thus the sacramental principle, which affirms the revelatory power of all that exists, and human immersion in this complexity, provides the grounding for an interrelational attitude toward the nonhuman world.

Ecofeminism provides a welcome understanding of the relationship between human beings and the "natural world." Like feminist theology and ethics, it stresses the values of embodiment and relation, and extends these broadly, to the nonhuman world and to the cosmos itself. But ecofeminism is not explicitly concerned with the ways in which this attitude is reflected in the life of worship, although it has pointed to the power of images in shaping human attitudes toward nature. Sacramentality as a principle is affirmed, but ecofeminism's aim is not sacramental transformation, but with understanding and relating to the world we live in.

All these approaches stress important dimensions of the relation between sacraments and ethics: the need for justice not only in word but in deed, a recognition of the formative power of worship, the need to broaden sacramentality beyond the human to the wider world. But attention to gender issues is nearly absent in the first two, while the third is less concerned with worship than with the integrity of the natural world. An adequate approach to relating sacraments and ethics would include all three of these concerns: the practice of justice, the moral power of symbols and rituals, and the need to extend sacramentality broadly. In what follows, I will suggest that feminist reflections on the family offer such a focal point: they question the divisions between private and public life, they reexamine the ways that the work of women and "family" is understood, and they give examples of the moral dimensions of sacramentality.

---

27. Ruether, *Gaia and God,* 237.
28. Ibid., 253.

FEMINIST ETHICS AND THE FAMILY

In a recent article, Sally Purvis has remarked how relatively little attention has been paid by Christian feminists toward the family. Feminist theologians, she writes, have devoted more attention to particular issues within the family that concern women — reproductive rights, sexuality, domestic violence, gender roles — while the general tone of theological writings on the family has defended the priority of the traditional model of the heterosexual couple with children. Proponents of this model have tended to extoll "family values" often hostile to feminism, and have also decried feminism's critique of this "traditional" family.[29] But it is time, she says, "that we reclaim the territory from a feminist normative position."[30]

Purvis's basis for a Christian feminist understanding of the family is that of Christian love: the dual command to love God and to love others as oneself. Building on this foundation, she develops two major points: first, "the feminist insight that persons are constitutively relational" and, second, "the Christian communal values of diversity and inclusivity."[31] In discussing the meaning and importance of Christian love, Purvis notes the many debates that have surrounded the topic of "love," especially as *agape*. Traditionally, *agape* has been understood to be self-sacrificing and disinterested, two characteristics that have proven to be problematic for feminists.[32] Feminist critiques and developments of the idea of Christian love have instead stressed mutuality, passion, and unconditionality, drawing on women's experiences as well as traditional Christian sources, such as the Bible and tradition.[33] Given these emphases, the traditional "problem of the family" for Christian ethics — that is, how to reconcile family

---

29. Sally Purvis, "A Common Love: Christian Feminist Ethics and the Family," in *Religion, Feminism, and the Family,* ed. Anne Carr and Mary Stewart Van Leeuwen (Louisville: Westminster John Knox Press, 1996) 111–24.

30. Purvis, 112.

31. Ibid.

32. See, e.g., Anders Nygren, *Agape and Eros,* trans. Philip S. Watson (Philadelphia: Westminster Press, 1953); Gene Outka, *Agape: An Ethical Analysis* (New Haven: Yale University Press, 1972). Although she does not mention them, the recent work on Christian love done by Edward Vacek, "Divine Command, Natural-Law, and Mutual Love Ethics," *Theological Studies* 57 (December 1996) 633–53, and Stephen Pope, "Love in Contemporary Christian Ethics: Christian Neighbor Love," *Journal of Religious Ethics* 23 (spring 1995) 167–97, have much to contribute to this ongoing discussion, especially as they take note of the issue of partiality.

33. Purvis, 114–15.

love and personal obligations with the ideal of Christian love as disinterested — "shifts," with the result that "the challenge is not renunciation of affect and intensity [according to the traditional model of *agape*] but rather the development of wider and wider circles of intense, passionate love."[34] In addition, self-sacrificial interpretations of *agape* are also subject to intense feminist criticism.[35] I would add to Purvis's understanding the feminist ethical emphasis on embodiment, which has also emerged as a central theme.[36] Embodiment grounds the understanding of the family in part in the "givenness" of our biological and cultural heritages, and stresses the concreteness and particularity of life and its moral obligations as well as the particular social contexts in which it is experienced.

One aim of Purvis's essay is to show how, for Christians, the values of the family are extended beyond their biological and cultural limitations to the wider society. She remarks that "extravagant outpourings of concern...are surprising only because they occur in relations with strangers as well as friends and family."[37] Thus a Christian feminist understanding of the family is one that emphasizes passion, relationship, and diversity, not just within the nuclear family, but in all of one's relationships. In other words, a Christian feminist perspective on the family builds on its basic values of affection, relationship, and embodiment, and extends them to the world. Christian ethics thus grows out of the family; it does not impose an alternative set of values, opposed to the family. In Catholic terms, one might put this in the familiar phrase "grace builds on and perfects nature, it does not destroy it." There is, then, a continuity between "family ethics" and "social ethics." Women's traditional association with the family does not relegate family to a private, domestic sphere, but proves to be the basis for the expansion of the Christian understanding of love. Thus a Christian feminist ethical perspective on the

---

34. Ibid., 115.

35. Andolsen, "Agape in Feminist Ethics," (see n. 2, above).

36. For ways of noting this: *Embodied Love: Sensuality and Relationship as Feminist Values*, ed. Paula Cooey, Sharon Farmer and Mary Ellen Ross (San Francisco: Harper & Row, 1982); Margaret Farley, "Feminist Theology and Bioethics," *Theology and Bioethics: Exploring the Foundations and Frontiers* ed. Earl Shelp (Boston: D. Reidel Publishing, 1989) 163–85; Cahill, "Notes on Moral Theology," n. 3, above. Purvis notes that the family has a biological basis but is also a sociological reality. Catholic feminist authors may tend to emphasize embodiment or positions more sympathetic to natural law than Protestant feminist theologians do.

37. Purvis, 114.

family stresses mutuality, criticizes exclusivity, and broadens the extension of family relations.[38]

The feminist focus on the family as a resource for the moral life is reflected as well in secular feminist literature. A number of prominent theorists have argued that the relegation of the family to a private sphere, beyond the moral demands of the public arena, impoverishes both the personal and the social dimensions of moral life.[39] By bringing the concerns of the family into the public sphere — gender justice between spouses, the rights of children, the division of labor in the home, the care of the elderly — feminist theorists have shown how these so-called domestic or private issues reveal deep and significant issues going on as well in the public sphere.[40] The feminist slogan "the personal is the political" says in essence that there is no hard-and-fast division between issues of social and personal ethics: rather, they contribute to and affect each other. An issue such as domestic violence reveals not merely what is going on in private disputes between couples in the privacy of their homes. It is also symptomatic of a culture that tolerates violence against women and children in its advertising and media images, promotes violence as a means of "solving" disputes, and implicitly supports the rights of men to treat their partners and children as their personal property.[41]

Political theorist Susan Moller Okin argues that the separation of family from public life has had a negative impact not only on women, but also on society as a whole. In her important book *Justice, Gender and the Family,* Okin argues that the moral division between the public and the domestic (a terminology she prefers to public/private) hides impor-

---

38. Cristina L. H. Traina is at work on a book that argues for maternal experience as a resource for Christian ethics. See her essay, "Passionate Parenting: Toward an Ethic of Appropriate Parent-Child Intimacy," *Annual of the Society of Christian Ethics* 1998 (forthcoming).

39. See, e.g., not only Susan Moller Okin, whose work I draw heavily on below, but also Sara Ruddick, *Maternal Thinking: Towards a Politics of Peace* (Boston: Beacon Press, 1989); Mary Belenky and Mary Field, *A Tradition that Has No Name: Nurturing the Development of People, Families and Communities* (New York: Basic Books, 1997).

40. See Susan Moller Okin, *Justice, Gender and the Family* (New York: Basic Books, 1989); Bonnie Miller-McLemore, *Also a Mother: Work and Family as Theological Dilemma* (Nashville: Abingdon Press, 1994); Don Browning and Ian S. Evison, ed., "The Family, Religion, and Culture," Series (Louisville: Westminster John Knox Press, 1996).

41. Note the voluminous literature on domestic violence; see, e.g., Myriam Medzian, *Boys Will Be Boys: Breaking the Link Between Masculinity and Violence* (New York: Doubleday, 1991).

tant connections between the two areas. First, she writes, domestic life is strongly affected by the dynamics of power in the public sphere. Far from being a "safe haven" from the cold world, the family is strongly affected by social power relations, as is evident in the issue of domestic violence. The kinds of relationships that one sees in the family often mirror those seen in the wider society, where men wield proportionately more physical and financial power than do women. Second, she writes that the very existence of the "domestic" sphere is itself an invention of the public arena, and the public continues to have a strong influence, for example, in the ways that the state regulates family life. Third, the domestic arena is where human beings are socialized for life, in both its public and domestic dimensions, a point I emphasized in chapter 5. Thus the distinction between the two raises questions about the differences between appropriate norms of behavior and standards operative in the two spheres. Fourth, because of the division of labor in the public arena, it is more difficult for women's voices to be heard, both in public and private. Women's traditional place in subsidiary areas of work (for example, the "helping" professions) tends to mute their voices in public, and affects their voices in private as well. Okin argues that all these factors work against a realistic division between the public and the domestic.[42]

The point is not that there should be no distinction at all between the two areas. It is, rather, to challenge the traditional way of having separate standards in the public and domestic spheres. A more just society, Okin argues, will be a society that is just both in the family and in the public world.[43] Okin writes, "I have suggested that, for very important reasons, the family *needs* to be a just institution, and have shown that contemporary theories of justice neglect women and ignore gender."[44]

Moral philosopher Joan Tronto develops a related thesis in her book *Moral Boundaries: A Political Argument for an Ethic of Care.*[45] While her book is not directly about the family, and indeed, while she is reluctant to align care and family, Tronto's book has important implications for a feminist perspective that seeks to take the family seriously. Tronto's

---

42. See Okin, 132–33

43. Ibid., 109.

44. Ibid., 170–71. See also Jean Bethke Elshtain, *Public Man, Private Woman: Women in Social and Political Thought* (Princeton, NJ: Princeton University Press, 1981), who makes a similar argument about the public/private relationship.

45. New York: Routledge, 1993.

first point is that the relegation of emotion, and practices of caring, to the "private" moral arena, and the consequent understanding of public morality as universal, rational, and disinterested, has its roots in the En-lightenment. At a time when the world was becoming both larger and more accessible to the West, through new geographic and scientific dis-coveries, and as the West was embracing democratic forms of government, "the spheres of domesticity and production separated. The family became a private sphere."[46] Morality became located in universalistic reason (Kant) and sentiment came to reside in the household, now the sphere of women. Tronto's aim is not so much to argue against this development, but rather to reveal its historical — thus not ahistorical or essentialist — dimensions.

The consequence of this development in moral theory was a separation of the private realm of sentiment, caring, emotion — the home — from the public realm of reason and justice. As Tronto puts it, "in separating the moral actor from cultural influences, the Kantian position also makes it difficult to explain how the concern for universal rights and equality is to be made part of people's everyday moral lives."[47] Thus feeling, sympathy, and especially caring are reserved for those closest to us, while the more rational concerns for rights and justice are played out in the public arena.

The challenge, then, Tronto writes, is to "conceive of a way to think of morality that extends some form of sympathy further than our own group...[this is] perhaps the fundamental moral question for contempo-rary life."[48] That is, the problem is two-dimensional: concerns for justice do not sufficiently extend to the realm of the private, as Okin has stressed, while concerns for care of others do not sufficiently extend to the realm of the public. The traditional "moral boundaries" that have arisen between morality and politics, the engaged and the disinterested moral perspectives, and between public and private life, serve not only to keep reason and emotion separate, but also "block the effectiveness of women's morality arguments,"[49] because they relegate care only to the sphere of the per-sonal, rather than that of the social and political. Thus it is important to "redraw" moral boundaries, and Tronto's main effort is to argue that "care" needs to be understood and practiced within a political as well as a

---

46. Tronto, 34.
47. Ibid., 58.
48. Ibid., 59.
49. Ibid., 10.

private context.[50] Given the changes of the twentieth century, where "capitalism has continued to spread to all corners of the globe," where "women have also joined the labor force and the traditional distributions and patterns of care have been transformed," and where "functions of care have increasingly fallen into the purview of the state and caring functions have also been moved into the market," care needs to be seen as a common and universal moral demand.[51]

For Tronto, *care* can be defined as "*a species activity that includes everything that we do to maintain, continue, and repair our 'world' so that we can live in it as well as possible.* That world includes our bodies, our selves, and our environment, all of which we seek to interweave in a complex, life-sustaining web."[52] Tronto notes some important features of this definition: it includes the nonhuman world; it is not necessarily dyadic or individualistic; it is defined culturally; and it is ongoing.[53] It "is both practical and a disposition"; it excludes creative activity *per se,* and "what is definitive about care...seems to be a perspective of taking the other's needs as the starting point for what must be done."[54] Thus Tronto includes the concerns of ecofeminists in a larger context.

Tronto, like Okin, cautions that "there is a danger if we think of caring as making the public realm into an enlarged family. Family caring is a necessarily private and parochial understanding of caring."[55] The existence of hierarchies, partiality, and unity, basic to family life, are "anathema to a liberal, democratic society."[56] Tronto's reluctance to focus on connections between family and caring arises, I believe, from her criticism of some feminist theories of caring that see it as an activity that is done primarily by women in families. Since her point is to define caring as an activity that is as relevant in the public sphere as the private, associating caring with families may appear to undermine the political point she is mak-

---

50. Thus Tronto is very critical of the work of Carol Gilligan and Nel Noddings for their failure to extend care outside the realm of the personal. See Carol Gilligan, *In a Different Voice: Psychological Theory and Women's Development* (Cambridge, MA: Harvard University Press, 1983); Nell Noddings, *Caring: A Feminine Approach to Moral Education* (Berkeley: University of California Press, 1984).

51. Tronto, 150–51, and 153.

52. Ibid., 103. Emphasis in the original.

53. Ibid., 103.

54. Ibid., 104–5.

55. Ibid., 169.

56. Ibid.

ing. In addition, Tronto is correct in noting that there is an appropriate separation between the private and public. Families have a necessary hierarchical structure and concerns of partiality are appropriate. But while understanding the legitimacy of Tronto's caution about making too close a connection between caring and family, I would want to make two points in response. First, the understanding of family that has arisen out of feminist ethics has argued strongly against *certain* hierarchies, especially of husband over wife, and has undertaken a critical examination of some of the partialities extended to families, for example, when it might be necessary to challenge them, as in cases of abuse. Thus a feminist conception of family is not *wholly* private and parochial, as Okin has helped to show.

Secondly, the ways in which people learn to care inevitably arise, at least in part, out of their family contexts, as well as the public arena, which ideally supports the extension of the importance of caring. Hence, while there are some dimensions of caring that are relevant more to families than to the public — intimate relations between spouses, for example, or child-rearing, although both have public dimensions — it would be a mistake to say that these are two entirely different understandings of care. They are, rather, expressions of care that are appropriate in different contexts. There is, then, a *continuity,* although not an *identity,* between care as it is experienced and expressed in the private realm of the family and how it is expressed in our public morality.

Thus feminist ethics, both in its Christian theological and secular forms, has found in a revised conception of family, and in the virtues traditionally associated with the family (like care), valuable resources for challenging traditional moral boundaries between the private and the public, and between women's and men's moralities. Both Christian and secular feminist approaches argue that the (revised) virtues of the family need extension to the public sphere, not containment in the private. I want to suggest that using the family as a bridge between these boundaries might also be helpful in bridging the analogous boundary between sacraments and ethics.

IMPLICATIONS FOR CATHOLIC SACRAMENTAL THEOLOGY

Feminist family theory shows that the roles of family in relation to the sphere of moral reasoning and of sacraments in relation to the sphere of ethics share an analogous structure. For both, as I have already anticipated, feminist approaches to the family offer ways of relating the spheres more adequately than is presently understood. As we have already seen, feminist ethicists are critical of moral views that see family as a private realm, apart from the public realm of "real" moral problems. In these views, moral persons are understood to be adults, usually adult men, and thus their development within a family context, nurtured (most often) by women is ignored. Because the family is seen to be a private realm, notions of justice and equity operative in the public sphere have not generally been applied to it. In addition, the family is understood to be a "natural" human organization, and thus its structure — usually patriarchal — is understood to be a given.

Part of the reasoning for the moral relegation of the family to the "private" has to do with its bonds of affection as "above" or "separate from" the realm of the truly moral. This separation further reflects the notion that the affective dimensions of human persons are not directly relevant to the moral. In fact, emotion can hinder moral reasoning because it introduces an element of "bias," which goes against the objective and rational ideal of public moral reasoning.[57]

In theological thinking about the family, many of the same issues apply. For example, in Vatican documents regarding the family, while there has been a welcome concern (at least in recent years) for issues of justice and mutuality to be operative in the family as well as in society, there is always a reservation that this concern for justice not override the "natural" place that women have in the family, and the concern, still found in recent writings, that women might "lose" their essentially maternal vocation by emulating the roles of men.[58] It is not entirely clear what elements of male behavior are found to be deleterious to women, but the concern that the "natural" and "essential" takes precedence over issues of (especially secular ideas of) justice is a prominent one.[59]

While there is an admirable concern to give the work that women do in maintaining a home and raising a family an equal value to the public work that men do, there is little, if any, recognition that, while childbearing

57. See Beverly Harrison, "The Power of Anger in the Work of Love," *Making the Connections: Essays in Feminist Social Theory*, ed. Carol Robb (Boston: Beacon Press, 1985) 3–21; Mary Ellen Ross, "The Ethical Limitations of Autonomy: A Critique of the Moral Vision of Psychological Man," in *Embodied Love*, 151–68. This theme is also developed in Okin.

58. See both *Familiaris Consortio* (the apostolic exhortation on the family) *Origins* 11/28–29 (December 24, 1981), esp. #23; and *Mulieris Dignitatem* (See chapter 4).

59. Especially when the issue of women's ordination comes up. See *Inter Insigniores*.

may be possible only for women, childrearing can be and is a task for both men and women.[60] It is simply assumed by the Vatican that women are "naturally" responsible for both. Further, women's capacity to bear children is understood to give women an innate receptivity and generosity that men intrinsically lack.[61] Thus, familial issues are seen to be women's particular moral realm, and this realm is bound to the natural in a way that men's more public work is not.

Ethical issues within the family, at least in Roman Catholicism, tend to revolve around the "natural" — largely sexuality — rather than around issues of justice. That is to say, there is understood to be a "natural order" established by God to which we are to conform. There is, indeed, a kind of "submission" to the natural order, as in the case of natural family planning, that supersedes concerns for justice related to men's and women's roles. Papal recognition of the "serious difficulties" that families may encounter in their use of natural family planning is one acknowledgment of this.[62] Thus the family is "naturalized" and ethical norms for the natural follow an eternal law, set by God and reflected in nature. Given that the natural order is established by God, it is also understood to be intrinsically just. In the public sphere, however, justice issues are subject to more complex, and changing, historical forces. The public sphere — the worlds of work, associations, government, and the like — is a socially constructed one. While related to "natural" understandings of social organization, the public sphere is guided more by rationality than by nature.

But the public sphere is "socialized" and thus follows more complex historical and particular processes. Because of this distinction, applying norms of justice to the family can raise the charge that one is making a category mistake. Doing "family ethics" does not necessarily mean raising questions of justice and mutuality within the family context for Vatican thinking on the family, as it does for feminists, but, instead, it means following the natural law — or, at most, raising questions of justice up to the point where issues of natural law override them. This is how the issue of women's "equality" has been treated by the church. Women possess an

60. See Okin, 171; Dorothy Dinnerstein, *The Mermaid and the Minotaur: Sexual Arrangements and the Human Malaise* (New York: Harper & Row, 1976); Nancy Chodorow, *The Reproduction of Mothering* (Berkeley: University of California Press, 1978).

61. See *Mulieris Dignitatem*, #18.

62. See Pope Paul VI, "Humanae Vitae," *The Papal Encyclicals 1958–1981,* ed. Claudia Carlen (Raleigh, NC: McGrath Publishing, 1981) n. 25, 230.

"equal dignity" to men, but it is not the same as men's, and has to do with women's "unique" and "natural" gifts, bestowed on them by God.[63]

There is a similar dynamic at work in the relation of the ethical to the sacramental. Since the sacraments are grounded in the realm of the natural, but given a supernatural significance through their divine institution, they are, in effect, twice removed from the social ethical requirements of justice and mutuality. In addition, the sacraments are also related to the area of the aesthetic, which also is seen to enjoy a kind of "exemption" from ethical norms.[64] So if one were to argue that the norm of justice ought to apply in the area of sacramental theology, as feminist theologians do in making the case for the ordination of women as a requirement of justice, one runs into the charge that the sacraments, as is the family, are of a separate sphere than secular society — the church is "not a society like the rest."[65]

As we have already seen, feminist theorists argue that this separation of spheres — of family from the public, of the personal from the political — has harmed not only women, but society as well. Recall Okin's four points disputing this separation: first, domestic life is strongly affected by the dynamics of power in the public sphere; second, the private and domestic is itself constructed by the public; third, the domestic arena is where persons are socialized *for* the public; and fourth, given the traditional division of labor in the public sphere, women's voices are far less likely to be given a public hearing. There is a similar dynamic at work in the relation between the sacramental and the moral. As the family is seen to be "natural," and thus either "above" or "beyond" judgments of justice, which operate in the public arena, so too is the sacramental seen to be in the realm of the "supernatural" and "eternal," and thus similarly beyond the claims of justice. Where justice is an issue, as in recent papal documents on the family, it is qualified by its "natural" basis.

----

63. See Christine E. Gudorf, "If you want a Seamless Garment, Use a Single Piece of Cloth," *Cross Currents* 34 (winter 1984) 473–91, and William P. George, "War and Other Moral Issues," Core Nine Lecture, St. Joseph College, Rensselaer, IN, March 1994.

64. See David Tracy, *The Analogical Imagination: Christian Theology and the Culture of Pluralism* (New York: Crossroad, 1982).

65. Margaret Farley makes such an argument for the ordination of women in her "Discrimination or Equality: the Old Order or the New," *Women Priests: A Catholic Commentary on the Vatican Declaration*, ed. Leonard Swidler and Arlene Swidler (New York: Paulist Press, 1977). The quote is from the Vatican declaration on the question of the admission of women to the ministerial priesthood, *Inter Insigniores*, 1976.

Thus, in relation to Okin's first concern about issues of power, it is often claimed by the magisterium that the priesthood is a vocation to service, not to power.[66] A vocation to the priesthood comes from a mysterious call from God to men. The sacraments are interpreted as loci of divine power (that is, grace), but human power is, in effect, denied as having any real bearing on the sacraments. Yet the very possibility of the exercise of any public power in the church (jurisdictional, sacramental) is grounded in the sacraments, particularly in holy orders, where the priest receives the power of sacramental ministry itself.[67] Further, the point that the church operates in a sacred and separate sphere provides one basis for its prohibition of women's full participation in sacramental ministry. Such an argument severely undercuts the church's own efforts to link more fully the sacramental and the ethical.

Yet if the two are "separate realms," how can there be separate norms of justice and equality operating in the two spheres, when truth is understood to be one? Of course, it should be noted that in the Roman Catholic tradition, natural law is understood to be at the same time both God's law and reflected in nature. In the best interpretations of natural law, there is real continuity between the realm of the supernatural and the realm of the natural. Problems arise where conceptions of natural law seem to run counter to human experience, as feminist and other critics of certain natural law positions charge they do, in areas relating to sexuality and gender justice. In these cases, revised conceptions of natural law, as developed by such scholars as Jean Porter and Lisa Sowle Cahill, seek to show how the "natural" is more ambiguous than it appears to be, and is thus open to wider interpretation.[68] Thus, the sacraments are, like the family, strongly affected by the dynamics of power operative in the church.

---

66. See Donna Steichen, *Ungodly Rage: The Hidden Face of Catholic Feminism* (San Francisco: Ignatius Press, 1991) 309; Helen Hull Hitchcock, "Women for Faith and Family: Catholic Women Affirming Catholic Teaching," *Being Right: Conservative Catholics in America,* ed. Mary Jo Weaver and R. Scott Appleby (Bloomington: Indiana University Press, 1995) 165.

67. This point is strongly emphasized in the November 1997 Vatican statement on the laity's collaboration with the work of priests.

68. See especially Cahill, *Sex, Gender and Christian Ethics;* Cristina L. H. Traina, *Undoing Anathemas: A Feminist Retrieval of Natural Law Ethics* (Washington, D.C.: Georgetown University Press, forthcoming); Jean Porter, *The Recovery of Virtue: The Relevance of Aquinas for Christian Ethics* (Louisville: Westminster John Knox, 1990).

Okin's second point is that the public arena defines and regulates the domestic; thus, the two spheres are not really disconnected. A similar point can be made in relation to the sacraments. The sacraments are human ritual and symbolic constructions, emerging out of a human response to the belief that the divine operates in all areas of life; sacraments also draw on the social, cultural, and historical dimensions of human society. Thus the argument that one cannot change the "nature" of the sacraments — as in the case of ordination — because they have been "instituted by Christ" is, in fact, disingenuous. This claim allows "separate" moralities to operate; indeed, it perpetuates a selective method of biblical interpretation, furthering the separation between sacraments and ethics. Appeals to the institution of the sacraments by divine mandate overlook the work of historical scholarship, particularly biblical scholarship, which, especially over the last two centuries, has transformed the ways that educated Christians regard the Bible. While I concede that far too often biblical scholars have shied away from making any kind of theological judgment on the impact of their historical-critical work, an uncritical approach to biblical narratives of "institution" is even more dangerous, as it further perpetuates a division between sacred and secular.[69] In other words, appeals to the divine institution of the sacraments without sufficient historical-critical grounding is, in effect, calling on the Bible as a *deus ex machina* to solve a contemporary problem. The Protestant tradition has argued (not without justification) that only two sacraments — baptism and Eucharist — can be definitively rooted in the bible. Older Catholic treatments of the "institution" of the sacraments drew on such passages as Jesus' breathing upon the apostles as the moment of the institution of confirmation, for example. Thus Catholicism opens itself to the charge of its own "selective" biblical interpretation.

Third, Okin observes that the family is where human beings are socialized. That is, the family is the "school" of social relations, and these relations are lived out not only in private, but in public. A similar dynamic is in operation with the sacraments, where there is a "formation" of personhood, where one receives, in the case of some of the sacraments, a "sacramental character." Recall the liturgical approach to linking sacra-

---

69. See Sandra M. Schneiders, *The Revelatory Text: Interpreting the New Testament as Sacred Scripture* (San Francisco: HarperSanFrancisco, 1991), as a welcome exception to this characterization of biblical scholarship.

ments and ethics, that liturgy forms and shapes us. Here, a consideration of gender dynamics again reveals a separation between sacramentality and the secular world. The community that is celebrated at the Eucharistic table is one in which all are meant to be servants to each other, where the last is to be first and the first is to be last. But the equality that should be celebrated at table is not present in the hierarchical structure of the church, where only ordained men have a voice of power or authority, where the celebrant priest communes first instead of last, where the appeal to the imagination perpetuates the exclusion of women. Sacramental practice is similarly a "school" of relations, where one learns one's place in the hierarchy, which — in the case of all women — is at the bottom.

Fourth, Okin notes that because of the division of labor in the public arena, women's voices are less likely to be heard even in the domestic sphere. The kinds of power relations operative in one arena will inevitably flow into the other. In the case of the sacramental and the ethical, women's voices are almost entirely — at least on the official level — silent in sacramental celebration. Women's voices are not at all silent, however, on the "unofficial" level. But because of the ways in which women's work and voices are unrecognized and unacknowledged, the impact of women's voices on sacramental praxis is yet to be fully developed. Women's voices and actions can help to bridge the gap between sacraments and ethics, yet the maintenance of separate spheres — of women's from men's, of the sacramental from the ethical, of the domestic from the public — prevents this from taking place.

Thus the moral implications of sacramental theology — of God's loving presence embodied in actions and relationships of justice and mutuality — lack development, in large part due to the exclusion of women from sacramental leadership. Two points become even clearer. First, the perpetuation of separate spheres of social and personal ethics, of the sacred and the secular, of men's and women's separate natures, all work against an organic connection of sacraments and ethics. To argue that sacraments and ethics are intimately linked, while maintaining clear divisions between these other related areas, is to undermine the potential linkage before it is even begun. Second, to make this connection real will require that women's involvement be central. An understanding of sacraments as emerging out of family/household life will move the two areas much closer.

WOMEN, FAMILY, CARING, AND SACRAMENTS

In a 1987 article, Christine Gudorf wrote:

> Limitation of sacramental administration to men functions as a claim for men that they — not women — have exclusive power to create and sustain real life, spiritual life, through representing Jesus, the source of life. This claim implements a separation between ordinary natural life nurtured by women, and spiritual life nurtured by a male elite who serve as symbols for all men.[70]

Gudorf notes that the sacraments, as rituals, are meant to "point our attention and appreciation beyond the ritual itself to the ongoing life processes they imitate."[71] Further, "the most interesting aspect of the ordinary human activities on which these sacramental rituals are based is the prominence of women."[72] For example, women give physical birth, but spiritual birth — "real" birth — is given by male clerics in baptism. Women are those who are most often engaged in the ongoing tasks of keeping families together: remembering and celebrating birthdays or anniversaries, bringing those at odds with each other back together. But "real" reconciliation, "real" healing, is done again by male clerics. Other cultures reveal a similar dynamic of exclusion of women from the sacred. Gudorf concludes that "the exclusion of women from sacred rituals is based in a fear of their power over life, and that this power over life is so central that men ritually claim it for themselves."[73]

Gudorf's suggestion is that men need to be included into more life-giving activities in daily life:

> Men need to be drawn into the ongoing work of giving life so that the rituals which celebrate this work do not carry the entire burden of satisfying male needs. Men must be drawn into the ongoing work of giving life so that their genetic contribution can be experienced by men themselves as symbolic of a lived commitment on their part rather than on an accident of sex.[74]

---

70. Christine E. Gudorf, "The Power to Create: Sacraments and Men's Need to Birth," *Horizons* 14/2 (1987) 296–309. The quote is from 297.

71. Ibid.

72. Ibid., 298.

73. Ibid., 301.

74. Ibid., 308.

If this were to be the case, men would not feel the need to monopolize ritual, as Gudorf argues is the case at present.

In this article Gudorf makes a number of important observations. First, the separation of ritual from ordinary life serves to unduly elevate the sacramental while unduly denigrating the ordinary. In the post–Vatican II reforms of the liturgy and sacraments, there has been a real effort made to overcome this separation. Nevertheless, Gudorf's point holds, especially when she observes that women who do offer blessings to the ill or listen to "penitential reflection" in the absence of a priest are "not really" doing anything sacramental, in the strict sense.[75] Second, her conclusion that men should be more involved in "life-giving activities" is crucial, and bears repeating. The relegation of feeding, nurturing, reconciling, in everyday life to "women's work" serves to perpetuate gender stereotypes as well as to place women under the bind of the "double shift," working both in the public arena out of economic necessity, yet also having to bear the burden of work at home.[76] Men indeed ought to be more involved in these activities. But the solution is easier said than done, and the difficulty of making this solution a real option reveals that the problem is a deep one. It is not that men simply "don't know" that life-giving work is as available to them as it is to women. It is that the culture perpetuates a division of the kinds of activities that women and men do, such as caring, to the private, and feminine, sphere, and "real," paid work to the public sphere. Such a division also reifies the latter and devalues the former. As Gudorf observes, men engage in "feminine" or "caring" activities when they are "elevated" beyond the ordinary to the supernatural.

But the problem is not only one of men's or women's work. What Gudorf points out is that the sacraments are separated from ordinary, domestic life. This separation is another way of expressing the separation of the ethical from the sacramental. It is also symptomatic of the way in which family concerns and caring activities are relegated to the sphere of the private and domestic, and excluded from the public and ritual sphere (except as they are "elevated," as Gudorf points out). The answer lies, I suggest, not in simply encouraging men to get involved in these activities, but in reconceiving the relation between caring and the public domain, in rethinking the relation of family to the public sphere. By applying the

---

75. Ibid., 304.

76. See Arlie Hochschild, *The Double Shift: Working Parents and the Revolution at Home* (New York: Viking, 1989).

insights of Okin, Purvis, and Tronto to the separation of the sacramental from the ethical, and by also including a consideration of the gender dynamics operative in the sacramental, we might come closer to a more adequate understanding of the moral dimensions of the sacraments, and the sacramental dimensions of the ethical.

Feminist theological ethics has highlighted certain values — relationship, community, embodiment — as central to the Christian understanding of human existence and its relationship to God. Feminists have also pointed out how these values need to be better incorporated into our personal, public, and political lives. As Okin, Purvis, and Tronto have suggested, from their differing viewpoints and concerns, the issues that have been relegated to the family and to private life (for example, caring, passionate love) need to be extended to the public realm, and those concerns that have been part of the public sphere (for example, justice) need more expression in the private.

Tronto's development of the need to care has many suggestive possibilities for a feminist ethical approach to sacramental theology. Not only are the components of caring helpful in showing the moral dimension of sacramental activity, as well as its gendered dynamics, but they also help to spell out what Purvis means by the Christian love command's relevance to the widening of family affection. The four "phases" of caring that Tronto develops offer some creative possibilities.[77]

The first phase of caring is "caring about." Caring is a disposition and "often involve[s] assuming the position of another person or group" in order to recognize the need. This first phase involves what Christian theologians have described as one of the most basic dimensions of *agape*, the attitude of "other regard." To be able to see the position of another, to take on another's situation or perspective, is essential to the meaning of *agape*. Gene Outka describes the first dimension of agape as "equal regard," and quotes Karl Barth in saying that it means "identification with his [the other's] interests in utter independence of the question of his attractiveness."[78] Tronto identifies "attentiveness," one dimension of "caring about" as "simply recognizing the needs of those around us...[as] a moral achievement."[79]

---

77. The following is taken from Tronto, 106–8.
78. Outka, *Agape*, 11.
79. Tronto, 127.

The second phase Tronto develops is "taking care of." This involves "assuming some responsibility for the identified need" and making some decisions on how this need is to be met. This is a crucial step, because it means that the person must take on some responsibility for the need identified in the first phase: not only to see the need as the other sees it, but also to decide that one has a responsibility to help meet that need. What is involved here is that taking the other's perspective in the first step is not simply a question of altering one's vision, temporarily. It involves first, an awareness of the other, and second, an identification that also sees the other's need as one's own need.[80] Thus personal involvement, in some way, follows from the initial shift in perspective. This point is reflective of the value of interdependence and relationship that feminist theologians and ethicists have stressed. The needs of the other are not the needs of someone utterly other than oneself, but of one with whom one is already in relationship. [81] It is important to stress, as Tronto does, that the one with whom one is in relationship need not be a human other. It can be an animal, and it can also be the environment. Thus relationship involves responsibility.

The third phase is "care-giving," that is, "the direct meeting of needs for care." It involves the actual work of meeting the needs of the one(s) to be cared-for. Tronto observes that this dimension of care is indicative of the "undervaluing of care-giving in our society," which all too easily equates giving money as a form of care-giving. Giving money, Tronto remarks, is more a form of "taking care of" (the second phase) than it is of direct care-giving.[82] "Direct meeting of needs for care" involves "physical work, and almost always requires that care-givers come in contact with the objects of care."[83] While it is frequently women who bear the burden of the physical work of care-giving, Tronto notes that "in fact, not just gender, but race and class, distinguish who cares and in what ways in our culture."[84] She further notes that "not only are these positions [of those who give care]

---

80. Tronto cites Simone Weil as one of the few who have noted the moral significance of attentiveness, 128.

81. This point ties in with the concerns of ecofeminists and others. See *Ecofeminism and the Sacred,* ed. Carol J. Adams (New York: Continuum, 1993); Lois K. Daly, "Ecofeminists and Ethics," *The Annual of the Society of Christian Ethics,* ed. Harlan Beckley (1994) 285–90.

82. Tronto, 107.

83. Ibid.

84. Ibid., 112.

poorly paid and not prestigious, but the association of people with bodies lowers their value."[85]

Again we find a connection with feminist concerns. The work that women and other oppressed groups do, and its frequent association with bodies, is seen to give it a lower value. But feminism is concerned with the intrinsic value of embodiment, not just as an abstract concept, but with its very real, indeed, its sacramental, dimensions. This is at the core of sacramentality and is why sacramentality invites, indeed, encourages, a feminist development. Being involved in embodiment, be it raising children, working with the environment, caring for an elderly parent, is recognizing the sacramental dimension of physicality. It is also absolutely necessary work.

The fourth phase of care is "care-receiving," that is, it "recognizes that the object of care will respond to the care it receives." This last point is, Tronto notes, "the only way to know that caring needs have actually been met."[86] This point also helps to show whether caring needs have been met well or poorly, as some ways of giving care may in fact make a situation worse. "Care-receiving" ties into feminism's emphasis on mutuality. Caregiving and care-receiving are activities that are done in the context of a recognition of the value of the other (the first phase) and the already existing relationship in which both exist (the second phase). Care-receiving builds on the second phase, of relationality, but extends it in the sense that there is a *responsive* relationship involved. It is not just the recognition of the *fact* of relationship, and the responsibilities that relationship entails, but a commitment to *maintaining* the relationship in a way that is responsive to the needs of both.

As is the case with the third phase, the fourth phase is most often experienced by the least powerful. Being the recipient of care is being in a position of dependence and vulnerability. But vulnerability, rather than being a part of life that we all experience at one point or another — as infants, as sick people, as elderly — is most often understood in the public arena as a threat to the ideals of autonomy, independence, and rationality. To be vulnerable is to be powerless, and as such it is a position that is to be avoided as much as possible. Tronto suggests that taking all of the dimensions of caring seriously will help to revise some of our assumptions about human nature, such as giving greater emphasis to

---

85. Ibid., 114.
86. Ibid., 108.

our interdependence, our vulnerability, our needs, our stance of ongoing moral engagement.[87]

Tronto's understanding of care can serve as a way of seeing more clearly the ethical dimensions of the sacraments, as well as the sacramental dimensions of the moral work often done by women. My intent is not to say that the sacraments are "only" moral activities, with no attention to their aesthetic, sociological, or theological dimensions. This would be a very truncated understanding of the nature of the "moral" or ethical dimension of human life — as if the aesthetic or sociological, not to mention the theological, were less than fully relevant. It is, rather, to see the sacraments as an extension of the work, largely (but not exclusively) done by women, in maintaining the world, in caring for the world. That they are more than "an extension" is a point that I will develop in the next chapter, which is more directly concerned with the distinct nature of worship, liturgy, and ritual. But the sacraments do involve a responsibility to care.

When we relocate the sacraments out of the specifically ritual, sacred arena, and bring them into the public and the domestic, we not only challenge the "moral boundary" that exists between the sacramental and the ethical, but we have also placed them within a new context of moral obligation. The sacraments are not solely acts that are performed by a ritual specialist, the priest, but are expressions of Christian faith lived in the family and in society. Thus they grow out of an understanding of Christian community as the place where we have obligations to others as we do to our own families. But similarly, when we relocate the activities that have been the province of women to the public sphere, *and include women in this process,* we challenge another "moral" and "religious" boundary: that is, the one between women and the sphere of the sacred.

Let us consider some of the moral and sacramental dimensions of these two related moves. If we were to consider the act of bringing a child into the world and into the Christian community as a sacramental and thus moral act, we would place more emphasis on the physical effort involved in childbearing, the importance of the community in taking responsibility for the life of the child. Our caring, as a way of living out the Christian love command, would include the demands not only to "care about" and "take care," as the present way of incorporating the community in baptism involves. It would also include the third and fourth dimensions,

---

87. Ibid., 162–65.

that is, physically caring for the children and families involved and being concerned about the results and reciprocity of this concern.

Using Tronto's four dimensions of care, it is possible to examine the sacraments to see where there might be other creative possibilities for enhancing the connection between church and world, between family and polis. Recall that "caring about" involves assessing a need, and frequently assuming the position of the other. This can mean, in the cases of the sacraments of initiation, the recognition of the need for a grace-filled community and the need to include the other. Thus a sacramental practice for a Christian community implies the recognition that human society is in need of redemption: that human beings cannot make it "on their own," without God's help, nor can they "make it" as individuals.

As Purvis has argued, the Christian command to love involves the values of relationality and community. The practice of "caring about" thus means that it is the responsibility of each member of the Christian community to see the diverse ways that this need is expressed: recognizing the needs of those in the community for reconciling and healing. This means recognizing basic needs for life, such as food and shelter, as well as needs for a sense of vocation, and nurturing these in the community. "Caring about" thus involves broadening one's sense of what needs are. Tronto remarks that this part involves "the recognition, in the first, place, that care is necessary."[88] Seeing the caring dimension of sacramentality means a real shift in perception, and implies a serious educational task on the part of the church, that these needs are not only to be met by a few — clergy, the "good women" who are always present to meet various needs — but are the responsibility of the entire community, and that they are a necessary consequence of sacramental participation.

Second, "taking care of" involves the assumption of responsibility for meeting the need for redemption in community. That there are processes in place to welcome strangers into the community, to educate, to feed, to heal, to foster a sense of vocation, is the responsibility of every member of the community, to greater and lesser extents, depending on one's situation. As noted above, this responsibility is the consequence of the realization of our interdependence, with others, with the environment, with God. It means that we recognize needs as if they were our own needs, and thus understand our responsibilities accordingly. Thus, "taking care

88. Ibid., 106.

of" is everyone's task. Such an approach ties in the need for community, reconciliation, food and shelter, and healing with the sacramental work of the church. And such work is not the exclusive province of the clergy but devolves upon all members of the community. Such a recognition implies a different approach to ecclesiology than the prevailing one, which sees the sacraments as under the power of the clergy.[89] Tronto notes that this stage of care involves not only assuming responsibility but also "determining how to respond to" the need at issue.[90] This determination cannot be made in a one-sided manner but involves careful consultation and co-operation on the parts of those requiring care and those who will give the care. And when the care-givers are increasingly members of the laity, their own experiences and perspectives will inevitably shape the ways that care is given.

Third, "care-giving" involves direct meeting of needs. As I suggested above, "care-giving" involves extending the first two points to the reality of embodiment. Our recognizing the needs of the other and our taking responsibility because of our interdependence also means that we see these needs in concrete ways and meet them, as best we can. There are a number of concrete ways of being involved, and here especially, as Tronto notes, the writing of a check is no substitute for hands-on care-giving. But it would be a mistake to think that only parish involvement would "count" for care-giving, or that sacramental ministry consists of the clergy "dispensing" the sacraments. When one takes into consideration the great amount of work that is done by women in various stages of sacramental ministry — preparation, education, community formation, cooking, sewing, cleaning, mystagogy — the direct meeting of needs as a dimension of sacramentality emerges as central. Broadening the recognition of the "sacramental moment" to a sacramental process would recognize the direct meeting of needs as a sacramental act.

Fourth, "care receiving" means the expectation of mutuality. This final point is significant. It means that the "recipients" of care are not merely passive but that their response is central to the practice of caring. Such a

---

89. "It is the priesthood which renders its sacred ministers servants of Christ and of the Church by means of authoritative proclamation of the word of God, the administration of the sacraments and the pastoral direction of the faithful." Eight Vatican Offices, "Some Questions Regarding Collaboration of Nonordained Faithful in Priests' Sacred Ministry," *Origins: CNS Documentary Service* 27 (November 27, 1997) 401.

90. Tronto, 106.

conception of mutuality works against an understanding of the laity simply as the receivers of the sacraments that are "dispensed" by the clergy. If responsiveness is essential to sacramental work, then those who are its recipients need to play more active roles in their responses. Further, as Tronto points out a number of times, it is impossible to divide up caregivers and care-receivers as permanent states in life, since all human beings require care at some point in their lives. Such a mutual understanding of caring serves to focus sacramental activity as the work of all together in the community, to highlight the point that all Christians are sacramental care-receivers as well as sacramental care-givers, that all Christians share in the "priesthood of all believers." This fourth stage means that sacramental ministry involves careful listening as well as preaching and instruction, a commitment to conversation, and a willingness to put oneself in the place of the other — a position basic to Christian ideas of *agape*. Such a commitment, then, involves attention to what we might term "the ethics of sacramental practice." That is, the practice of the sacraments must embody a concern for the vulnerable, a commitment to mutuality, an understanding that one's role could easily be reversed.

Tronto's four dimensions of care are helpful in expanding our thinking on the ways in which sacraments and ethics can be more closely connected. In addition, such thinking leads to more reflection on the nature of "women's work" and of the "natural," just a few dimensions of which I sketch out here. A greater recognition of the significant work that women do, not just in the public arena, but in the realm of the so-called private and domestic, is certainly called for by a consideration of sacraments in the context of "care." The domestic work that women do is not simply "natural" work, as if childbearing and childrearing were purely instinctive. The work of raising a family, of managing a household, involves a set of complex skills that is by no means "purely natural." Raising children, managing a household, is difficult work, involving not just love, but patience, negotiating skills, empathy, toughness, taking a long view, gratitude, and mutuality.[91] While there are also important physical dimensions to this experience, these physical dimensions are always experienced within a cultural context. Women reflect on their lives, as do men, on what they are doing and what it means. This has been one of the major efforts of feminist thought, in showing how the complexity of women's experiences,

---

91. See Miller-McLemore, *Also a Mother* (n. 40, above).

biological and social, have given women insights into human experience as well as into theological issues. Thus it is a fundamental error to relegate the work that is done in a family context as simply "natural."

Using feminist theory on the family to explore the connections between sacraments and ethics has been instructive. Such theories demonstrate that any discussion of the ethical dimensions of the sacraments will be fruitless unless there is an honest recognition of the ways in which the divisions of natural/supernatural, laity/clergy, private/public, and female/male are being continually perpetuated at both the theoretical and practical levels. While it is sometimes important to make a *distinction* between the two, *divisions* are seldom helpful. Feminist theologians have long questioned dualistic separations, showing how they have functioned frequently to exclude and divide. Although contemporary sacramental theology has challenged these separations, as chapter 4 demonstrated, by failing to note the use of gender, these theologians, as well as contemporary ethicists, have maintained these separations, and the consequent ethical problems of a two-sphere understanding of morality. Only by reconnecting these two spheres, as I have suggested here, will we overcome this separation and make the celebration of the sacraments genuinely relevant to human life.

CHAPTER SEVEN

Women, Worship, and the Sacraments: Toward a Feminist Theology of Worship

To insist upon construing eucharist solely as a symbol of male power is to squander a known source of spiritual vitality in the Catholic community.
— Mary Collins[1]

Our talk is our prayer. It is our faith.... We recognize our connections to women from the beginning of time. Women have rarely known primacy in temples or churches, and so we continue to find it at *other* altars, with our sisters, who have *never* lacked for words, only for voices and volume.
— Martha Manning[2]

We come to reflect on worship at the end of this journey of exploration into women and the sacraments. The traditional theological maxim *lex orandi, lex credendi* (the law of praying is the law of believing) says that worship precedes conceptual expression, that our faith is really expressed in our worship — more so than in our intellectual reflection. So it might seem that a chapter on worship ought to have come first in this book, if our worship is to inform our theological reflection. But the maxim, as it

---

1. Mary Collins, O.S.B., "Women in Relation to the Institutional Church," Leadership Council of Women Religious Address, Albuquerque, NM, August 1991.
2. Martha Manning, *Chasing Grace: Reflections of a Catholic Girl, Grown Up* (San Francisco: HarperSanFrancisco, 1996) 96.

is usually interpreted, overlooks the difficulties that feminist women have experienced with and in worship, especially in light of the women's movement for full equality in the churches. As the opening vignettes of this book illustrate, the traditional forms of sacramental worship have been found wanting by many women. Thus, for feminist theology, the question of authentic worship can only come *after* critical reflection, not only on the experience, but on the history and theology of the sacraments as well. We do not approach worship as if it were a blank slate; on the contrary, there is much already there, and what is there cannot simply be ignored.

Women's experiences of the sacraments have prompted hard questions about their meaning: of Eucharist as the sacrament of unity, since many experience it as one of exclusion; of baptism and confirmation, if despite the words of Galatians 3:28, differences of race and class do not matter in the Christian community, but gender does; of holy orders, if half the human race is deemed incapable of representing God incarnate; of marriage, if sexual complementarity is intrinsic to the church's understanding of committed partnership; of reconciliation and anointing, if God's healing and forgiving grace can only be mediated by male clerics. Yet the anger and frustration of many women has not prompted them into wholesale abandonment of the canonical sacraments, as one might think — although this *is* the case for those who have been embittered and exhausted by their experiences. Rather, many women's experiences have led them to keep one foot in the tradition while, at the same time, they experiment with newer forms of worship that lie on the margins or outside the official sacramental framework.

In sum, women's experiences of the sacraments are ambiguous and ambivalent. But these ambiguities and ambivalences are not entirely negative and have the potential to refocus and redefine the nature and experience of sacramentality itself.

BACKGROUND FOR THE CURRENT LITURGICAL SITUATION

Mary Collins has reminded her readers of the complexity of women's historical experiences of the sacraments, especially the Eucharist.[3] Daily

---

3. Collins, "Women in Relation." See also Mary Collins, "The Church and the Eucharist," and Gary Macy, "The Eucharist and Popular Religiosity," *Proceedings of the Catholic Theological Society of America* 52 (1997) 19–34; 39–58.

Mass was a central part of many of our mothers' and grandmothers' lives, as they slipped out of houses in the early morning dark for a short time with God, before the daily chores of working, cooking, cleaning, and raising families took over their days. This was true as well for women religious. I have vivid memories of worshiping with the community of nuns who taught at my high school at their 7 a.m. daily Mass and prayer. The priest was necessary, of course, for there to be daily Mass, but my memory is of a powerful sense of the community of women gathered together, a sense that I did not experience in Sunday Mass at my family's parish. I always felt that the celebrant was a guest in this community, and that his personal presence was far less significant than the opportunity for this community of nuns to experience the Eucharist together. While it is certainly the case that pre–Vatican II liturgies left much to be desired in terms of participation — not only of women, but of the laity as a whole — the sameness and regularity, especially of daily Mass, allowed for a different kind of experience of participation: one of something larger than this parish, this church, this city, but of the whole world, all worshiping in the same way.

My intention is by no means to romanticize the pre–Vatican II sacramental tradition. The routinization of liturgy, the passivity on the part of the congregation, the objectification of grace, all countered the intent of eucharistic liturgy, which is to celebrate together the heavenly banquet at which God gives us God's very self, and where we are invited to go and do likewise for our neighbor. But the very routinization of the Mass made the ritual, not the participants, the central feature. For the worshiper, it mattered not where one went: it was always the same. The person of the priest did not really matter, either, since the whole point was to perform the rubrics exactly, and the sermon (only on Sundays, and one could skip the sermon without "missing Mass") was (unfortunately) far less significant than the consecration or communion. The Mass was neither the possession of the clergy nor of the people: it was simply *there,* and everyone knew what was expected.

The liturgical changes of Vatican II revolutionized the liturgy, and I need not rehearse all the many changes that transformed the experience of the sacraments, and especially of the Eucharist. The point of these changes, as the constitution on the liturgy phrased it, was the "full and active participation" of the laity in the liturgy.[4] The non-Eucharistic devo-

---

4. The constitution on the sacred liturgy (*Sacrosanctum Concilium*), #14: "Mother Church earnestly desires that all the faithful should be led to that full, conscious, and active

tions of forty hours, benediction, the nine first Fridays, novenas, rosaries, and processions, at least in the U.S., received much less attention as the Eucharist became the chief focus of the church's liturgical life. Indeed, in many parishes, especially Anglo parishes, these devotions disappeared entirely as the Eucharist took on enhanced significance.[5] These changes also entailed a greater sense of personal participation on the part of the celebrant, as well as the laity. Now that the eucharistic liturgy was at center stage, celebrated in the language spoken by the people, the ways in which that language was used became more important, and the personality of the celebrant took on a significance that it did not have prior to the council. The result has been a much greater emphasis on the centrality of the eucharistic liturgy, and on the role of the presider. While the laity have come to play a much more active role in Eucharistic liturgies — as readers, cantors, planners, ministers of communion, and so forth — they are "supplementary" to the priest's role, at least in the official understanding of the Eucharist.[6] But the fact that the laity have taken on more important roles has also affected the way that sacramentality is increasingly understood.

As I argued in chapter 4, the issue of gender in the developments in liturgical and sacramental theology following Vatican II was never explicitly addressed. Indeed, the laity were, and still are, "feminized," in the sense that they are to play the receptive, not the active, role, in relation to the clergy and hierarchy.[7] But as the women's movement gained momentum

---

participation in liturgical celebration which is demanded by the very nature of the liturgy, and to which the Christian people, 'a chosen race, a royal priesthood, a holy nation, a redeemed people' (1 Pet 2: 9, 4–5) have a right and obligation by reason of their baptism. In the restoration and promotion of the sacred liturgy the full and active participation by all the people is the aim to be considered before all else." in *Vatican Council II: The Conciliar and Post-Conciliar Documents,* ed. Austin Flannery, O.P. (Collegeville, MN: Liturgical Press, 1975).

5. Such a statement might not be so true of primarily Hispanic communities, where processions and other forms of "popular religiosity" have not experienced the decline that they have in Anglo communities. For literature on popular religion, see, e.g., Juan José Huitrado-Rizo, MCCJ, "Hispanic Popular Religiosity: The Expression of a People Coming to Life," *New Theology Review* 3 (1991) 43–55; Orlando O. Espín, "Popular Religion as an Epistemology (of Suffering)," *Journal of Hispanic/Latino Theology* 2/2 (November 1994) 55–78.

6. See "Some Questions Regarding Collaboration of Nonordained Faithful in Priests' Sacred Ministry," *Origins* 27/24 (November 27, 1997).

7. There are any number of ways to illustrate this. One would be in the insistence that the bishops are to teach, not to learn from others. This was made especially clear during

in Catholicism in the years following Vatican II, and in other denominations and traditions as well, the question of women's sacramental roles emerged, with the issue of ordination being the primary one. Women and men sought full equality in the church, and this meant that women sought to be ordained alongside men. And given Vatican II, with the church's new understanding of its relation to the world, and of the significance of the secular world itself, it was only to be expected that women sought full equality in the role of the priesthood.

Since the first Women's Ordination Conference (WOC) meeting in November 1975, the issue of the ordination of women in Roman Catholicism has increasingly shifted to the question of the nature of the priesthood itself. In its promotional material, WOC advocates "a renewed priestly ministry,"[8] which would incorporate a more service-oriented understanding of priesthood and a stronger emphasis on the "common priesthood" of all believers. Indeed, a number of texts written by sacramental theologians since Vatican II have stressed a servant-oriented model over a cultic model of priesthood.[9] Moreover, the issue of whether even to pursue ordination at all has become a critical question; it was strenuously debated at the November 1995 WOC meeting. But it is clear that the Vatican's understanding of priesthood remains a sacerdotal, cultic one, and a theology that maintains an "essential" difference between the ordained and common priesthood is still very much in force.[10]

My point in rehearsing some of this background is to provide a context for making a few important points. First, that the long experience of Eucharist, of sacramental worship, and of popular devotions, has not always been as clerically centered as it has come to be in the present. Much,

---

the discussions on the four drafts of the U.S. Bishops' pastoral letter on women's concerns, which was finally tabled in the fall of 1992. For a reflection from the tradition on this question, see John Henry Newman, *On Consulting the Faithful in Matters of Doctrine* (New York: Sheed and Ward, 1962).

8. A recent Women's Ordination Conference brochure (1994) contains the following mission statement: "The Women's Ordination Conference is an international grassroots movement of women and men committed to the ordination of Roman Catholic women to a renewed priestly ministry."

9. See Bernard Cooke, *Ministry to Word and Sacrament: History and Theology* (Philadelphia: Fortress Press, 1976; Edward Schillebeeckx, *The Church with a Human Face: A New and Expanded Theology of Ministry,* trans. John Bowden (New York: Crossroad, 1988).

10. See David N. Power, *The Sacrifice We Offer: The Tridentine Dogma and its Reinterpretation* (New York: Crossroad, 1987), esp. chapters 5 and 6.

although not all, of the alienation, anger, and frustration of women concerning ordination has arisen from an understanding of worship, especially of eucharistic worship, that places the priest-presider at the center. The success, or failure, of eucharistic worship is often almost entirely in the hands of the priest-presider: for setting the tone of the liturgy, for the ways in which the prayers are said, for the sermon, and, most importantly, for uttering the words of consecration. The Eucharist has, at its worst, become, unfortunately, a one-man show. Efforts to redefine the nature of priesthood in more servantlike metaphors run up against clerical dominance in the sacraments, especially the Eucharist. Thus many women quite justifiably feel excluded in eucharistic worship: not only is the language overwhelmingly male, but the iconic significance of the priest as representative of God incarnate leaves them feeling far less than the image of God. They turn to noneucharistic worship, develop their own eucharistic worship practice, move on to other denominations which are more inclusive of women, or they abandon the church's sacramental life altogether.

One central dimension of this problem is that, officially, it is the priest who gives legitimacy to the Eucharist and assures the "real presence" of Christ in the community. According to this view — the official view of Roman Catholicism — without the priest, there is no real presence. In the light of this point, it is interesting to note that so many of these now neglected religious devotions were really not clerically centered: in benediction it was the real presence in the monstrance that was the center; rosaries were recited by anyone; processions might have been led by a priest, but it was the people's participation that was central. Often priests were invited to lend a sense of legitimacy to a service, but they did not have the same kind of centrality that they have today — or, if not centrality, what they represent is how the church sees legitimacy, but not how many people are seeing it. The increased emphasis on the priest's importance — as developed, for example, in the November 1997 Vatican statement — is in large part a result of the increased participation of laity in ministry.

A second dimension is that, given the decreasing numbers of active clergy, the laity who remain active in parish life, especially women, are moving increasingly into quasi-clerical roles: as pastoral associates, liturgy directors, or ministers of communion. As they move into these roles, they are challenging prevailing understandings of clerical dominance, in their efforts to include the congregation in the activities surrounding the sacraments (for example, in sacramental preparation and education) and in their development of "alternative" (that is, noneucharistic) worship ex-periences.[11] Because there are fewer priests available to "administer" the sacraments, lay ministers — largely women — are extending sacramental-ity beyond the strict confines of canonical sacraments: in communion services, in praying with the ill and those in need of reconciliation, in preparing families for the canonical sacraments, in working with youth groups and marriage preparation classes. In doing this work, they are both reclaiming a broader sense of sacramentality that was nearly lost after the refocusing of Eucharist as the center of church life in Vatican II as well as reinventing the very ways of celebrating the sacramental life of the church.

I should note here that many priests welcome these changes and work hard to accommodate themselves within a new understanding of the sacraments that emphasizes community and not clerical control. Many priests ask how they can better serve their communities, be they parishes, women's religious groups, college and university centers. But these priests work against the official model of the priest's role in sacramental worship: a role that is distinguished by its uniqueness and irreplaceability.[12]

Thus the question of a feminist perspective on sacramental worship is not so much whether women can or ought to participate in the existing sacramental life of the church — a feminist version of "how can we sing God's song in a foreign land?" — or even whether alternative worship is the only route for feminist women to take. It is, rather: How is women's practice of worship in relation to community and church *already* redefin-ing what we mean by the sacraments? I will argue in this final chapter that the *practice* of the sacraments, as witnessed in women's involvement in parish ministry, in alternative worship groups, and in women's family and community activities, reveals a renewed sacramental theology: one that is open to and appreciative of ambiguity, one that honors women's embodi-ment, one that is sensitive and aware of the multivalency of symbols, and one that seeks to do justice.

---

11. See Barbara Brown Zikmund, Adair T. Lummis, and Patricia M. Y. Chung, "Women, men and styles of clergy leadership," *Christian Century* 115/14 (May 6, 1998) 478–86.

12. See November 1997 Vatican statement, "Collaboration," for comments on uniqueness and irreplaceability. In my own experience of lecturing to priests' groups, parishes, and making presentations at conferences, the priests who have attended have been concerned to be as open as possible to a communally centered form of sacramental worship. They are at a loss, however, in adequately responding to these concerns since neither their training nor diocesan governance emphasizes a collaborative style of leadership.

WOMEN AND SACRAMENTAL PRACTICE: THE PARISH

In the years since Vatican II, new forms of ministry have developed in parish structures. Prominent among these are the roles of pastoral associate, liturgy director, and religious education director. Overwhelmingly, these are women's roles and they are also almost exclusively oriented toward the sacraments. How do women in these positions understand their ministries? Given their sacramental orientation, how do these ministers see themselves as ministers of the sacraments?

It will come as no surprise to anyone knowledgeable about the contemporary Catholic Church that, even as the magisterium has hardened its official line opposing the ordination of women, women are, in increasing numbers, taking on leadership roles in parish communities. The illuminating study by Ruth Wallace, *They Call Her Pastor,* documents the experiences of a group of women who have taken on leadership roles in so-called priestless parishes.[13] The author found that these parish leaders, who, from an official perspective, are not canonically pastors but lack any other appropriate name — indeed, they *cannot* be called pastor, according to the most recent Vatican directives — are changing the face of parish life and are presenting a challenge to the institutional church. That is, as the numbers of ordained clergy continue to decline, and women take on more positions previously held by priests, women will no longer be simply substitutions or exceptions to the norm: *they* will increasingly be the face of parish leadership.

In this section, I will reflect on the results of interviews that I have conducted with eighteen women who are involved in parish work. While only one of these women was herself a "pastor," all of the women, who were pastoral associates, directors of liturgy and religious education, and teachers of ministry students, repeated themes that have serious import for sacramental theology. The interviews that I conducted with these women were intended to obtain some concrete information on how women involved in parish work understand the sacraments. But as the interviews progressed, it was increasingly difficult to confine the issue to sacraments alone. For these women, sacramentality is bound up with ecclesiology, in that their understandings of their sacramental ministry affect their understandings of their role in the church. In what follows, I will reflect on

---

13. Ruth Wallace, *They Call Her Pastor: A New Role for Catholic Women* (Albany: State University of New York Press, 1992).

five themes that have emerged from these interviews, and consider the implications of these themes for a contemporary understanding of the sacraments and for the church. These themes are, first, a broadening of the understanding of sacramentality; second, an emphasis on the importance of the Sunday liturgy; third, a concern for hospitality; fourth, a continued commitment to the Eucharist; and, fifth, a sense of lived ambiguity.

The first point — and this is a theme that ran throughout all the conversations — is that women's involvement in ministry has led to a broadening of the meaning of sacramentality. When asked how they would define the sacraments, for themselves and for their ministry, the most frequent response I received was some version of "Do you mean a definition of sacraments canonically or experientially?" When pressed, these women said that their understanding of a sacrament was not, nor could it be, restricted to the "seven sacraments" as officially defined by the Roman Catholic Church. While the official sacraments were not at all to be dismissed, they served as the center of what I call a "constellation" of the official sacraments themselves and what one woman called "sacramental moments," times when these women's own pastoral skills were exercised in a way that they viewed as sacramental.

Let me share a few of the examples that these women gave. The celebration of a Hispanic girl's fifteenth birthday, the *quinceañera,* is not a sacrament by any official definition. Indeed the question of how to, or even whether to, celebrate this occasion in a parish context has generated many questions among pastoral workers, in part because of their concerns that the celebration, marking the girl's maturity, becomes an occasion for the family to spend money that they may not have, or that the church may simply be there as the location of a basically secular feast.[14] Two of the women I spoke with talked about how they worked with the girls and their families. Some of these girls had not received first communion nor had they been confirmed. But both of these pastoral ministers remarked that this occasion was a "sacramental moment," for the girls, their families, the parish staff, and the community. One church requires six weekly meetings in preparation for the girl and her attendants, while another hosts a retreat for girls from a consortium of parishes. The girls meet with parish staff at least two or three times before the actual celebration. In recognizing the importance of this feast for these families and for the community,

---

14. Note, however, the extensive literature on popular religion. See n. 2, above.

and in taking the celebration seriously, these women argue that the church is blessing the lives of these girls, acknowledging the sacramental character of their lives and of this particular moment. What is key here is that *the church makes itself available* to recognize the sacramentality of a girl's maturity into adulthood and offers the community a religious context in which to celebrate this occasion. The celebration, when it involved the girl, her family, and the church, is considered to be a "sacramental moment," an opportunity to recognize God's presence in a special way on this occasion.

Another example is how an RCIA (Rite of Christian Initiation of Adults) director planned infant baptisms in her parish. She, along with other members of the pastoral team, visited the families in their home, and involved a network of other families in the education process, so that the infant's baptism was a process that began with a ceremony of welcoming (in the home) and culminated in the actual ceremony of immersion in the church. The intent was to highlight the community's involvement and responsibility for new members of the parish, and for the family to connect with other parish members. Thus baptism was the beginning of a long-term relationship for the child and for the family with the parish. By turning this into a process, and not simply a one-time event, the sacramental quality of community was emphasized as well as the process by which one becomes a member of this community. For the pastoral minister and the families involved with this process, it was not really accurate to say that the "real" sacrament occurred only in the church ceremony; rather, the whole process was understood to be a part of the sacramental event.

I heard of a number of examples in which the *preparation* for the "official" sacrament was carefully ritualized. As Catherine Bell has argued, the process of ritualization is a strategy whereby one "dominate[s]...other, nonritualized situations to render them more coherent with the values of the ritualizing schemes and capable of modeling perceptions."[15] In these situations, the women who are engaged in these practices of ritualization are indeed making their values coherent and modeling perceptions as they develop new ways of including their parishioners' experiences into sacramental celebrations. I will return to Bell's theories below.

There are many other examples to note: how wake ceremonies, where the parish priest may be seldom present, are planned and led by the non-

---

15. Catherine Bell, *Ritual Theory, Ritual Practice* (New York and Oxford: Oxford University Press, 1992) 108.

ordained pastoral staff; how ministries of care to the ill and housebound are understood as sacramental. Many of the women related experiences where parishioners asked, "Why can't *you* anoint me?" "Why can't *you* give me absolution?" What I see in the broadening of this definition of sacrament is an intent to see sacraments as actions *of the community*. What they are not is even clearer: sacraments are not purely priestly actions; they are not restricted to the actual moment when the sacrament is "conferred." They are linked to an ongoing process of recognizing God's presence in all of life, and most particularly, within the community. Thus, ironically, while the magisterium's understanding of priesthood and of sacrament is increasingly termed in cultic and sacerdotal language (I am thinking here of the magisterium's discomfort with general absolution services and its making strong distinctions between communion services and Eucharists),[16] the actual practice, given the numbers of clergy, works very much against this trend. The sacraments are increasingly in the hands of the community, not solely in those of the priest, and, thus, the institutional church.

A second theme that emerged, which may at first appear to go against this trend, is a sense of the weekly Eucharist as the main celebration of the "gathered community." This also ties into the clergy shortage, in that there are fewer weekday Masses — indeed, in some parishes, there are no longer masses seven days of the week — and often there are fewer Sunday Masses as well. Recall the familiar focus of Vatican II on the Eucharist, and the decline, in the last thirty years, of noneucharistic devotions such as first Friday, litanies, rosaries, benedictions, novenas, and the like. But what has happened in parishes is a reassessment of the meaning of daily and weekend liturgies. There is a greater focus on the Sunday (or weekend) liturgy as the one time when the whole community comes together. Most often, people tend to go to one particular liturgy and find a community there, although the place and time of the liturgy make it open to anyone who comes, a point I will return to below. What this means is that the communal dimension of the weekend liturgy is enhanced, as at the same time, there are opportunities for different kinds of liturgical celebrations, some more individually oriented, for the whole congregation at other times. This focus on the weekend liturgy works to establish a strong sense of identity on the part of the parish. So, while sacramentality

---

16. "Directory for Sunday Celebrations in the Absence of a Priest," *Origins* 18 (1988) 321–27.

is broadened, as we have seen, it is also *intensified* in the weekend liturgy (or, in some cases, the monthly liturgy, depending on how often a priest is available).

The women I spoke to saw this as a positive move. The purpose of the weekend liturgy is then clearer: it is not expected to bear the weight of *all* of the community's liturgical needs. These can be met elsewhere: in small faith-sharing groups, in women's groups, meditation groups, or in some of the other devotional practices that have arisen, or have been revived, in response to people's needs for a stronger focus on spirituality. The Sunday Eucharist is a time for the whole community, when not only is the Eucharist celebrated together, and when the results of parish liturgy planning are seen (in the involvement of readers, communion ministers, the choir, and others), but also when the particular concerns of the parish are raised to the community as a whole. This can be seen in how the parish prays for those who are ill, for the dead, and how some special concerns (care of refugee families, staffing the soup kitchen, asking for volunteers for RCIA) are brought up.

While this may seem to paint an idealistic picture, it is certainly not my intent. I will comment below on how the poor quality of liturgies was also frequently mentioned by these women. But this does mean that a great deal hangs on the ability of the pastor or presider and the parish staff to foster this sense of community: when it works well, it draws people into a greater commitment to the parish. When it does not, the Eucharist is lifeless and so too, often, is parish life. In a way, the Sunday Eucharist is really the litmus test for gauging the life of a parish. When there is a strong sense of community, it will be reflected in the weekend liturgy; it will also be evident when it is lacking. Thus there is a direct relationship between the community's life and its weekend Eucharist.

How does this relate to the first theme? I suggest that the metaphor of "constellation" helps to understand this process. The Eucharist is still central to a Catholic sense of the sacraments, and it is from the "light" of the central star of Eucharist that the other ritual practices draw their initial power. But the engagement of the community in eucharistic liturgy has empowered many to extend this sense more broadly. Weekend liturgies are not so important because they are the "real" Eucharist, but rather because it is the time when the community as a whole affirms its identity in a sacramental context.

A third theme is the significance of hospitality. Every one of the women I spoke with mentioned the importance of hospitality. This is also a central theme in Wallace's study. There, the women pastors comment how important it is that they learn the names of the people in their parishes so that they can personally welcome them, ask about them and their families, relate to them in a personal way. The women I spoke with frequently commented that the clergy — and men in general — are not socialized to be welcoming, to be nurturing, to their congregations. Some of them commented that this was something that came "naturally" to women, that the lives of diocesan clergy were isolated, and that many priests didn't know how to relate personally to people, that clergy were often afraid to "break the rules" so as to foster a stronger sense of community.

A phrase that I heard repeatedly from this group of women was the need to "meet people where they are." This meant that whenever people requested the services of the church, no matter what their circumstances, they were to be welcomed. There were stories of couples who had lived together for years, and came requesting sacramental marriage; of respecting the different kinds of time frames experienced by different cultures in relation to church ceremony; of the need to do a lot of "bending" to meet pastoral needs. These women stressed the importance of making the church a welcoming community, of being a presence for people, of responding to needs both expressed and unexpressed. This was not only important for those in parish staff positions, but also for those who had any involvement in parish ministry. The church is a servant, not an institution for itself, these women stressed. The role of the church is to serve the community, and the role of the parishioners is to serve each other. Where hospitality is lacking, so also is a strong sense of community. But this hospitality is not merely a politeness accorded to other people: it is a responsibility of a sacramental community.

When I asked why these women felt that men were, on the whole, less able to be welcoming, they responded that women performed a similar role in families: women are the ones who remember birthdays and anniversaries, who keep the family social calendar, who are the unofficial "greeters" in family life. And there is a profound way in which these women see their role in the parish as analogous to family life. I do not mean here that these women readily accept a traditional understanding of "family values," where they are the "angels in the house," ready to warm up the cold, uncaring atmosphere in public or parish life. I think it is rather that these women sensed a real lack in the ways that parishioners were (or, more likely, were not) "welcomed" into parishes and sought to be as inclusive as possible in the ways that their ministries were carried out.

What hospitality meant for these women was a process of personalizing, as much as possible, the meaning of parish membership. These women modeled their understanding of hospitality both on the ministry of Jesus as well as on an understanding of family that went beyond kinship.

That Christianity is a "family" was a point expressed by a number of these women who also commented on the Christian's obligation to see others as members of their own, extended families. They were also able to draw on family metaphors for understanding the dynamics of parish life and the church's institutional life. These included descriptions of parish and institutional life as being like healthy or dysfunctional families, as examples of the need to extend the real life experiences and values of families to the "real world" of business as well as the often "unreal world" of the institutional church.

A fourth theme was, that while just about every woman with whom I spoke complained about the poor quality of the liturgies (except the liturgy directors!), mentioning the often unprepared preaching, poorly chosen and performed music, and intrusive presiding styles, there remained a sense that the eucharistic liturgy was something that they "stayed with," that it still had the capacity to "hold" them, that it was, for better or worse, one place where they had continuity. Some of the women had been or were still involved in alternative worship communities. Because of their time commitments to the parishes and often to their families as well, they tended to have little time for this kind of worship experience — and, as anyone who has been involved in one of these worship groups knows, they can be extraordinarily time-consuming. The bottom line is that these women are not ready to give up on the Eucharist. They are trying to make it more inclusive, better able to meet the needs of the communities, but there is what I can only call a gut-level Catholic sense that one can let go of a lot, but not the Eucharist.

When pressed on this, some of these women commented that the Eucharist would not let go of them. Historical scholars, notably Miri Rubin and Carolyn Walker Bynum, have noted that women's experiences of the Eucharist are not restricted to the official meanings that are bestowed on them by the magisterium.[17] Recall Mary Collins's observation that, for women in the pre–Vatican II church, going to daily Mass was something

---

17. Carolyn Walker Bynum, *Holy Feast and Holy Fast: The Religious Significance of Food to Medieval Women* (Berkeley: University of California Press, 1987; idem, *Fragmentation and Redemption: Essays on Gender and the Human Body in Medieval Religion* (New York: Zone

that they were able to do on their own, for themselves, often before the work of the day was underway.[18] This was also true for women in religious communities, who may have had to call in a local priest to preside, but for whom their daily liturgy was their own expression of their community's sacramental life together. Thus, *despite* the fact that the priest has, ironically, become *more* important in the post–Vatican II liturgy (often because he mistakenly thinks that the success of the liturgy depends on him), the sense that the Eucharist is much *more* than the priest's performance is something that remains. Thus there is a need to recognize the tensions in the contemporary church between Vatican II's emphasis on the community and the clerico-centrism of the magisterium's understanding of sacramentality and of priesthood. This recognition of the transcendent dimension of the Eucharist — and I mean this in the best sense of the term, that there is more to this than may appear — is very important.

The fifth theme that emerged is that these women live with, are aware of, and wrestle with, ambiguity. The sacraments are not neat and clean; these women meet people in the messiness of their lives; they live in and sometimes battle with an imperfect church, but these women refuse to make dualistic choices: either WomenChurch or the Roman Catholic Church, either feminism or the patriarchalism of the parish clergy, either in or out. For a variety of reasons these women remain committed to parish life. They deal with the contradictions of the church every day: of their roles in ministry, of people's relation to the church, of the role of the clergy, and they have learned that you have to roll with some punches but not others. They have come to see, often by getting together with women clergy of other denominations, that women's ordination does not solve the problems of institutional sexism and clericalism. They realize that the world itself is complicated; that there are many ways of meeting the needs of the community; that some approaches to solving problems will work in some instances but not in others. In other words, they are aware of the dimensions of metaphysical, expressive, and moral ambiguity.[19]

Books, 1991); Miri Rubin, *Corpus Christi: The Eucharist in Late Medieval Culture* (Cambridge and New York: Cambridge University Press, 1991).

18. Collins, "Women in Relation."

19. See chapter 3. See Ruth Page, *Ambiguity and the Presence of God* (London: SCM Press, 1985); Donald N. Levine, *The Flight from Ambiguity: Essays in Social and Cultural Theory* (Chicago: University of Chicago Press, 1985); David Tracy, *Plurality and Ambiguity: Hermeneutics, Religion, Hope* (San Francisco: Harper & Row, 1987).

This ambiguity, though it includes tension, is not one of vagueness or moral indecision, but rather of a determination to honor the complexity of their own lives and those in their parishes, and to recognize that there are few simple solutions. This is evidence, I think, of a real maturity on the part of women who are on pastoral teams in parishes, and their maturity is not uncommonly in contrast to a less mature and often more rigid approach to things on the part of the clergy. Many of these women told me that they viewed their work as one of educating both the laity of the parish and the clergy, too many of whom have an inflated sense of their own importance. This acceptance of ambiguity is not a despairing one, but one that includes much humor and an acknowledgment of their reliance on others. These women frequently commented on the lack of a sense of ambiguity on the part of those clergy with whom they had worked unsuccessfully.

What are some of the implications of these findings? First, what I have called the broadening of sacramentality has led to a real sense of empowerment on the part of many of these women. They feel that they know their parish communities well, often better than some of the clergy. There is a real loyalty on their part to their community, more so than to the institutional church. Where they find community is in the particular, not in the institutional. There is a strong participatory sense and a concern that their voices be heard. Many of these women have basically given up on any hope that the institution will respond to their gifts in a significant way in the near future, but they gain their sense of affirmation from the parish community, supportive clergy, and their colleagues in similar situations. This empowerment leads them to claim sacramentality as a dimension of their own lives, whether the clergy participate or not.

A second point is that the institution fails to recognize sufficiently the work that these women are doing. The institution's insistence on the primacy of the priest and the "supplementary" nature of the ministry of the faithful works to alienate those who are in service to the church.[20] Many of these women told me of times when they were not invited to meetings, or, on the few occasions when they were, when their presence was virtually ignored by the clergy present. There remains a strong clericalism within institutional culture and the work that is being done on the parish level is often not recognized on the diocesan level. Clerical culture

---

20. See "Collaboration," Article 8 (*Origins* edition, 406).

thus works to strengthen the bonds of lay ministers to the local community and weaken those to the institutional church. As people's loyalties are more often to their parishes than to the institution as a whole, the church risks losing talented people if their gifts are not recognized. Thus, as sacramentality has been broadened and even heightened, these women encounter the very real "stained-glass ceiling" of institutional clerical culture. The ecclesiological implications here are very serious, where the risk is of disaffecting local congregations with the diocese.

Third, as Catholicism's face grows more diverse, and as greater attention is being paid to local customs (in Chicago, this is especially true of Hispanic culture), this broadening of sacramentality will increase. On the first Sunday of November each year, my own parish celebrates the "day of the dead" with a procession of children in their Halloween costumes, carrying skeletons and other vivid symbols of death. It is most often women who are engaged in passing on their own family and ethnic traditions, and while there is loyalty to the church, it is not in the terms of the pre–Vatican II homogeneous U.S. church. The work that has been done by, for, and among Hispanic women, for example, has encouraged them to honor their own traditions and to see their own work as part of the sacramental mission of the church. Unless the sacramentality of these ethnic traditions is given greater recognition, the church stands to lose much in richness and diversity.

Fourth, while these women do "hold on to" the Eucharist, and as it "holds on" to them, this connection is by no means fixed or secure. Nearly all acknowledged that they continuously struggle with their loyalty. Women in religious communities wrestle with the role of the Eucharist in the context of their lives (since, as Collins observes, the Eucharist is part of their constitutions). Many of these women religious also work in parish situations. While the Eucharist remains central, it also remains painful. I heard stories of women needing to "take a sabbatical" from parish liturgy because their limits of tolerance (of exclusive language, of clerical domination) had been reached. Will these women "return" from their "sabbaticals"?

My point is that the centrality of the Eucharist is very real and significant, but it is also fragile, as women seek to have their ministerial skills recognized and affirmed. They are dependent on sympathetic and intelligent pastors, and bishops who are willing to welcome them. They have some power — I think here of the pastoral coordinator in Chicago who got her position by giving Cardinal Bernardin an ultimatum: another bishop had promised her a place if she couldn't get one in Chicago. Within six weeks, she had a parish. For some of these women, Eucharist is no longer the possession of the institutional church, and they are claiming it, even if it means leaving the institutional church.

My interviews confirmed that sacramentality and community are closely bound together in the experiences of women in pastoral leadership. They are influencing their own parishes and suggesting new ways for their parishioners to understand the nature and purpose of the sacraments, as well as their membership in the church. Empowered by their experiences, these women are increasingly changing the face of parish leadership. But their loyalty is less to the church as an institution than it is to their own vocations and the perceived needs of their own communities, and their sense of the mission of the church. Their sacramental and communal understanding of parish leadership and their sense of empowerment are already having a strong influence on the ways that their parishioners understand membership. But there are very real tensions with the institutional church's failure to take women's ministry seriously, as more than a stopgap measure until there are more ordained clergy. These women are, at present, able to live with the ambiguity of being on the margins of official ecclesial structures and to create a sense of community with a equally ambiguous sacramental ministry. I hope that the future will show a church where the margins will encroach more and more on the center.

WOMEN AND ALTERNATIVE WORSHIP PRACTICE

Women now have other avenues for worship that go beyond the parish and official liturgy. Women's worship groups have arisen as alternatives to the clerical domination of the liturgy, as ways of recognizing women's distinct experiences, as refuges from an androcentric church. Most importantly, women's worship groups have empowered women to "take ownership" of their worship and to put into practice their understanding of Vatican II's acknowledgment of the priesthood of all believers.

In an important 1993 article, Mary Collins described five characteristics of women's liturgical practice. Women's rituals, she wrote, ritualize relationships that empower women; they are collaborative, and not the product of experts; they serve to critique patriarchal liturgies; they draw

on a distinctive repertoire; and they produce events, not texts.[21] Women's
ritual groups are no longer the new and exotic experience that they were
twenty or more years ago, when women in such groups felt like the early
Christians who gathered secretly despite threats and fears of persecution. I
can recall vividly my first experience with such a group. In the early 1970s,
a friend who was then a member of a religious community invited me to
join her and some of her community members to read the scriptures, to
share reflections on them, and to bless bread and wine, all without the
presence of a priest. We deliberately modeled our ritual on the Eucharist
and celebrated, nervously but also excitedly. When I later told a fellow
student, who was a priest, what we did, he commented that whatever it
was that we did, it was not a Eucharist, and there was no "real" presence
because of the absence of a priest. Yet the group of women of which I
was a part felt that this ritual was profoundly eucharistic: we had shared
together, felt among us the presence of Christ, acted in continuity with
thousands of years of the same actions.

In the years since, women's worship groups have sprouted all over this
country and others, as women come together in intentional communities,
to share weekly, monthly, or just occasionally, significant events of their
lives and to worship together. WomenChurch Convergence, an umbrella
organization of women's groups, and WATER (Women's Alliance for Theology, Ethics, and Ritual) are examples of how the movement for women's
worship has even become somewhat "institutionalized."[22] A recent book,
WomenEucharist, describes the development of these groups, and includes
narrative accounts of women's experiences in forming and maintaining
these groups.[23]

One of the most dramatic examples of an alternative Eucharist took
place in October 1997, when a "Critical Mass" was celebrated publicly in
Oakland, California. "Critical Mass" involved an elaborate ritual in which
a traditional "Mass" was dramatically interrupted by a group demanding
greater participation. The celebrant threw off his vestments, and declared

---

21. Mary Collins, "Principles of Feminist Liturgy," in *Women at Worship: Interpretations
of North American Diversity,* ed. Marjorie Procter-Smith and Janet R. Walton (Louisville:
Westminster John Knox Press, 1993) 9–26.

22. For WomenChurch Convergence, contact the Eighth Day Center, 205 W. Monroe,
Chicago, IL 60606; for WATER (Women's Alliance for Theology, Ethics and Ritual), see
Diann L. Neu, *WomenChurch Sourcebook* (Silver Spring, MD: WaterWorks Press, 1993).

23. Sheila Durkin Dierks, *WomenEucharist* (Boulder, CO: WovenWord Press, 1997).

that the Mass was open to all. What followed was a deliberate alternative eucharistic celebration. This ritual action was planned months in advance, and unlike most women's ritual groups, involved hundreds of people, publicity, and deliberate drama. The sensitivity of the issue was underscored by the fact that only a few of the organizers were willing to give their names to the press. Reaction to "Critical Mass" in the Catholic press was mixed. Susan Wood, associate professor at St. John's University, commented that because "Critical Mass" lacked an ordained minister and because it used a sign of unity as a protest "over and against the rest of the church," it was inherently problematic.[24] Mary Collins, of Catholic University, on the other hand, while remarking that the ritual might have been "bad liturgy," noted that "it was driven by women's frustration and inattentive bishops" and that "such public liturgies were bound to proliferate" unless the bishops took women's concerns seriously.[25]

Most meetings of women's worship groups are far less dramatic than was "Critical Mass." Indeed, as Dierks's *WomenEucharist* shows, many of the women who belong to such groups are also more or less active participants in traditional parish communities. The author herself writes that she continues to participate in the life of her own parish while also active in a women's group, and notes that parish and diocesan clergy are often well aware of these groups, and of staff members' participation. These groups meet weekly, or monthly, most often in members' homes, and constitute intentional communities where Eucharist is celebrated by women.

Such groups have come to serve as "church" for many women, many of whom are too discouraged with the institutional church's position on women to stay with it. While some miss the structure of parish communities, the opportunities for singing and for family participation, these groups are evidence of women's claiming the sacraments as their own, apart from the church's institutional structure. For most of these women, women's worship groups provide a place where women's experience is taken seriously, where there is a commitment to inclusive language and images, where Eucharist is frequently celebrated, but most importantly, where there is a sense of shared community. Many of these groups had their beginnings in women's discussion groups, often originating in parishes, and members found that they wanted to continue

---

24. "Critics, Sponsors Size up 'Critical Mass,'" *National Catholic Reporter* vol. 34, no. 2 (October 31, 1997) 6.
25. Ibid.

meeting, but in a way that included some ritual dimension. Central to many women's experience of forming women's worship groups was a need to deal with their anger and frustration toward the institutional church. Dierks quotes one response to her question on how groups came into existence: "We're mostly Catholic women who were frustrated and felt the pain of non-inclusion."[26]

Only recently have such groups begun to attract serious scholarly attention.[27] The articles and books written about women's ritual groups have emphasized a number of common themes, including an emphasis on immanence as characteristic of the deity's presence, circular and horizontal use of spaces, deliberate attention paid to nature, the body, and women's embodied experiences, a focus on community, the extended use of narrative.[28] It is not my intent here to provide a study of women's ritual worship nor to contrast it to the involvement of women in more traditional sacramental worship. Rather, my aim is to argue that what women who remain connected to the institutional church are doing in parish sacramental ministry and what women are doing in women's worship groups are not completely at odds with each other. They are, instead, reinforcing common patterns that together are challenging sacramental life and practice. Even more, however, women's work in parish ministry and women's alternative worship practices are providing critical insights into sacramental worship that can prove to be both enriching and challenging, to each other, and to the wider church. Catherine Bell provides a helpful framework for making this case.

In her important and influential *Ritual Theory, Ritual Practice*, Bell argues against the standard approach to theories of ritual that reinforce dichotomies of mind and body, theory and practice. Ritual, she observes, has long been understood as a way of "acting out" what is believed, or as

---

26. Dierks, 46.

27. See, e.g., Rosemary Radford Ruether, *Women-Church: Theology and Practice of Feminist Liturgical Communities* (Boston: Beacon Press, 1985); Lesley A. Northup, *Ritualizing Women: Patterns of Spirituality* (Cleveland: Pilgrim Press, 1997); *Women and Religious Ritual*, ed. Lesley Northup (Washington, D.C.: Pastoral Press, 1993); Susan Starr Sered, *Priestess, Mother, Sacred Sister: Religions Dominated by Women* (New York: Oxford, 1994); Charlotte Caron, *To Make and Make Again: Feminist Ritual Thealogy* (New York: Crossroad, 1993). Northup's 1997 study has a helpful bibliography.

28. These examples are drawn from Northup's 1997 study. A similar list of component characteristics can be found in the table of contents of Caron's book, which includes beauty, survival and safety, embodiment, healing, vulnerability, play and humor.

the "practical" or embodied dimension of a religious belief system. Such a dichotomy (ritual = practice; belief = thought), she contends, is both a product of, as well as the means to perpetuate, the very dichotomies that it is claiming to resolve (mind/body, belief/action).[29] Rather than attempt an alternative theory that continues to reify ritual, Bell proposes an approach to ritual as a "strategic practice," and uses the term "ritualization" to "draw attention to the way in which certain social actions strategically distinguish themselves in relation to other actions."[30]

Central to Bell's approach to ritual is an appreciation of the significance of power in ritual practice. As she remarks, "closely involved with the objectification and legitimation of an ordering of power as an assumption of the way things really are, ritualization is a strategic arena for the embodiment of power relations."[31] Certainly the issue of power is significant in the practices of women's alternative worship groups, since most of these groups see themselves as places of empowerment for women. And especially for Roman Catholic women, who have been socialized in a church that has excluded women not only from ritual leadership but also from ritual space, claiming a ritual role is an empowering act.

Women involved in women's worship groups understand themselves as deliberately taking on a role that has no official status or recognition. In learning how to organize and develop their groups, they take their cues from works in feminist theology and spirituality, others experienced in women's worship, and from their own experiences. But their aim is to provide a ritual experience that is otherwise lacking in their tradition. The women who are involved in women's eucharist groups and the women who work in sacramental ministry in parish contexts have a great deal in common. Both groups of women are engaged in "strategies of ritualization," which serve to define their own roles as well as redefine the sacraments. These strategies also serve to open up and celebrate difference and particularity among women, which are erased in the traditional placing of women in relation to sacramental practice.

Bell's theories also help to reveal how women's relation to sacramentality is not adequately covered by an approach that includes only women in official parish work roles and women in "women-Eucharist" groups. While such groups may appear to be those that issue the most explicit

29. Bell, *Ritual Theory,* part I. See, e.g., 21, 25, 74.
30. Ibid., 74.
31. Ibid., 170.

challenge to the traditional sacramental structure, they conceal the involvement of the majority of women who have maintained a powerful sense of
sacramentality in their families and community lives.

Not even the institutional church would deny the "sacramental" dimensions of women's family rituals, of home altars and personal devotions,
of the implicit sacramentality of the family and the home. But the self-
conscious awareness that has developed among women of the importance
of these activities in relation to the mission of the church as a whole has
prompted them to adopt new "strategies of ritualization" that position
these activities differently and thus challenge the institutional ownership
of the sacraments. These strategies involve a deliberate adoption of the criteria that I discussed in chapter 2: that is, a tolerance and appreciation for
ambiguity; a critical understanding of embodiment and its use in the sacraments; a critical approach to the uses of symbols; and a concern to link
sacraments and justice. This "self-conscious adoption" is the intentional
"making public" that ritualization itself involves.

"Making public" the kinds of activities that have been formerly seen as
private is a common practice of women's ritual groups. This practice is
a kind of "naming" of reality, the kind that arose, for example, in "rap"
groups in the civil rights movement, which was taken up by women in
"consciousness-raising" groups, and described through educational practice
by Paulo Freire and his understanding of "conscientization."[32] In the first
chapter of this book, I included Ada María Isasi-Díaz's description of the
"rosary protest" at the third national Hispanic pastoral encuentro in Washington, D.C., in 1985. Isasi-Díaz describes this "simple ritual [of praying
the rosary], for so long the mainstay of Hispanic women," as something
that "had successfully relocated the sacred" out of the cathedral and onto
the steps outside where the people were gathered.[33]

The women who celebrate a Eucharist among themselves, by coming
together and sharing bread that they have baked, transform the meaning
of the simple act of making and sharing food by their "ritual strategy" of
setting this meal aside as different from others, and naming this Eucharist.
The women who work in pastoral situations where the work of education
and formation are central have come to ritualize these situations as well,

---

32. Paulo Freire, *Pedagogy of the Oppressed,* trans. Myra Bergman Ramos (New York:
Herder and Herder, 1970; new revised twentieth anniversary edition, Continuum, 1993).
33. Ada María Isasi-Díaz, *Mujerista Theology: A Theology for the Twenty-First Century*
(Maryknoll, NY: Orbis Books, 1996) 199–200.

thus giving them a public and sacral character that "religious education" has largely lacked. By making these "private" activities "public" — that is, saying the rosary in public, ritualizing a shared meal, making the act of teaching and forming a ritual event — these women are transgressing the traditional boundaries between "sacrament" and "sacramental," and thus challenging clerical ownership of the sacraments. This is not a question of women "playing Mass," as some skeptics have suggested, but of challenging the powers that have tried to keep the sacred bottled up in expensive bureaucratic and clerical jars.

Through these ritualizing activities, the strict boundaries of "sacrament" and "sacramental" — what has traditionally had official status between real sacrament and what is unofficial — become blurred. Ambiguity then becomes a lived reality, not just a theory. The more serious question then becomes whether there ought to be any boundaries at all: Is there *any* difference between a shared Eucharist among an intentional community of women and a traditional Mass in a parish? My own sense is that the criterion for authentic Eucharist ought not so much to be location or whether there is an "official" presider but rather to what extent the Eucharist "effects what it signifies" — that is, unity, community, a sense of radical inclusion, a concern for feeding our many hungers and thirsts, a living out of the real presence of Christ in the midst of human life. While parish liturgies suffer all too often from routinization, clerical dominance, poor liturgical planning, and lack of participation, they are, at least in principle, open to all who come in the doors of the church.

There is something very important to be said about worshiping alongside those with whom one passionately disagrees, those among whom one would not choose to live, those whom one might never encounter except for shared membership in a parish. Intentional communities, on the other hand, have the advantage of being self-selected groups who share common values, views, and commitments, and provide identity and nurturing, but by definition they lack a radical openness to the wider community. A tolerance and appreciation for ambiguity allows one to recognize that it is hardly ever the case that any one religious community will meet all one's spiritual and communal needs. But such an appreciation for ambiguity ought to function in such a way that criticism can be leveled at oneself as well as the other. Thus women's ritual groups challenge communities to be intentional and active in their work of community development, while parishes challenge intentional communities to be open to the stranger, to practice hospitality, to look beyond themselves to the wider society and its needs.

Women's sacramental practice has sought to be inclusive of women's embodied concerns and to value the distinctive experiences of women that have not received sacramental recognition by the tradition. My effort in chapter 4 was to suggest that embodiment be understood within both a physical and a social context: that of the family, and ultimately, of the family that constitutes the body of Christ. Women's worship groups have provided an opportunity for women to honor experiences that cry out for some kind of ritual acknowledgment, as well as to place their embodied selves within roles of ritual leadership.[34] These groups correctly point out how women's bodies have been excluded from sanctuaries and ritual leadership in traditional sacramental observances. Such ritual attention to women's embodiment fills a deep and longstanding need, as such experiences as pregnancy loss, menopause, and relational transitions are given their ritual due.

But here again, women's celebration of embodiment needs to be seen in a context that includes its social, political, and economic dimensions. To the extent that ritual celebration of embodiment incorporates such dimensions, it will be attentive to the sacraments as revealing God's presence, especially where there is hunger, lack of clothing and shelter, racial and economic injustice. Feminist, and particularly womanist and *mujerista* theologians, have been critical of traditional sacramental theology for its "essentialist" focus on women as mothers without giving sufficient attention to the contexts in which some women live as mothers, and others live as sisters, daughters, and partners within their own communities. The temptation of women's worship groups, to the extent that they focus on the body, is to fail to put those bodies into real social and economic contexts. The longstanding criticism made by womanist and *mujerista* theologians of (white) feminist theology is that white middle-class women take for granted a stable social and economic context for their lives and can think about celebrating the body without worrying about where the next meal is coming from or whether the bodies of their sons are safe on the streets.

A critical understanding of the embodied context of the sacraments includes attention to all material dimensions of human life, including not only sex, but also race, ethnicity, social and economic class. Women's worship groups thus need to scrutinize their practice for their embodied inclusiveness as parishes need to ask how the concerns of their members,

---

34. One form of women's ministry to women is the "Elizabeth" ministries, which are directed toward women's experience of childbirth and pregnancy loss. I am grateful to Mary Stimming for drawing this to my attention.

in all their diverse embodied needs, can be met. Understanding the family, as I suggested in chapter 4, as a goal for which we struggle, not as a reality we take for granted, prompts us to be clearer about bodily and family needs, and their role within the Christian community.

Critical attention to the function of symbols in the sacraments was the major concern of chapter 5, particularly the ways in which the symbolic function of language is based on the exclusion of women. Women's worship groups serve to position women as "speaking subjects" and not the objects of the language of men, as well as to draw attention to the powerful effects that exclusive language and images have on women and on those who do not see or hear themselves in liturgical language. Claiming the power of language, of naming, is a powerfully liberating experience. The traditional symbols and language of family relationships, I argued earlier, can serve to perpetuate an understanding of family role and language that excludes the experiences of women as subjects. Thus a new and more inclusive approach to language and symbols is imperative in sacramental worship.

Women's involvement in parish ministries makes the issue of language and symbol somewhat more complex than it is in women's alternative worship groups. In the parish, these concerns include not only the ways in which gender-inclusive language is a factor, but also the ways in which racial and ethnic groups are (or are not) involved in ritual planning and practice as well as the ways in which religious symbols operate within cultural contexts. Thus the issue of subjectivity becomes not simply whether women qua women are included as ritual leaders and speakers but also how relationships are symbolized within worship practices.

My concern in chapter 5 was how women's presence helps to embody God's presence in the community: how God is not the "absent other" but present in and through the concrete and mundane, as well as the sacred. The emphasis that women have placed on active and visible presence within the worshiping community — in the use of language, in women's taking on roles of ritual leadership — is crucial, since otherwise our symbols for God's presence limit and constrict our possibilities for seeing God in a woman's face.

But women's presence in and of itself is not sufficient to guarantee that God's dynamic presence within the community will be more visible. While some feminist theologians are justifiably wary of women's movement into parish leadership roles out of a concern for their being co-opted by the church's hierarchical structure, it is also important to recall that the presence of any minister is to make the extravagant affections of God for humanity, and ours for each other, more visible, more active, in the life of the church.[35] Thus, while the nature of the symbol itself is crucial, ultimately it is the symbol's effectiveness in mediating God's love to the community that is the real test.

The issue of sacraments and justice, the theme of chapter 6, is also close to the heart of both women in parish ministries and women in alternative worship groups. My concern there was that the sacramental arena ought not be exempt from the concern for justice in the wider community, that sacraments not be "privatized" and "naturalized" so that they operate under their own particular set of rules. The feminist emphasis on care, especially as it is seen as a political as well as personal act, can help to extend the embodied context of sacramentality in ever-widening ways. Using the model of "family" makes more vivid the point that the Christian community calls all of its members to a just love for each other that extends beyond kinship and personal affiliation.

Women's worship groups challenge the institutional church to be a church of justice and provide models of collaborative leadership and inclusive liturgies. But women in parish ministry are called to live out this just and inclusive love in a worship context that includes those both favorable to and hostile to feminism, where concerns for just wages and living conditions may at times overshadow concerns for gender-inclusive language in the liturgy. Worshiping alongside those with whom one disagrees, alongside those with whom one would not ordinarily associate, is a crucial test for the sacraments' effectiveness: they are thus *not* dependent upon the presider's charism (or lack), or the worthiness of the community. If the sacraments are effective, they work to unite rather than to divide.

WOMEN'S WORSHIP AND SACRAMENTAL THEOLOGY

The activities of women in sacramental pastoral ministry, the practice of women's worship groups, and the work of women in families and commu-

---

35. Mary E. Hunt has expressed this concern. See, e.g., "Medals on Our Blouses: A Feminist Theological Look at Women in Combat," in *Feminist Theological Ethics: A Reader*, ed. Lois K. Daly (Louisville: Westminster John Knox Press, 1994) 315–25, esp. 316–17 where she compares the experiences of women taking on leadership roles in the military with women taking on leadership roles in the church.

nities, raise important questions about the nature of the sacraments, their place within the church's worship tradition, and women's participation in sacramental leadership. The liturgical context of the sacraments, as they are presently officially practiced, does not always provide the opportunity for reflection on ways in which new practices may reveal grace-filled ways of sacramental encounter with God, or how those who are alienated from liturgy may come to a renewed sense of the sacraments. What the practices described in this chapter reveal is that the sacraments have slipped out of their institutional and liturgical confines and established themselves in the practices of women and men who seek to celebrate God's presence in the midst of life. Such practices eventually push the question of the sacraments to the forefront: What are sacraments for? What does feminist theology find of value in the sacraments? Does feminist theology push beyond the sacraments to a new understanding of worship, symbol, ritual action?

Feminist theology, by pushing the questions of the relation of women and nature, of the sacraments and nature, of the power of language, of the roles of women and men in families in relation to society, of women's role in worship, forces the tradition to face fundamental questions. We have only begun to ask these questions and to push for answers. But the energy of women in asking these questions and, even more, in challenging the tradition to be faithful to the message of Jesus, insures that such questions will continue to be asked. I believe that the women's movement in theology constitutes a prophetic grace to the church, and to the world. I do not believe that feminist theology can provide all the answers, or that it will, in the words of a friend, "usher in the new millennium," wipe all tears away, and make possible the new heaven and earth. Women-defined theologies, to use Janet Kalven's term, are *part* of the workings of the Spirit in our time. Each new movement of the Spirit reveals heretofore hidden places where God is to be found.

But this does not answer some of the hard questions that are posed about women and the sacraments. Women in religious communities continue to wrestle with the often divisive question of community Eucharists. Women and men in parish contexts wonder about their continued attendance at liturgies that they find uninspiring or even alienating. I believe it is necessary not only for the institutional church to undertake a serious and self-critical examination of its use of symbols, its reliance on canonical validity, its focus on traditional forms of worship, as much of these preceding pages have tried to do. But it is also important for those, like myself, who are critical of the tradition, to ask whether an exclusive focus on the presence of women, of inclusive language and symbols, can also obscure what it is that the sacraments are really about: making God's presence a living reality in the world.

The toleration of ambiguity that I have suggested is so important to a full appreciation of the sacramental tradition also serves to remind those working for reform that no liturgy will ever be perfect and that the eucharistic table is for all, especially sinners. The challenge that a feminist perspective on the sacraments offers is, fundamentally, whether the sacraments are indeed "occasions of grace," whether they "effect what they signify," in making God's love for humankind concrete and available to all, whether Christ becomes "really present" in the midst of those who celebrate together. This book has asked whether women's experiences make a difference in the theology and practice of the sacraments. The answer is that they do, to the extent that they make more concretely present God's gracious and all-embracing love.

*   *   *   *   *

At the end of *Final Payments,* Isabel Moore leaves the home of the woman she forced herself to live with in an unsuccessful attempt to "love purely." She found that she could not. Her life and love would inevitably be filled with joy but also loss, with good works as well as sin. In the company of her friends Liz and Eleanor, Isabel goes forth, not knowing what the future will bring, only that she will no longer live in her self-imposed prison. She "opens her jar of ointment" and resolves to live with her extravagant affections for those she loves, for her faith, and for herself.

The women and men who see in the sacraments the possibilities of God's extravagant affections for us, and ours for others, as well as the pain, hurt, and loss that accompanies the tradition, are already breaking open these alabaster jars of ointment. Their work, within parishes, women's groups, families, and communities, is making the presence of God in our lives a reality.

Index